The Shadow
of
Extinction

Europe's Threatened Wild Mammals

By the same author
Okavango Adventure
Earning Your Living With Animals
Modern Classic Animal Stories (*editor*)

The Shadow of Extinction

Europe's Threatened Wild Mammals

by
Jeremy Mallinson

Foreword by
Professor François Bourlière M.D. D.Sc.

M

The publishers gratefully acknowledge the assistance of the Council of Europe in the preparation of this book. Data on distribution and status, together with map references for 25 of the 33 species covered here, are drawn from the Council of Europe report prepared for the European Committee for the Conservation of Nature and Natural Resources, Strasbourg, by the State Institute for Nature Management, Netherlands: C. J. Smit and A. van Wijngaarden (1976), 'Threatened Mammals – Mammals in Need of Special Protection in Member States of the Council of Europe'.

First published by
MACMILLAN LONDON LIMITED
London and Basingstoke
Associated companies in Delhi, Dublin,
Hong Kong, Johannesburg, Lagos, Melbourne,
New York, Singapore & Tokyo

Illustrations by Don Cordery
Maps by R & B Art

Typeset by
Santype International Limited,
Salisbury, Wiltshire

Printed in Great Britain by
Lowe & Brydone Printers Limited,
Thetford, Norfolk

British Library Cataloguing in Publication Data

Mallinson, Jeremy
    Threatened mammals.
    1. Rare animals — Europe   2. Mammals —
    Europe
    I. Title
    599   QL726

    ISBN 0-333-19214-1

'What is man without the beasts? If all
the beasts were gone, men would die
from great loneliness of spirit, for
whatever happens to the beasts also
happens to the man.'
*Chief Seathl, in a letter to
the U.S. President, in 1855*

Author's Acknowledgements

A book of this nature could never be as comprehensive and include such a cross-section of data had it not been for the availability of a great many authoritative works and the assistance of a number of people who provided me with a great deal of advice on the subject matter. For this I am grateful to the following individuals: Dr G. K. Godfrey (Wildlife Preservation Trust, Jersey), the late Dr W. C. Osman Hill (Royal College of Surgeons), Dr David Jenkins (Banchory Research Station, Kincardineshire), Dr R. D. Martin (Wellcome Institute of Comparative Physiology, London), Judith Rowe (Forest Research Station, Farnham, Surrey), Dr R. E. Stebbings (Monks Wood Experimental Station, Huntingdonshire) and Roger J. Wheater (Royal Zoological Society of Scotland).

It is also my duty and pleasure to acknowledge the unstinted help received from my friend and colleague Dr Michael Brambell (Zoological Society of London), who has not only gone through the text with a 'tooth-comb' but has also provided me with many helpful suggestions and given immense encouragement throughout the book's gestation.

The splendid drawings of Don Cordery do more to illustrate the detail of the mammals covered than could any verbal description, and my thanks are due to R & B Art, who prepared the artwork for the maps. I should also like to thank Miss Rachel Dickens for her forbearance in typing and re-typing from some untidy manuscripts during the preparation of the diverse information contained in this book; my wholehearted thanks go to Mrs Joss Pearson for pulling the whole text together.

Finally I should like to thank Professor François Bourlière for writing the Foreword to this book and Mr Gerald Durrell for his guidance and friendship over the past eighteen years, as well as for providing me with every encouragement throughout my studies of the Animal Kingdom.

JEREMY MALLINSON
Wildlife Preservation Trust
Jersey, 1978

Map sources Pyrenean Desman, Greater Horseshoe Bat, Beaver, Common Hamster, Tundra Vole, Crested Porcupine, Right Whale, Wolf, Brown Bear, Polar Bear, European Mink, Wolverine, Otter, Wildcat, Lynx and Pardel Lynx, Walrus, Ringed Seal, Mediterranean Monk Seal, Red Deer, Reindeer, Wild Goat, Alpine Ibex, Spanish Ibex, Mouflon: after Smit and Wijngaarden (1976), with additional data. Large Mouse-Eared Bat, Mountain Hare, Red Squirrel, Dormouse, Pine Marten, Badger, European Bison: after van den Brink (1973), with additional data. Lesser White-Toothed Shrew: data supplied by Dr G. K. Godfrey. British distribution of species checked against recent data of the Biological Records Centre, Huntingdon.

Contents

Foreword

Except for the disappearance of the aurochs or wild ox (ca 1627) and of the European wild horse (at an unknown but early date), no native wild European mammals have become extinct in recent centuries. In contrast, the West Indies have lost at least 10 full species since 1800, Australia 9, Africa, Asia and North America 2 each, and South America one. Yet during the nineteenth century the area of western and central Europe was the cradle of the modern industrial world, after supporting for many centuries some of the densest and most active of human populations. Furthermore our native continent has been the stage of many of history's bloodiest conflicts, which have involved extensive environmental disturbances, as well as wholesale human slaughter.

How can such a paradox be explained? The main reason for this quite unexpected survival of Europe's native wild mammals undoubtedly lies in the existence, since mediaeval times, of extensive refuge areas in most European countries. These areas include mountainous regions and marginal lands in which large mammals were left free to roam and breed. Many people still do not realise that in western and central Europe deforestation was a much more serious problem from AD 1400 to 1700 than in recent times. The use of coal for iron smelting and other industrial processes did not become general until the beginning of the eighteenth century. Before that time wood and charcoal were the major sources of energy in the home as well as in the factory. It is thus not surprising that the amount of wooded land constantly diminished up until the middle of the last century, but then slowly began to increase again. At present forests cover about 22% of western Europe, and 50% of northern Europe. Needless to say these, present-day forests are by no means comparable to the pre-neolithic wilderness. For example, many are tree plantations of exotic species. Most of these forests have, however, provided a refuge for our large wild mammals. A recent study by G. H. Parent has convincingly demonstrated how the reafforestation of the 'red zone' around Verdun, between the two World Wars, helped the wildcat to multiply and initiated its recent and spectacular comeback in north-east France and Belgian Lorraine.

The second cause of this survival in Europe of a relatively rich mammalian fauna is the early conservation efforts of a number of political leaders. In mediaeval times some ruling monarchs laid down various laws designed to preserve forests and game for the aristocracy. In Germany, royal and baronial decrees from the Middle Ages onward regulated forest usage and grazing rights, thus protecting at least some areas from excessive lumbering and their game from poachers. The present-day *Administration des Eaux et Forêts* in France was established in AD 1291 with Philip IV's organisation of 'Masters of Streams and Forests, examiners, inquirers and reformers'. If so many forest belts are still found close to the large capital cities of Europe, it is because most of them were for centuries considered royal forests where the ruling monarchs and the nobility preserved large animals for the pleasure of hunting. In the last 150 years this policy was continued by some private landowners, foresters and hunters' organisations who established 'forest reserves' and 'hunting reserves' many years before the first 'nature reserves' and 'wildlife refuges' were ever conceived. At first the management policies of these areas were sometimes questionable from an ecological point of view, but in some countries these policies progressively improved. The concepts of forest and game management were actually coined by foresters and hunters long before naturalists and ecologists initiated the conservation crusade.

An exception to this general policy is the treatment of predators. It is not by chance that a third of the threatened large mammals of Europe that are dealt with in this book are carnivores. Our forefathers had little sympathy for the wolf, the brown bear or even smaller 'vermin', which were considered competitors for game, livestock and fowl.

The encouraging fact that not a single species of our native mammalian fauna has become extinct during the last hundred years does not mean that the future of the wild populations of these species is bright, or even satisfactory. Quite the contrary: the 'species richness' of western and central Europe may have remained the same since the seventeenth century, but the populations of most large and middle-sized mammals have been considerably depleted in numbers, and their initial wide areas of distribution broken up into a number of small more or less isolated populations. Both these effects represent a serious threat for the future, as such 'relict' populations are not only more vulnerable to poaching, accidents or disease but, because of increased inbreeding, are also less able to adapt to environmental changes. Even the larger and apparently more stable populations could be threatened by unexpected change in land-use policy, hunting regulations and pressures, or even by public health campaigns. The programme for 'eradication' of foxes and badgers, now under way in some countries to counter the spread of rabies epidemics, is a case in point. Furthermore, pollution of the major European rivers, with resulting changes in their invertebrate and fish fauna — a major factor in diminishing the numbers of otters in most European countries — is far from being efficiently controlled. Even small rivers and streams are now being polluted, with already serious consequences on the distribution of small amphibious mammals, such as for example the Pyrenean desman. Thermal pollution, which will result from the multiplication of atomic power-plants in the forthcoming decades, will certainly turn most of the large rivers of Europe into open sewage systems and drive out what remains of the native amphibious mammals, with the Norway rat being perhaps the sole beneficiary. Finally the competition with some recently and successfully introduced 'exotics', like the muskrat and the coypu, might well have some unexpected long-term influence upon the distribution and abundance of small native animals, which until now were considered more or less safe from human interference.

What then is to be done to safeguard our European mammalian heritage? There is plainly no single answer to this question. It is obvious that the first step should be to increase the number of protected areas and the size of those already existing. Some areas should be established in each of the major climatic and vegetation zones of Europe — especially in the Mediterranean zone where the number of adequately managed natural reserves is alarmingly small. This is the only possible way to assure the future of threatened habitats and their vegetation and fauna, including their small mammals. Such nature reserves must, however, be ecologically self-supporting, i.e. large enough to support adequate populations of both plants and animals, in order to avoid random genetic drift and even accidental extinction. As 'islands' in the midst of agricultural land or industrial areas, nature reserves in Europe have to be properly managed and their plant and animal populations constantly monitored in order to prevent immigration, over-population and subsequent destruction of the original habitat.

The preservation of an adequate stock of carnivores in natural reserves and national parks raises some difficult problems. Since carnivores are at the top of the 'feeding pyramid', they are much less numerous than the herbivorous species upon which they prey. Such small populations are always very vulnerable. This is particularly true for species whose individuals are large in size, such as the brown bear and even more the wolf, which normally wander over very large home ranges. In this case, the protected areas must be extensive and surrounded by a buffer-zone in which compensation should be given to the local people for the harm eventually done to their domestic stock by large predators.

The future of ungulates, the horned species — which are by no means restricted to national parks and nature reserves — will largely depend, as in the past, upon sound management policies for game animals. This implies closer and more confident relationships between hunters' associations, foresters and conservationists. Although it is not easy to agree on common policies, a consensus must be achieved before it is too late — and the quicker the better. The large-scale introduction of exotic ungulates, like the Sika deer, the fallow deer, and even the Corsican mouflon, should not be undertaken on a haphazard basis. Rather, such efforts should initially be focused on selected experimental areas, until we know more of the impact on different habitat types of these introduced species, and of their possible forms of competition with native species.

Finally, every effort should be made to improve and extend public education in the field of nature conservation. Every wild creature, large or small, is in the long run man's direct or indirect rival in terms of space and food. This means that we have to find a compromise between our needs and theirs. There is no conservation policy entirely 'free of charge'. In order to accept the few necessary constraints which will ensure a peaceful coexistence between wildlife and industrial man, everyone has to understand the basic needs of the wild animals. In this way the average citizen will gradually learn first to tolerate their presence, then to realise their usefulness and finally to enjoy their companionship. This book should represent an important step towards such a future.

FRANÇOIS BOURLIÈRE M.D., D.SC.
Past Chairman, International Union for Conservation of Nature and International Biological Programme

Preface

This work makes no pretence of ranking as a scientific treatise, being essentially popular in its treatment of the subject matter. As there is not sufficient room within the text to include a monographic coverage of each animal species discussed, it is recognised that there are sure to be points that, to the specialist, require further elucidation.

Only 33 species (which includes 3 sub-species) have been chosen here — out of the 150 or so mammal species and sub-species represented in Europe. The species chosen are not necessarily the most threatened, but rather constitute a series of examples aimed at acquainting the reader with important insights into the general biology of the animals, as well as up to date evaluations of their present population and distribution, and hence an understanding of the factors crucial to their survival.

Twelve of the 33 mammalian forms chosen are listed in the Survival Service Commission of the International Union for the Conservation of Nature and Natural Resources (I.U.C.N.) *Red Data Book* as in danger of extinction — the Pyrenean desman, the North Atlantic right whale, the brown bear sub-species, the polar bear, the Pardel lynx, the Atlantic walrus, the ringed seal sub-species, the Mediterranean monk seal, the red deer sub-species, the European bison, the Spanish ibex, and the mouflon. Fourteen more — the greater horseshoe bat, the European beaver, the common hamster, the northern vole, the crested porcupine, the wolf sub-species, the European mink, the wolverine, the otter, the European wildcat, the European lynx, the reindeer, the wild goat, and the Alpine ibex — along with 11 out of 12 of those already listed by I.U.C.N., are described by C. J. Smit and Dr A. van Wijngaarden (1976) in 'Threatened Mammals', a report on mammals in need of special protection in member states of the Council of Europe — the European bison is not included in the latter. The remaining 7 of the 33 species included in the text — the lesser white-toothed shrew, the large mouse-eared bat, the mountain hare, the red squirrel, the dormouse, the pine marten, and the badger — help to illustrate further the variety of species and sub-species that belong to the 8 different mammalian orders (not including the order Primates) represented in Europe.

In order to facilitate direct comparisons between one species and another, each animal has been presented in the same way: description — habitat — behaviour — diet — breeding — population — distribution — conservation — literature cited (full details of the latter will be found in the Bibliography). In some cases I have dealt in detail with such subjects as taxonomical differences, behavioural characteristics, dietary essentials, delayed implantation, development of young, population dynamics, and estimations of age — to mention only a few of the intriguing factors that afford insight into the general biology of the varied collection of mammalian species described in this work.

The literature cited in the text ranges from a translation of a Latin bestiary of the twelfth century, through Topsel's mid-seventeenth-century history of four-footed beasts and serpents, and late nineteenth-century and early twentieth-century literature by such great Victorian naturalists as Richard Lydekker and J. G. Millais, up to the present time of the 1977 editions of The Fauna Preservation Society's Journal *Oryx* and the 1976 report by C. J. Smit and Dr A. van Wijngaarden listing European mammals in need of special protection.

For up to date information concerning status and distribution of species I have relied heavily on the researches of previous authorities. Apart from specialist books about the various species, I have taken advantage of recent general natural history publications by authors such as F. Bourlière, G. B. Corbet, F. H. van den Brink and E. P. Walker. Furthermore, in order to glean as comprehensive a picture as possible of each particular mammal species, I have corresponded with scientists who have specialist knowledge about the animal concerned.

My personal acquaintance with the animals described is by no means equal throughout, for in some cases, due to the scarcity of the animal, the species is not known to me 'in the flesh'. However, with those mammal species or related forms that I have had the privilege of observing, I have interwoven into the text certain episodes that are considered to be both relevant and of interest.

The Survival Service Commission reports that from AD 1600 there were approximately 4226 living species of mammals in the world. Since then 36 have doubtless become extinct, and today at least 120 more are in some danger of extinction.

Different conservation bodies and international organisations, as for example the I.U.C.N. and the World Wildlife Fund, have already achieved encouraging successes in the more conventional conservation methods of saving habitat as well as in the creation of reserve areas. In some cases, the last hope for preserving threatened animal species lies in an attempt to maintain and breed them in captivity. Some zoological institutions, for example Basel, Cologne, Frankfurt, Jersey, New York, Slimbridge, to mention only a few, have already attained promising results in this respect and conservation captive breeding programmes have proved to be responsible for the survival of some species, as is strikingly well illustrated in the story of the European bison (page 188).

Local extermination is especially characteristic of Europe, and a true reconciliation of man and nature is essential if man's tendency to threaten wildlife and upset the harmony of his whole environment is going to be overcome. It is undoubtedly a sad reflection on mankind that the thirty-three mammals covered in this book have to be described, in the first place, as 'threatened' with extinction. It is therefore my hope that, in the future, an enlightened public will do everything in its power to ensure the survival of these irreplaceable forms of animal life so that future generations can still benefit from sharing this planet with them.

Lesser White-Toothed Shrew

Crocidura suaveolens

Status: Considered as a relict species in some parts of its range, and scarce in others, the disappearance of suitable habitat is the crucial factor governing whether it can be supported in some regions

Description   Although shrews superficially resemble mice, they are more closely related to the mole and the hedgehog than to rodents, and in the zoological classification they are placed in the Order Insectivora. They are easily recognised by their sharp snout and small eyes and ears. The widespread family of shrews contains a multitude of forms. Three sub-families are recognised, although the groups appear to be very difficult for systematists to sort out, which has resulted in wide variations between the 'splitters' and the 'lumpers'. In one sub-family are grouped all those species of shrews whose teeth contain reddish pigment: these include the genus *Sorex*. Another sub-family, *Crocidurinae*, contains the white-toothed shrews, whose skull is distinguished by lack of red pigment on the tips of the teeth. *Crocidura* is the largest genus of the white-toothed shrew, and includes several ground-living species. The lesser white-toothed shrew itself, *Crocidura suaveolens*, is very similar to the common white-toothed shrew, *Crocidura russula*, but is slightly smaller and has a more variable dental structure; it is much less well known than the common white-toothed shrew, and is consequently easily overlooked.

The lesser white-toothed shrew's close velvety fur has greyish dark brown upper parts, sharply contrasting with the paler under parts which some authorities consider to distinguish this species clearly from the other white-toothed shrews. It is characterised by having more prominent ears and a more foxy appearance than the *Sorex* shrews, as well as prominent scattered vibrissae (stiff, bristly hairs) on the tail, and three upper single-pointed teeth.

Shrews have a characteristic musky odour: it is caused by the secretions of glands on the flanks, and its function appears to be social. Experienced field researchers have taken advantage of this musky odour, for when they detect it during field work they realise that shrews are in the vicinity and set their traps accordingly. On the basis of numerous observations it has been established that the best developed sense in the lesser white-toothed shrew is hearing, which primarily keeps it safe from its enemies and is made use of in the search for its food. The hearing response of this species of shrew is excellent: it responds very sensitively, even at a distance of several metres, especially to high-pitched sounds. It is, however, of interest that in searching for food the animal does not respond via its hearing to objects more distant than 10–15 cm. Thus, in the search for food, smell and hearing play approximately equal parts. In some cases touch seems to be more significant than smell: there are cases where a hungry animal may pass, even several times, a prey that is not moving and eventually respond to it upon direct touch only. The most useful tactile sense organs are the prominent vibrissae which fan forwards and outwards from the muzzle. The part played by the sense of sight in the search for prey is irrelevant in shrews of this species: they do not respond markedly even to moving mealworms placed behind glass.

The head and body measurement of the lesser white-toothed shrew has a range of 6.0–7.6 cm (average 6.8 cm); the tail 3.5–5.0 cm (average 4.3 cm); the length of skull is usually under 1.9 cm, and the length of mandible usually under 1.0 cm. The weight range is 5–11 g, with pregnant females weighing up to 15 g.

Habitat   Detailed ecological studies on the genus *Crocidura* are lacking, for the majority of the published work to date has been largely taxonomic. However, a number of researchers have recorded trapping a quantity of specimens in habitats ranging from a dry locality of steppe character in the close vicinity of residential houses in Prague, to the top of beaches on an island environment. Whilst collecting shrews for laboratory breeding in Jersey, Channel Islands, G. Godfrey trapped 40 *Crocidura* in about 30 localities; the largest catches were obtained from the beaches, in hedgebanks, meadows and woods. Similarly, whilst trapping *Crocidura* in the Scilly Islands, Y. Spencer-Booth found that the population was more dense at the top of the beach than further inland. J. P. Rood, working in the Scilly Islands, found that shrews were trapped in a variety of habitats on the five inhabited islands, but were usually more abundant in fields of bracken.

Behaviour   The members of the shrew family are hard to detect in their natural habitat and there are considerable difficulties involved in studying shrew behaviour in anything but a captive environment. However, shrews are considered to be solitary creatures and their reaction to others of their own kind is either to run away or to fight. Petr Vlasak has recently given a detailed description of the development of the 'caravan-forming' instinct, which occurs only when the nest is in danger. The young are then led by their mother so that they form a kind of chain behind her in which each young individual holds with its teeth the fur at the root of the tail of the preceding one; the young either follow the mother in two chains on each side of her tail or they form a single chain. The transport of the young by means of the 'caravan' is thought to be restricted to representatives of the sub-family *Crocidurinae*.

The small size and rapid metabolism of the shrew have forced it to·wake and sleep about every one and a half hours; that is, to adopt a short-term activity rhythm of about three hours. It is known that the shrew is in general more active in the early morning than in the early afternoon, and that the total amount of its activity during the hours of darkness is greater than that during the day. Nevertheless, even during the day shrews will be abroad at any hour.

Diet   Shrews are carnivorous predators to almost the same extent that lions and tigers are, and in their miniature jungle they devour whatever small animals they can overcome and eat. Insects and their larval stages undoubtedly form a substantial part of their food; but as P. Crowcroft has pointed out, it must be remembered that the term 'Insectivore' refers only to the place of shrews in the formal classification: the bulk of their food probably consists of arthropods. The insects that are taken most readily include sandhoppers and woodlice; small crustaceans are also one of their favourite foods. In captivity, the white-toothed shrews are considered to be easier to keep than *Sorex* species; they can survive longer and recover more quickly if short of food. Godfrey has fed an extensive breeding population of the lesser white-toothed species on a diet which has proved to be of the utmost success: raw minced meat (calf brain, heart, liver, kidney, muscle) to which calcium phosphate is added. Mealworms are also given twice weekly, and water is provided for drinking.

Breeding   It is well recognised that when dealing with such a diminutive and secretive mammal there are considerable difficulties in managing to obtain any reliable data as to the species' reproductive biology. Therefore the information that has been collected is the result of laboratory breeding programmes, not observation of the wild state.

Petr Vlasak, in Czechoslovakia, found that the breeding season falls into the period from March till September, predominantly from the end of April or the beginning of May until the end of August. Reproduction was found to take place only after the animals' first winter.

The process of mating and the behaviour at the period of mating in *Crocidura suaveolens* differs in many features from that in other shrews. The females may initially try to escape from males but behave quite passively during the mating itself. During copulation, which occurs in most cases 5–20 minutes after the female in oestrus is joined by a male, the male holds the female with his teeth by the fur in the region of the nape of her neck. At the end of the mating, the female begins to be rather aggressive towards the male again, and the latter gradually loses interest in her and departs.

After a gestation period of 26–28 days, the births occur, mostly between 6 and 11 pm, and in the morning hours between 6 and 10 am. The litter size varies from 2 to 6 infants and it has been recorded that females can have up to 5 litters per year. Lactating females are frequently found to be pregnant, for conception often takes place within 24 hours of a delivery. Since second litters can be conceived soon after birth, at the post-partum oestrus, and implanted without delay, it follows that the period of gestation and the period of lactation (and milk-feeding of young) must be about the same, otherwise the second litter would not be able to compete for milk with the first litter. This period is about 21 days. Towards the end of lactation the young of each successive litter are forced to turn to other food by the falling-off of the milk supply.

At birth the ash-grey pinkish young shrew is blind and weighs only about half a gramme; it reaches the adult weight at the age of 40–60 days. A male attains sexual maturity at an early age, and a female can become pregnant at less than two months. It has not been established how soon the shrew family breaks up, but it

3

probably depends upon the state of the food supply and whether or not the female is pregnant again. However several eye-witness accounts of shrews hunting in packs suggest that the solitary habit does not always develop immediately after weaning.

As is the case for the majority of the smaller mammals, the lifespan is often greatly increased by captive conditions. In a laboratory the maximum age for a lesser white-toothed shrew so far recorded is 792 days for a female and 750 days for a male.

Population   As shrews are seldom seen, living as they do in undergrowth, amongst boulders, and in other such concealed habitats, population densities are almost impossible to establish. Some evidence as to the presence of shrews is sometimes apparent when their bodies are found on paths and other open places during autumn time. Otherwise, we have to rely on researchers trapping shrews for specific research projects, to provide us with any type of insight as to the species' numerity and whereabouts.

Distribution   The lesser white-toothed shrew is distributed over central and southern parts of the Palaearctic Region, occurring throughout the Mediterranean, steppe and deciduous woodland zones, including these zones in eastern Asia. Although present throughout southern and central Europe, it is absent from most of the Iberian peninsula and northern parts of France and Germany. In the British Isles, it does not appear on the British mainland or the Normandy coast; however, it is present in Jersey and Sark of the Channel Islands, and on the Scilly Isles in a form originally named as a separate species but now reckoned to be a sub-species, *Crocidura suaveolens cassiteridum.*

Conservation   Shrews are preyed upon by owls, kestrels, weasels and to a lesser degree by domestic cats. Other predators include foxes, otters, stoats and the European wildcat.

Although the lesser white-toothed shrew does not qualify as an endangered species, it should however be treated in some parts of its range as a threatened one. The disappearance of suitable habitat for it to live in is undoubtedly the crucial factor governing whether the shrew can be supported in some regions.

The life-cycle and ecology for this species is as yet so poorly known that no useful assessment can be made to determine how numerous it still is throughout its considered range and how many related forms are in competition with it.

Until comparatively recently there were considerable difficulties involved in catching live specimens and keeping them in a captive environment. But during the last decade, great progress has been made in research on shrews under laboratory conditions.

Considered as a 'relict' species in some parts of its distribution, and scarce in other regions, it is important to draw attention to this often overlooked form. Further investigations on the biology and development of the lesser white-toothed shrew should be carried out to serve as a basis for a deeper knowledge of its true status.

Corbet, G. B. (1966): *Terrestrial Mammals of Western Europe*, pp. 116–18. **Cranbrook**, Earl of and **Crowcroft**, P. (1968): 'The white-toothed shrews of the Channel Islands'. **Crowcroft**, P. (1957): *Life of the Shrew*; (1963): 'Shrews',

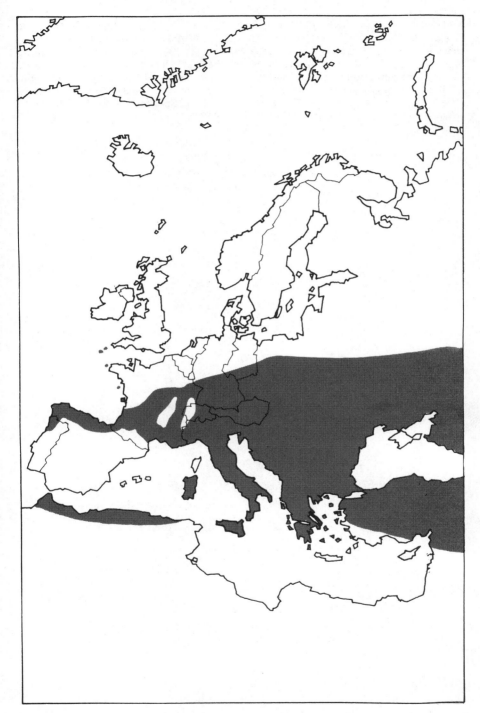

in *Animals of Britain, No. 17.* **Godfrey**, G. K. (1976): 'The ecological distribution of *Crocidura suaveolens* in Jersey'. **Millais**, J. G. (1904): *Mammals of Great Britain and Ireland, Vol. 1*, pp. 140–53. **Pernetta**, J. C. (1973): 'The ecology of *Crocidura suaveolens cassiteridum* (Hinton) in coastal habitat'. **Rood**, J. P. (1975): 'Observations on population structure, reproduction and moult of the Scilly shrew'. **Smit**, C. J. and **Wijngaarden**, A. van (1976): 'Threatened mammals'. **Southern**, H. N. (1964): *Handbook of British Mammals*, pp. 222–3. **Spencer-Booth**, Y. (1963): 'A coastal population of shrews'. **Vlasak**, P. (1972): 'The biology of . . . *Crocidura suaveolens*'.

Pyrenean Desman

Galemys pyrenaicus

Status: A relict species that could be on the way to extinction, should its restricted range not be properly safeguarded from the desmans' chief adversity, the menace of water pollution

Description   The very existence of this Insectivoran species was not known about in the scientific world until 1811. Its general appearance is more that of a shrew than a mole; and although it belongs to the mole family Talpidae, it is regarded as the connecting link between shrews and moles. Internally, desmans are fairly primitive, having the full complement of 44 mammalian teeth, and a skeleton that shows certain ancient features.

The most remarkable thing about the appearance of the desman is its long and extremely mobile naked snout which has a trumpet-shaped end to it; hence it was originally known as the 'Trumpet Rat'. Structurally the desman is adapted to an aquatic species: the long tail which has a web of stiff hairs is laterally compressed at the end to act as a rudder; the legs and feet are proportionately very long, powerful and 'disengaged' from the body; the hind feet are webbed and all the feet bear fringes of hairs; the nostrils open on the upper surface of the snout and are protected by valves; the ears can shut on submersion; and the pelage consists of a dense underfur and flattened, water repellent guard-hairs.

Whereas the Pyrenean desman's tail is laterally flattened only at the end, in the other species, the Russian desman *Desmana moschata*, it is compressed for most of its length. The latter species is a much bigger animal, being twice the size of the Pyrenean desman.

The remarkably soft, thick glossy fur is completely waterproof. It is made up of two layers: down that is tightly packed and waterproof, and the outer layer of long hair which facilitates the running-off of water. The fur ranges from dark brown to a shiny anthracite grey, becoming lighter to a dirty white under its stomach, and even appears shiny silver in some lights.

On the ground its body is more often hunched up, forming a ball of fur from which one can only see emerging the tail, the snout and the feet armed with strong white curved claws. Its head is sunk deep into its shoulders. The eyes are minute, and due to the perpetual movement of the animal are almost invisible. The ears are buried in the fur. It is probable that the desman hardly perceives more than a general variation of light. Its hearing, on the other hand, is extremely acute. The front of the face is almost hidden by a mass of whiskers; the whiskers on its trunk-like muzzle are probably tactile organs used to locate underwater prey. The mouth is like a small round hole. There are large glands opening under the tail that let out an odour causing the animal to smell strongly of musk.

The Pyrenean desman's body length is 10.0–13.5 cm; the tail length 13.0–15.5 cm, the snout about 2.0 cm and the hind-foot 3.1–3.8 cm. The weight varies between 50 and 80 g.

Habitat   The Pyrenean desman is found in fast-flowing mountain streams, clear well-oxygenated rivers, lakes, marshes, clear mill-streams and canals. In large rivers it is confined to places where the bank is steep and covered with vegetation. Cover is important, in the form of crevices in rock or holes under roots of trees. It is found in altitudes ranging from 65 to 1200 metres; and it burrows in the banks of water-courses. In summer it has been found in tussocks of grass and under haycocks.

Behaviour   In the water the desman comes into its own. It can float like a cork, with its body held so high that the paws often beat the air when it is searching for foodstuff in the moss of surrounding rocks. Sometimes it dives vertically, bounding out of the water in order to leave the surface. Sometimes it swims slowly just under the surface with only its trunk showing above. At other times it descends to the bottom, crossing the depth of water like lightning. Then it will follow the river bed, which it apparently works over with its trunk, as if it were walking with its front paws, with the back paws paddling or holding the body by opposition between two objects. Sometimes it will come up like a cork, bounding from the surface straight to the top of a rock which is sticking out of the water.

In spite of its incontestable adaptation to aquatic life, the desman is not unendowed with means for operating on land. It is perfectly capable of moving itself rapidly and climbing along the river banks. A desman has a peculiar gait, with the front legs being slightly bowed, and its movement is reported to be somewhat rolling and relatively slow. It walks on its toes, and has proved to be more of a skilful acrobat than a good walker.

8

Since desmans do not travel far from water they are dispersed along rivers. They probably lead predominantly solitary lives. They are nocturnal, only occasionally active in daytime during cloudy and dull weather. They are very agile animals and can become agitated very easily. That remarkable snout is reputed to be responsible for all their sensitive contact with the Universe!

Diet Water provides the desman's main hunting area, but it is also known to hunt on land. Its voice is a characteristic high-pitched humming. It swims with its hindfeet and feeds almost entirely on the riverbed, its movements on the bottom having been likened to those of a mole in soft soil.

Due to the difficulty of observing the animal in the wild state, feeding behaviour can only properly be observed in captivity. The desman does not eat under water but on dry land; although it frequently wets larger prey while eating it. When eating, it sits on the solid tripod formed by its back feet and tail. Its forepaws are then used either to hold its prey to the ground, or to direct it towards its mouth, or else to remove from its mouth some awkward piece. However, food is usually held with the trunk, which is used just in the same manner as the trunk of an elephant — for feeding, directing, holding or pushing things into the mouth.

Desmans usually prey upon aquatic insects, crustaceans and alevins. Richard and Viallard often discovered that when trout were caught in the same nets as a desman, the trout were never attacked; it was the same in an aquarium. However, when the fish is in poor condition and of a small size, the desman may attack it, but will only eat it if it can bring it to dry land, which is only possible with small prey. In captivity the desman has shown signs of a preference for small aquatic fauna, of which it breaks the most fragile shells. It accepts fauna ranging from worms to arthropods. When very hungry it may devour all sorts of animal foods, even giblets of meat from butchered animals: but it is quite probable that these last two items of diet do not agree with it and that these have been responsible for losses during the breeding season. The quantity of food taken in is very large, as one would expect for a small insectivore. Recently captured animals, who may have had to fast for several hours, are quite capable of engulfing the equivalent of their own entire weight in a very short time.

Breeding Desmans of both sexes, like most insectivores, are very aggressive. It is probable that the aggression only disappears during the rutting period, which is considered to be very brief (as is also the case with other insectivores: several hours for the mole and the European shrew), and of course during milk-feeding between the female and the young.

In the male, sexual activity begins in November, reaches a peak between January and May and subsides slowly to complete quiescence between August and September. Oestrus in the female begins in January and is protracted. The first pregnant female appears in January, the last in June. A gestation period has not been firmly established; but parturition occurs between March and July with 1—5 young being born, although 2—4 is the most frequent litter size. The young weigh less than 50 g. The females are polyoestrous and can bear 2—3 litters a year.

Population Because of its tendency to conceal itself, no estimates of the numbers of the animal living in the distribution area can be made. However, one indication as to a population density was recorded by A. Peyre in 1955 when 79 individuals were trapped in the French Pyrenees; thirteen years later Richard and Viallard, who systematically trapped desmans in the same area, only took 31 animals of which 17 were males and 14 females.

Distribution   The desmans reached their apogee during the Miocene period. The majority of the various species have since disappeared, and the two that remain are localised relict forms, widely separated from each other.

The Pyrenean desmans are distributed along streams on both sides of the Pyrenean Mountains and in the mountainous regions of northern Spain and Portugal. In general, the same area is still inhabited, for the species is confined to the Pyrenees and the north-western half of Iberia. The canals of the French Pyrenees seem to be particularly favoured habitats.

The other species, the Russian desman, is found in the basins of the Volga and Don and on some Siberian rivers.

Field researchers have never been able to find the least trace of the desman's presence in its natural surroundings without having to resort to trapping. After a year of such systematic trapping and banding in the Pyrenees, it was found that the Pyrenean desman is very attached to a definite area (of which the greatest length varies from about 30 metres to 200 metres at the most), and one finds it there throughout the year. When removed from its original home range and placed elsewhere, it is capable of returning to it: one female returned from about 1500 metres; another female in the month of March covered 450 metres in 7 hours.

Conservation   Because this species is bound to a very vulnerable habitat in a very restricted area, its food supply is menaced by water pollution and its habitat by the construction of hydro-electric plants. As G. B. Corbet has summarised: 'The desmans are clearly not a very successful group. The restricted range can probably be attributed to the high degree of specialisation for a habitat that is itself discontinuous and is more than usually dependent upon climatic conditions; it must be montane without being extremely cold'.

The importance of getting to know an animal well in its natural habitat is well recognised. Once having achieved an understanding of the complexity of its relationship to its habitat, one should be able to emulate natural conditions in a controlled environment, in order to facilitate successful breeding. But regrettably, in the case of the desman, because it lives mostly in mountain torrents it passes almost unnoticed from the river banks and so escapes the observation of naturalists. It is for this reason that systematic trapping has proved to be necessary.

Initially, scientists encountered considerable difficulties in studying this animal's behaviour because of its inability to withstand captivity. However, now that the desman's life history and habits are more fully understood, it is hoped that experimental breeding programmes will soon get under way in places like the National Centre of Scientific Research at Moulis (Artiège), where a breeding nucleus has already been established.

In 1973 it was reported that P. B. Richard, who for the previous two years had been ringing the Pyrenean desman at Artiège in the French Pyrenees, had then found that the desman had ceased to exist in the area – the cause of this being completely unknown. It is therefore of crucial importance to draw attention to the plight of this relict species: soon it will disappear, if it cannot be assured waterways free of pollution, and other necessary environmental safeguards.

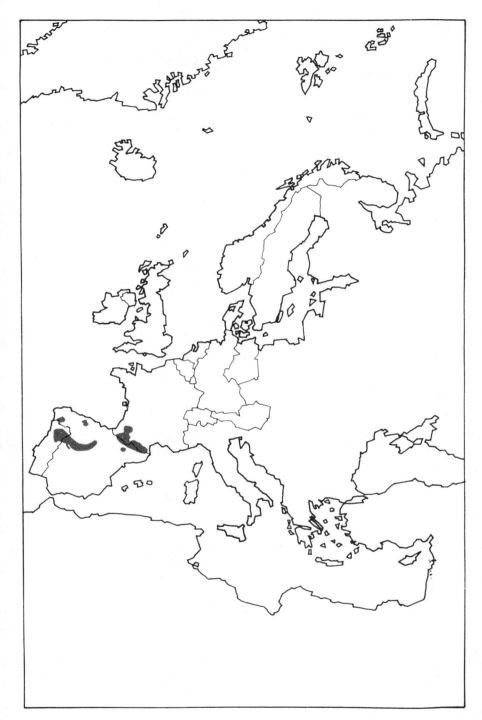

11

Collins (1975): *Collins Encyclopedia of Animals*, pp. 598—9. Corbet, G. B. (1966): *Terrestrial Mammals of Western Europe*, pp. 100—1. Larousse (1972): *Encyclopedia of Animal Life*, p. 492. Oryx (1973): *Vol. XII*, No. 1, pp. 27—8. Peyre, A. (1956): 'Ecologie et biogeographie du desman'. Puissegur, C. (1935): 'Recherches sur le desman pyrénées'. Richard, P. B. and Viallard, A. V. (1969): 'Le desman des pyrénées'. Richard, P. B. (1973): 'Le desman des pyrénées'. Sanderson, I. T. (1955): *Living Mammals of the World*, p. 52. Simon, N. (1969): *Red Data Book: Mammalia*, *Vol. 1*. Smit, C. J. and Wijngaarden, A. van (1976): 'Threatened mammals'. van den Brink, F. H. (1973): *A Field Guide to the Mammals of Britain and Europe*, pp. 42—3.

12

Greater Horseshoe Bat

Rhinolophus ferrum-equinum

Status: Rapidly declining in western Europe, having virtually died out in the north-western regions. In Great Britain, its population has declined by at least 90% within the last 25 years

Description Bats are one of the most distinctive groups among mammals and have many affinities with the order Insectivora. They are an extremely old group, fossil bones of recognisable bats having been found in the Middle Eocene rocks which were formed on lake bottoms at least fifty million years ago, and other remains that are almost certainly those of bats in the Palaeocene rocks which were first formed soon after the age of the dinosaurs.

A bat is the only mammal capable of true and controlled flight, for it has true wings consisting of flexible membranes of skin which are attached to the sides of the body and also to the arms, the legs and sometimes the tail. The forearm and four of the fingers are greatly elongated, supporting the wing-membrane. The first digit of the hand is always free of the membrane and bears a claw which is used mainly for climbing. The hind-toes are always free and bear long, curved claws, which are used for combing the fur as well as for hanging from a support during resting periods. The head may be short and broad, with powerful jaws and teeth; or long and slender, with weak teeth and a long tongue.

The order Chiroptera, meaning 'wing-handed', represents the various families of bats. It is divided into two suborders: Megachiroptera, comprised of only one family, Pteropidae – the common fruit bats or 'flying foxes' of Asia, Africa, and Australasia to the Pacific; and Microchiroptera, which embraces the rest of the order, divided into 16 families which are world-wide in distribution.

John Hooper remarks that to the uninitiated, many bats look remarkably alike, and identification involves a detailed knowledge of facial and other characteristics. But with the horseshoe bats there is no problem. The grotesque nasal membrane, or nose-leaf, is unmistakable. This most prominent feature, just above the upper lip, is a flattish disc of skin, shaped like a horseshoe – hence the name of the species. The two nostrils form conical depressions in the centre of the horseshoe and immediately above them and projecting forwards is a wedge-shaped protuberance known as the sella. Above this, but pointing upwards, is a slender spear of tissue known as the lancet. This description serves for both the greater and the lesser horseshoe bats, although there are minor differences in shape. However, there is no need to confuse the two, as their difference in size is very obvious: the forearm of the greater horseshoe bat is over 50 mm, whereas the forearm of the lesser is under 41 mm.

The ears of the horseshoe bat are large, broad at the base, tapering to a sharp point, the front edge being curved so that the point is directed backwards. The mouth is large and has 32 teeth, the canines being particularly conspicuous; the upper incisor and the first upper and second lower premolars are minutely small.

The eyes are set close in to the nose-leaf and are small in comparison with those of some other species. How much it uses its eyes, or how good are its powers of definition, is a matter for conjecture, but scientists have established that a horseshoe bat can certainly distinguish light from dark. However, in darkness the bat avoids obstacles with uncanny skill, relying on its powers of hearing (see **Behaviour**, page 15). The fur is thick, and woolly to silky in texture, and extends a short distance on to both surfaces of the wing membranes. The colour of the fur can vary considerably from one bat to another. The dorsal surface is usually ashy brown, the underside pale buff, although it is considered that a good general description is 'tawny-brown'. Immature specimens are much greyer than the adult, although grey adults are not uncommon. The wings are brown and have a pinkish cast to them. The females are usually larger than the males.

The head and body length of the greater horseshoe bat is about 65 mm (up to

68 mm); forearm 54 mm (up to 58 mm); tail about 40 mm; and it has a wingspan varying from 330 to 385 mm. In the British Isles, H. N. Southern records that the weight varies considerably throughout the year, with a maximum in December when an average male weighs 20.6 g (heaviest 23.4 g) and an average female 21.6 g (heaviest 27.3 g). By April, the male's weight has decreased by approximately 25% and the female's by approximately 28%.

Habitat   During the winter, horseshoe bats tend to seek out underground passages, ruins and caves, since these provide seclusion, darkness and an even temperature to hibernate in. Limestone rock is often deeply pierced by natural caverns, and these are constantly inhabited by the bats. Man-made tunnels are equally acceptable, such as mines, stone quarries and so forth.

Colonies sometimes occur in the roofs of houses, barns, cathedrals and in other types and parts of buildings, including cellars. There are also records of horseshoe bats in the summer utilising the cavities provided by hollow trees.

Behaviour   The species is usually gregarious; however, the greater horseshoe bat sometimes sleeps as a solitary individual as well as in the familiar clusters. These latter may comprise just a handful of bats or they may be big groups of a hundred or more. J. Hooper records that in such clusters, the bats pack themselves tightly together into an almost amorphous mass of wings and fur and noses; on one occasion he counted 45 bats in an area little larger than a page in a book. This gregariousness occurs more frequently during the colder spells, but the bats show no particular consistency over their sleeping habits, and a greater horseshoe found in a cluster one week may be in an entirely different group the following week, or could equally well be found hanging quite alone. These clusters are considered to be in fact merely temporary groupings. An individual horseshoe bat will sometimes return many times to the same tunnel, or even to the same patch of roof, but usually it appears to settle more or less at random. Whilst sleeping, the bats wrap their wings tightly round their bodies, rather like dark silken cloaks, and when seen from a distance, give the impression of some strange brown fruit hanging from the rock by their toes.

The most spectacular behavioural characteristic of bats is undoubtedly their development of sonar. Through experiments it was long ago noted that covering the eyes of bats did not impair their powers of flight nor cause them to collide with things whilst in the air. They maintained their uncanny and unerring ability to avoid even hundreds of piano wires stretched at all angles across a small room. But if one ear of a bat was taped down, it flew round in circles and bumped into obstacles; and if both ears were taped down, it could hardly fly at all and crashed into the first obstruction.

It has been found that most species of Microchiroptera bats find their way predominately by echo-location. The horseshoe bat is highly specialised in this sense. During flight it emits high-pitched sounds, at a frequency of about 80,000 cycles per second; these are directed forward and focused by the curiously shaped 'horseshoe' around the nostrils — and usually above the limit of human hearing. The sound waves reflected by obstacles or prey are perceived by the ears. When a horseshoe bat is in flight, it continuously turns its head from side to side and up and down. At the same time, its ears swivel rapidly from side to side also, sometimes together and sometimes independently, so that its sensitive hearing system can derive the maximum of information from the returning echoes. Evidently it knows where it is so exactly that it can turn upside down while still in flight, and skilfully hook on, head downwards, just at the instant of coming to rest. In addition to its high frequency sounds, the horseshoe bat can also produce lower frequency noises which are perfectly audible to man: these are squeaking or 'chittering' sounds.

Results of bat banding show that they move only over small distances, and their movements are usually local; the longest flight recorded in England for this species is 40 miles. It usually flies low (2–3 ft), but sometimes higher (10 ft). The flight is heavy and butterfly-like, with frequent glides. The bats emerge from their roosting places rather late and fly at intervals throughout the night. Even during hibernation, which lasts from October to the end of March, the bats often shift their quarters within the hibernation caves at intervals during the winter; it is possible that at these times they feed upon insects in the caves.

Diet   Horseshoe bats hunt only in the dark. Their food consists of beetles, moths, other nocturnal insects and spiders. Larger prey is pouched against the wing membrane during manipulation in flight (unlike some bats the horseshoe has no tail membrane to be folded forwards to form a pouch), and is often taken to the roost to be eaten; small insects are devoured on the wing. Some prey is caught by the bat dropping on the ground with outstretched wings; in other cases the flight is only a few inches above ground level and wingless and other insects are picked up off it as the bat passes.

Under the feeding haunts of the horseshoe bat one can find discarded wings, wing cases, legs and other indigestible insect remains. Studies of these insect remains have shown that the summer diet of this species includes many large insects such as cockroaches, various large black dung beetles and ground beetles, as well as moths and spiders. Some authorities record that the lesser horseshoe bat tends to go for slightly smaller 'game', even as small as gnats, but also eats many moths.

Breeding   Mating occurs in the autumn and there is no permanent pairing. The sperm is stored during the winter in the uterus, also in a white jelly-like plug which completely occludes the vagina. Ovulation occurs once the female starts to become active again after hibernation, usually about April, with subsequent fertilisation by the stored sperm from the uterus. Thus, the weather conditions in the spring not only affect the time when the bats emerge from the caves, but can advance or delay the date of birth of the young.

The breeding rate of horseshoe bats is low: only one offspring is born every year, between mid-June and mid-July, more usually in July. The young bat is blind at birth, clinging helplessly to its mother with feet, claws and mouth. The eyes open at 10 days, and it is able to fly short distances when it is about 22 days, just prior to being weaned. By mid-August most juveniles are independent. By the autumn, they have grown to adult size and, apart from their slightly darker fur, are not easy to distinguish from the adults when they all begin to gather in their winter haunts.

Some segregation of sexes is apparent in the nursing colonies, where it is reported that young-bearing females are usually accompanied by non-breeding immature females and a few immature males. The mean lifespan is put at about 7 years, although many live to 15 years and recent reports of ringed individuals have recorded ages of up to 24 years.

16

Population   The overall size of greater horseshoe bat populations is decreasing. P. A. Racey and R. E. Stebbings state: 'the only objective evidence of population changes comes from observations made on bat roosts where individuals can more easily be identified and captured.'

In Britain, for example, the greater horseshoe bat's main area of distribution is now bounded by Devon, Dorset, Wiltshire and Gloucestershire. The British Mammal Society has had the three main centres of population under continuous observation: in 1971, the total number of this species was estimated (by mark and recapture methods) to be about 500. Estimates made in 1955 indicated that colonies were then at least five times the size of the colonies in 1972. In a more recent estimation, R. E. Stebbings goes on to report that in the United Kingdom between the years 1950 and 1975, the greater horseshoe bat population has declined by at least 90%.

Distribution   The greater horseshoe bat ranges over central and southern Europe, eastward through southern Russia and Asia Minor, and also occurs in Palestine, Persia, the Himalayas, China, Korea, Japan, Algeria and Morocco.

In Great Britain, it is locally common in the south-west of England, and south and west Wales, and occurs in most southern counties eastward to Kent. It does not occur in the north of England, and is absent from both Scotland and Ireland. It is present in the Channel Islands, although considered to be quite rare there.

C. J. Smit and A. van Wijngaarden record that in France the species occurs all over the country except in the mountains of the Massif Central. In Luxemburg, it is found everywhere, especially in the old fortifications of the city of Lumerburg. In Belgium, it is found only in the south-eastern provinces of Luxemburg and Namur; in the Netherlands, only in the southern part of the province of Limburg. In Spain and Portugal it occurs throughout the Iberian peninsula and on the Balearic Islands. In the Federal Republic of Germany, it occurs in rather low numbers in the Rhine Valley between Kaiserstuhl and the Mainz basin, and more numerously in a few places in Bavaria. In Poland it has been observed in recent years, as a straggler. In Switzerland, it occurs in the western, central and south-eastern parts of the country. In Austria it is common in some areas and is ringed regularly. In Italy, it occurs over the whole country, as well as on Sicily, Sardinia, Capri, Elba and other islands. In Czechoslovakia, relatively small populations occur in caves in the southern part of Slovakia. In Hungary, it is found in the Karst mountains in the north-eastern part of the country. In Rumania, it occurs in the central and southern parts of the country. In Yugoslavia, it is common in some regions, and on islands in the Adriatic. In Albania, it is recorded to be the most common bat species in the country. In Bulgaria, it occurs in caves throughout the country. In the U.S.S.R., it is found along the southern coast of the Crimea, in the Caucasus, and in the eastern part of the province of Baku. It occurs on the island of Cyprus, and in Turkey is found on the northern and southern coasts of Anatolia and along the Bosphorus.

Conservation   Horseshoe bats have few natural enemies, although the examination of pellets from barn and tawny owls has shown that hibernating bats form a large part of their diet in the months of December and January. But the species has virtually died out in north-west Europe, and in Great Britain is now considered to be an endangered species.

The numbers of almost all bat species are rapidly declining throughout western

17

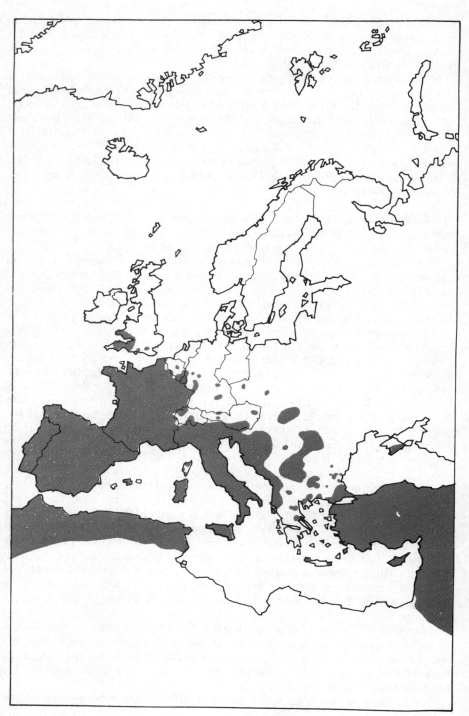

Europe. This is considered to be mainly due to the widespread use of insecticides, to which they are highly susceptible and which also reduce their food supply. Other reasons are the increasing popularity of caving as a sport and the demolition and restoration of old buildings: both of these give rise to the general disturbance of bats during hibernation, as well as depriving them of suitable habitats to roost in.

In 1970, R. E. Stebbings reported that the need to protect bats was becoming increasingly important. He listed the main causes for the decline in bat populations, as well as some conservation proposals. In 1972, with P. A. Racey, Stebbings summarised the status of bats in Britain as follows: 'Of the 14 species, the status of two, the greater horseshoe and mouse-eared bats, is precarious. The survival of these and other cavernicolous species depends on the availability of underground roosts, many of which are being destroyed, or rendered uninhabitable by extensive disturbance during hibernation. There has also been a trade in cave-dwelling bats for museums, schools and research. Where such disturbance is prevented by a grille at the cave entrance, the number of bats using the roost increases. More recently, the World Wildlife Fund has given support for this species by providing money for protective grilles to be put on the entrance of known roosting sites. An appeal in 1975 in connection with the sponsorship of bat boxes has also been most successful.'

Bats are protected by law in the majority of European countries, the exceptions to this being Norway, Belgium, France, Spain, Greece and Turkey. In Rumania it is reported that this species will receive this protection in the near future. With the mouse-eared bat, the greater horseshoe species is one of six wild creatures protected in Great Britain by the Conservation of Wild Creatures and Wild Plants Act 1975.

Legal protection for this species throughout Europe is highly desirable, and the management by nature conservation organisations of caves and subterranean quarries where appreciable numbers hibernate is imperative. The chief objectives of the International Council for the Protection of Endangered Bats are: (1) to obtain a representative in each country/region; (2) to obtain and disseminate information and to provide material for public education; (3) to serve as a consultatory body to organisations and governments on matters relating to bats; (4) to obtain governmental support for programmes sponsored by this council; (5) to publicise problems of worldwide importance such as the effects of pollution; and (6) to formulate codes of conduct for research.

Allen, G. M. (1939): *Bats*. **Baal**, H. J. (1950): 'Some bats of Jersey'. **Burton**, M. (1962): *Systematic Dictionary of Mammals of the World*, pp. 52–3. **Harrison Mathews**, L. (1952): *British Mammals*, pp. 122–3. **Hooper**, J. H. D. (1962): 'Horseshoe bats', in *Animals of Britain, No. 2*; (1964): 'Bats and the amateur naturalist'. **Millais**, J. G. (1904): *Mammals of Great Britain and Ireland, Vol. I*, pp. 24–30. **Racey**, P. A. and **Stebbings**, R. E. (1972): 'Bats in Britain – a status report'. **Smit**, C. J. and **Winjngaarden**, A. van (1976): 'Threatened mammals'. **Southern**, H. N. (1964): *Handbook of British Mammals*, pp. 232–3. **Stebbings**, R. E. (1970): 'Bats in danger'; (1975): *in litt*. **van den Brink**, F. H. (1973): *A Field Guide to the Mammals of Britain and Europe*, p. 47. **Walker**, E. P. (1964): *Mammals of the World, Vol. I*, p. 252.

Large Mouse-Eared Bat

Myotis myotis

Status: Its numbers have decreased alarmingly in recent years and it has now virtually died out in north-west Europe

Description   From earliest times the peculiar traits of bats have aroused the imagination and interest of mankind; indeed as an order, they represent one of the most distinctive groups among mammals. Information concerning the general characteristics, affinities and biology of bats has been explored in some detail in the account of the other bat species included in this book — see **Greater Horseshoe Bat**, p. 13.

The mouse-eared bat belongs to the genus *Myotis* which contains more species than any other genus in the order Chiroptera; the genus is the least specialised of the family Vespertilionidae. Vespertilionid bats have a well-developed lobe in the ear, known as a tragus: it looks somewhat like a small second ear or earlet, and its shape and size are often an aid to species identification. They also have a simple nose, without a nose-leaf, and a fairly long tail with a well-developed inter-femoral membrane (the stretched skin between the thighbones and the tail). The third digit has three phalanges, the second digit is vestigial.

All members of the genus *Myotis* have a slender muzzle, ear and tragus. The average size of the mouse-eared bat makes it larger than any native British species; after the European free-tailed bat *Tadarida teniotis*, it is the largest of the European bats. Its colour is medium-brown, with the dark coat on the back contrasting strongly with a greyish-white underside. There is a clear line of demarcation from the base of the ear to the shoulder.

H. N. Southern records the measurements for the large mouse-eared bat as follows: head and body length 65—79 mm; forearm 57—64 mm; length of ear 27—28 mm, width 17.5—19.0 mm (when laid forward, ear extends about 5 mm beyond muzzle); wing-span 355—412 mm (exceptionally 450 mm). Its weight is put at 18—45 g.

Habitat   The mouse-eared bat chiefly confines itself to buildings and caves, usually living in attics during the summer and hibernating in caves during the winter months.

Behaviour   It is not uncommon for several species of bats to live in the same cave, although in these cases it is usual to find each kind in a separate part of the cave by itself, so that all seem to get on happily together without interference. It is also the case that some species may vary somewhat in preferring either very moist or drier situations. Thus, the barbastelle seem to like the drier parts of caves, while the large mouse-eared bat and its smaller relative Daubenton's bat have been recorded hibernating in such damp places that their fur may be beaded with drops of dew.

The flight of the mouse-eared bat has been described as slow and straight. On the Continent it has been known to travel considerable distances, up to 260 km. It utters a loud strident shriek when either handled or alarmed.

Diet   The bat's diet consists of insects, its nocturnal feeding flights usually alternating with periods of rest, during which time it hangs upside down by its hind feet to digest its catch.

One report recorded by G. M. Allen refers to some *Myotis myotis* being kept in Germany for a period of three months on a diet of mealworms and flies, of which they would at times consume prodigious numbers. For though they ate on average about 20 mealworms a day, they would, if very hungry, take as many as 75 or 80 at a single feeding, and in one case a famished bat consumed over 100.

Breeding   Since in winter the bodily activities of hibernating bats are reduced to a very minimum, it is not surprising that this state extends to the reproductive cells as well. Only a few European bats have been carefully followed through this period, all of which are members of the Vespertilionidae, and in all the process is reported to be essentially the same. During the winter the egg follicle in the ovary slowly enlarges, while the vagina becomes filled by a plug formed from the mucous secretion of its walls. When spring arrives and the bats again come into regular activity, the plug is cast, ovulation takes place, and the egg starts down the oviduct, into which meanwhile the spermatazoa have made their way, and thus fertilisation is effected by means of the stored sperm. The gestation period for *Myotis myotis* has been recorded as 70 days.

The young are born blind and hairless, the eyes opening after about the seventh day. Although there is no exact date for most species, the first flight is taken at about 20—22 days old; the age of sexual maturity is considered to be attained in the second autumn. The lifespan for the genus has been put at 7—12 years.

G. M. Allen relates the classic account by Rollinat and Trouessart (1896) of the breeding habits of *Myotis myotis* which describes parturition as taking about half an hour: 'The first part of the young to appear was its left knee, then the body appeared and was nearly free in twenty minutes more, and completely exuded in another ten minutes. The young in this case is born feet first and is received into the apron formed by the membranes of the mother as she hangs upside down from all four feet; or she may cling upright from the wires of the cage.' These authors found that the female pulls out the placenta, which is eaten, and meanwhile the young one attaches itself to a teat. It is not until the thirtieth day that it hangs itself up beside its mother.

Some further interesting observations on the birth of young in a small brown Myotis bat *Myotis austroriparius*, common in Florida, was reported by H. B. Sherman. Some two dozen pregnant females were secured from an old building. Contrary to the usual rule in this genus, two young were produced by most of these females instead of a single one.

Population   Little is known about the overall status of bats in Europe. Racey and Stebbings report that the mouse-eared bat was common on the continent of Europe until about 1950, but its numbers have decreased alarmingly in recent years. R. E. Stebbings remarks that in the late 1940s there used to be very large colonies of mouse-eared bats in the Netherlands, but by 1970 the species had virtually become extinct there. In the British Isles, its status is uncertain. At the beginning of this century, the naturalist J. G. Millais considered the claim of this large bat to be included in the British list to be so slender that he thought it wisest not to describe the species in full; however, more recent authorities conclude that there were authentic occurrences in Cambridgeshire in 1888 but these could easily have been imported. In more recent years it has only been recorded in Dorset between 1956 and 1966, and in Sussex since 1970.

Distribution   Apart from occasional occurrences in the British Isles, Belgium and the Netherlands, the distribution ranges through Germany, Switzerland, France, Spain and Portugal, Italy, the Balkans, eastern Europe to southern Russia, China, Persia, Afghanistan and Israel. (It is not found in northern Europe.)

Conservation   One of the main reasons for the threatened status of the mouse-eared bat is the same as that endangering the greater horseshoe species; for as both are cave dwellers, they are both suffering from extensive disturbance, exploitation and loss of roosts. Otherwise, in keeping with almost all bat species, whose numbers are rapidly declining throughout western Europe, the mouse-eared bats' decline is mainly caused by the widespread use of insecticides, to which they are highly susceptible.

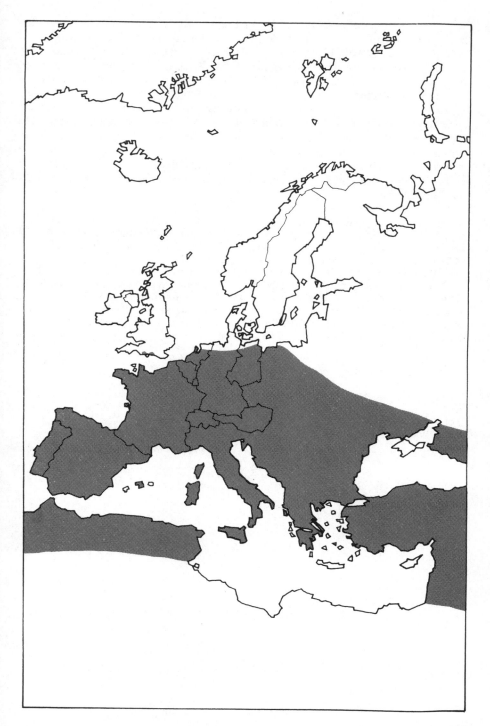

23

Although bats are protected by law in the majority of European countries, they have virtually died out in the north-west part of the Continent. The Conservation of Wild Creatures and Wild Plants Act 1975 includes the mouse-eared bat as one of the six wild creatures afforded protection in Great Britain, for authorities have stated that the chances of it surviving in England are precarious unless roosts are adequately protected.

The aims of the International Council for the Protection of Endangered Bats are all highly desirable: namely to obtain a representative in each country or region; to obtain and disseminate information; and to serve as a consulting body to organisations and governments on matters relating to bats. It is also essential that legal protection throughout Europe be obtained, and that nature conservation bodies organise management of caves and subterranean quarries where appreciable numbers hibernate.

Allen, G. M. (1939): *Bats*. **Blackmore**, M. (1963): 'Bats — noctule, leisler's and serotine', in *Animals of Britain, No. 18*. **Harrison Mathews**, L. (1952): *British Mammals*. **Millais**, J. G. (1904): *Mammals of Great Britain and Ireland, Vol. I*, pp. 105—6. **Racey**, P. A. and **Stebbings**, R. E. (1972): 'Bats in Britain — a status report'. **Sherman**, H. B. (1930): 'Birth of the young of *Myotis austroriparius*'. **Smit**, C. J. and **Wijngaarden**, A. van (1976): 'Threatened mammals'. **Southern**, H. N. (1964): *Handbook of British Mammals*, pp. 234—9. **Stebbings**, R. E. (1975): *in litt.* **van den Brink**, F. H. (1973): *A Field Guide to the Mammals of Britain and Europe*, pp. 56—8. **Walker**, E. P. (1964): *Mammals of the World, Vol. I*, p. 337.

Mountain Hare

Lepus timidus

Status: Extremely common in some regions, although becoming restricted in range and reduced in numbers in others

Description   Hares and rabbits, with pikas, were for a long time lumped together with rodents, and were only distinguished in a distinct suborder, the Duplici-dentata, because they have a small second upper incisor (there is also a third one which only appears in the milk dentition). Perhaps the most important difference is that the incisors of rodents have enamel on the front only, whereas in Lagomorpha (the order that now embraces hares, rabbits, and pikas) it is found on the backs of the teeth as well. As a result hares and rabbits have inferior gnawing abilities to rats and mice. However, as with both rodents and rabbits, the hare's incisor teeth have hard sharp enamel edges for cutting, and, since they grow continuously, never wear out. The molars, broad with hard ridges on their surface, are well adapted for chewing hard vegetation.

All hares are distinguished from rabbits by relatively long ears, long hindlegs and a loping gait. Although considerably bigger than a rabbit, the mountain hare, or blue hare, *Lepus timidus*, is a good deal smaller than the brown hare, *Lepus capensis*. It also has shorter ears, a greyer coat in summer, and at all seasons lacks the black tip to the tail which is characteristic of the brown hare. The coat colour varies in different individuals from a dark grey-brown to a light sandy brown. The ear tips are always black.

There appear to be three annual moults: from white to brown in spring: from brown to brown in autumn; and from brown to white in winter. The Irish race in summer and autumn is more russet than the Scottish race and, especially when the hair is worn, may appear almost foxy red. A yellowish variety is not uncommon in either race.

Watson and Hewson record that Pliny considered mountain hares became white by eating snow! However, experiments show that the winter moult is triggered off by a reduction in day length and conversely that an increase in day length will cause white hares to begin their moult to brown. Once under way, however, the rate of moulting is influenced by prevailing temperatures. The descendants of mountain hares which were transported from Norway to the milder climate of France, in the space of about 40 years ceased to turn white, but became merely blue-grey in the winter. Mountain hares at high altitudes in Scotland remain white for a longer period in winter than those living on lower moors.

The head and body length ranges from 57 to 61 cm in the Alpine race; 46—56.5 cm in the Scottish race; 52—56 cm in the Irish race; and 52—60 cm in Northern Europe. The tail length ranges are 5—6.5 cm, 4.5—7 cm, 4—8 cm, and 5—7 cm respectively. Hind foot 14—14.5 cm, 12—14 cm, 14—15.5 cm, 15—16.5 cm respectively. Ear length 8—9.5 cm, 6—8 cm, 7—8 cm, 8—9.5 cm respectively. Weight 2—3.5 kg, 1.7—4 kg, 2.7—4.2 kg, 2.5—5.8 kg respectively. The males of the Scottish race weigh on average 198 grams less than the females.

Habitat   In the British Isles, G. B. Corbet remarks that the existence of both the mountain hare and the brown hare constitutes the only example of a pair of closely related species with mutually exclusive ranges to be found within the mainland.

H. N. Southern reports that in Scotland the mountain hare is usually found on open moorland and rocky slopes from 1000 to 4000 feet (300—1200 m) but thinly above 2500 feet (750 m). In hard winters it may descend to woodlands and the coast. The tendency to seek cover has been described for Finland, where it prefers boggy willow and birch forest during the winter months. In Ireland it inhabits all relatively open habitats, and in mountainous areas it resorts especially to rock crannies for shelter.

Behaviour   Hares are solitary except in the breeding season and during heavy snow. However, Watson and Hewson record that when a hare runs away from danger, other hares, seeing it running, often join in; but they quickly split up as soon as they are well away from danger. During storms the mountain hares are often known to move to the lee side of a ridge and sit with their backs to the wind — where as many as forty have been known to gather together.

The mountain hare is active mostly just after dawn and in the late afternoon to evening, as well as during the night. It lies up during the day in its 'form' or some other rudimentary shelter, of which it uses several scattered over its home range. It generally crouches low and motionless with its ears down when any type of predator approaches, and does not rise till danger is past. Sometimes it allows a man to come within a few yards, and will allow a dog to come within a foot, generally not moving until the dog pounces. It relies for escape on speed and endurance and especially on intimate knowledge of its own home range, which is traversed by well-used 'pads', passing through hedges and walls by customary known gaps. It swims well, although not unless pressed to do so.

When hurt or terrified, its voice is like a shrill penetrating scream: the sound has been likened to a wailing child. Both sexes make low grunts and the doe has a 'gutteral' pipe to her young. One report alleges that an alarm call is given by grinding the teeth.

Coursed and hunted hares usually cling to their intimately known home range, perhaps 1–2 miles (1½–3 km) in diameter, with great adroitness: when driven out of this area they may then run straight for a distance of 5 miles or more. Their long hind-limbs make them least efficient going downhill, so they usually descend diagonally across the contours. Hares are so vigilant, and have so keen a sense of hearing, that their eyes are nearly always wide open when they are observed by a human. A most attractive report about a tame hare in captivity, published by a Mr Drane in 1894–5, was perhaps the first to record that hares sleep with their eyes closed. Mr Drane recalled: 'One of my first errors was a belief that the hare sleeps with its eyes open, for by no artifice or arrangement could I catch my hare with closed eyes. That was because we had not grown sufficiently intimate to lay aside our "society manners"; but now my hare will sleep, and sleeping dream, with closed eyes, not only in the room where I am but on my lap — nay even in bed with me, for where I am the hare likes to be, if there is no intruder'.

Diet The mountain hare feeds predominantly on heather, and in winter this makes up about 90% of its food. In summer, much of its diet consists of moorland grasses, along with cotton grass, but although the stomach contents when examined vary greatly from hare to hare, heather still remains the predominant food plant. Flowering shoots of cotton grass are keenly sought after in early spring, when they provide the first new growth. In other months food preferences may vary. In winter the hare scrapes away shallow snow with its forepaws to get at the vegetation; and in fact, hares will sometimes eat almost any plant growing on or near moorland, in difficult times.

Hares do not eat such a great variety of food as rabbits, and in comparison are considered to be somewhat selective in their diet. Refection, in which the food is passed twice through the body, occurs in the mountain hare as in other Lagomorpha. During the day the hare produces soft rather moist faeces which it immediately eats. These soft faeces are the end product of the first passage of the food through the digestive tract, particularly the large intestine where minor organisms play an important part in breaking down the plant fibres and releasing their nutrients. During the second passage of the food through the digestive tract the hare's enzymes can reach the nutrients and break them down into an absorbable form. At the end of the second passage through the large intestine most of the water has been extracted, so the faeces are passed as rounded rather dry pellets.

Breeding The mountain hare starts breeding early in the year. Watson and Hewson record that most mature bucks are already in breeding condition by the end of December, and pregnant does are found from February onwards. Some of the earliest litters conceived may not be born, as the small embryos are completely resorbed by the female. Alternatively, some of the embryos of a litter may be resorbed, but the remainder survive to be born. Resorption, which occurs in other hares and in rabbits, spares the female the heavy burden of nourishing embryos or feeding young during bad weather or food shortage.

After a gestation period of 50 days, up to 4 young per litter may be born, but usually only 1–2. During March or April the litters are smaller than in June, when 2–3 young per litter is more common, and 4 occasional. Then litters become small again, until breeding ends in August. This is reported to be a shorter breeding season than for the brown hare; but young born later than August grow slowly and so are less likely to withstand the rigours of an upland winter.

In contrast to the rabbit, which is sparsely covered with fur at birth and has its eyes open at 10 days, the leveret has a thickly-covered pelage, having its eyes open from the start. The number of litters per year has been recorded as 4, but 3 in the doe's first breeding season. No breeding has ever been reported to have taken place in the year of birth: the leverets take about 8 months to attain sexual maturity. They are able to run within a day, are weaned within the first week and become independent soon after.

During the period of lactation the leverets keep close to their hiding places and do not leave them until they are able to nibble vegetable food. Bourlière makes reference to the positions assumed by the mother during lactation. Whereas the wild rabbit may lie on its back, the doe hare sits on its hind-quarters while nursing its young. As soon as the young are able to feed properly the mother will not allow them to suck, and is said to drive them off her regular beat.

Until Professor Hediger's comprehensive work in breeding brown hares at the Basle Zoological Gardens, Switzerland, the details of the breeding processes in hares were not in any way so well known as those of rabbits. In 1944 Hediger built the first breeding station for the hare in captivity. His preliminary trials established that the main difficulty in rearing the brown hare would not be food, but the hare's extreme tendency to flight — i.e. the proverbial fear of the hare — on the one hand, and the fight against parasites on the other (the hare has a susceptibility to coccidiosis, a disease caused by intestinal parasites). Of the dozens of births observed, the size of the litter was never more than 3. Weights of new-born leverets were: single births, 135–170 g; twin births, 100–145 g; triplets, 110–140 g.

More recently, an interesting and valuable comparative study between the brown hare, the domestic rabbit and the endangered volcano rabbit *Romerolagus diazi* has been carried out at the Jersey Wildlife Preservation Trust. Here it was found that the gestation period and the development of young in the volcano rabbit fell between those of the other two species. The figures were, gestation period: domestic rabbit 28 days, volcano rabbit 38–40 days, brown hare 42–44 days; pelage at birth: sparsely covered, covered, thickly covered; eyes open: 10 days, 5–6 days, at birth; eating: 21 days, 15–16 days, 8 days; independent: 42 days, 25–30 days, 17–21 days respectively. We found, just as Hediger did with the brown hare, that the main problems with captive *Romerolagus* appeared to be parasitism (principally coccidiosis) and, to a minor degree, the psychological one of flight.

Hybridisation between the brown hare and the mountain hare has been recorded on numerous occasions. The lifespan of the former species is up to 12 years.

Population   At any one place, hares fluctuate greatly in numbers over a period of years. As far as records go there are two types of information about hare populations: general population trends over many years from series of game-bag records, and population estimates from estate owners and their keepers. The numbers of the mountain hare fluctuate greatly, more so than in the brown hare. Peak populations may be ten times the size of low populations.

Watson and Hewson record that hare densities of 1 per acre occur on a few grouse moors in Scotland, in Aberdeenshire and Banffshire, but densities of 1 per 5 acres are more common, and often only 1 per 10 acres. On the mountains and deer forests of north-east Scotland, hares are much scarcer, at 1 per 100 acres; and on the higher peaks 1 per 300 acres or more. In most of north and west Scotland hares are scarcer still.

H. N. Southern records that high numbers were recorded in Scotland in 1895, 1910, 1930 and 1948. In Inverness-shire, yearly bags can be as many as 550 per 1000 acres. Some reports infer that Irish hare numbers do not fluctuate as violently as the Scottish ones.

Distribution   The mountain hare's range extends over the whole of the Palaeartic Region with outlying populations in the Alps. The hares in North America have been classified as a different species from *Lepus timidus*, but resemble it in size and colour.

The Scottish race was originally confined to the Highlands, but has now been introduced into the Lowlands, the Hebrides, Orkney (Hoy only) and Shetland; also to the northern Pennines, the Peak district and North Wales. The Irish race occupies low as well as high ground, in the absence of the brown hare which, however, has been introduced a number of times and appears to thrive, at least temporarily, in competition with the mountain hare.

Conservation   The mountain hare is preyed upon mainly by golden eagles, foxes, wildcats, stoats and buzzards, but it is the leverets that are especially vulnerable. Sometimes many hares die during snowy weather when food is scarce. These dead hares are usually infested with coccidiosis, roundworms, tapeworms, or other diseases.

As a species they are extensively shot. Many shepherds and farmers on good hare ground add to their income by snaring and shooting hares in winter. Unlike sportsmen on the Continent, who regard the hare as almost equally important to the fox as an object of the chase, British shooters do not value the mountain hare for sport. It is reported that the hare is immune from myxomatosis; consequently hare populations increased in much of western Europe during the 1950s, when the rabbit population was decimated by this imported virus.

The mountain hare has been included in this book in an attempt to make the selection of species as much as possible representative of the zoological orders occurring in Europe. Once this order *Lagomorpha* is included, each of the European mammalian orders are represented in the book by at least one species.

30

Throughout the majority of the species' European range, it is afforded some type of protection through hunting legislation. The Irish race is coursed, and up until recently numbers have been imported into England too for this purpose. In October 1975, the British Government passed an Act making hare coursing matches illegal (Hare Coursing Act, 1975). This Act was promoted by a welfare lobby, as opposed to being a piece of deliberate conservation legislation. Nonetheless it is hoped that, should further inroads be made by man into the types of habitat where the hare is at present numerous, further legislation will be undertaken by governments in order to ensure that this well-known species may continue to enjoy its established status.

Bourlière, F. (1967): *Natural History of Mammals*. **Burton**, M. (1962): *Systematic Dictionary of Mammals of the World*, pp. 91−3. **Corbet**, G. B. (1966): *Terrestrial Mammals of Western Europe*, pp. 181−4; (1974): 'The distribution of mammals in historic times', in *Changing Flora and Fauna of Britain*, pp. 179−202. **Durrell** G. and **Mallinson**, J. J. C. (1970): 'The volcano rabbit . . . in the wild and at Jersey Zoo'. **Gray**, A. P. (1971): *Mammalian Hybrids*, pp. 90−2. **Harrison Mathews**, L. (1952): *British Mammals*, pp. 142−4. **Hediger**, H. (1947): 'The breeding of field hares'. **Lyon**, M. W. (1903): 'Classification of the hares and their allies'. **Millais**, J. G. (1906): *Mammals of Great Britain and Ireland, Vol. III*, pp. 1−37. **Smit**, C. J. and **Wijngaarden**, A. van (1976): 'Threatened mammals'. **Southern**, H. N. (1964): *Handbook of British Mammals*, pp. 259−62. **Watson**, A. and **Hewson**, R. (1963): 'Mountain Hares', in *Animals of Britain, No. 23*.

Red Squirrel

Sciurus vulgaris

Status: In some regions the competition for food during the hardest part of the winter has produced a significant replacement of the red squirrel by the grey; in other areas the disappearance of habitat has caused a substantial decline

Description   Of all mammalian orders, the rodents have the greatest number of different species. The squirrel family Sciuridae consists of a well-defined group that embraces well over 40 genera and something just less than 400 species. Squirrels are found throughout the world, being absent only from Madagascar, Australasia and the southernmost portions of South America. The European species belong to four genera which display most of the diversity to be found in the family. The red squirrel is the type species, with 42 forms described, although seven of these may be synonyms; size and colour characteristics distinguish these races.

The red squirrel is smaller and more delicately built than the American grey squirrel. Its bones and teeth are consequently smaller, it leaves smaller tracks, and there are some differences in the proportions of parts of its skull. Its hairs are finer and more silky, and in winter the underfur is far denser than in the American species. The two are closely related, separated at the species level only.

The feet of the red squirrel are long and pliant, as we should expect in an animal leading an arboreal life, whilst the tail is long and heavily plumed to help it in maintaining its balance. The characteristic bushy tail of a squirrel serves as a warm wrap in sleep, with the nose buried cosily into the fur. The hind feet have five toes, while on the front feet there are four, the first being a mere stump; they are all furnished with sharp well-curved claws.

The teeth consist of a single pair of incisors, heavily enamelled on the front and stained a reddish colour, in both jaws; one or two pairs of pre-molars in the upper jaw and one pair in the lower jaw; and three pairs of molars in both jaws.

It appears that the colouring of the red squirrel changes with the seasons; the colour is modified in the course of the year by moults in spring and autumn, which take place respectively in May and October; the same hair may pass through three distinct colour phases during its life. In full winter dress, the squirrel, both body and tail, is brownish-grey, becoming ash-grey by the time of the spring moult; the pelage is long and soft, whilst its ears are ornamented with long tufts of hair. In summer its coat is rufous with a dark stripe down the middle of its back. Woolly ash-grey underfur protects the squirrel against winter weather, and the white underparts are covered in finer, denser hair than that of summer. The soles and palms are thickly covered in fur. Hairs of the tail and ear-tufts are shed once a year; the new growth in the autumn is black, becoming brown, rufous and cream in turn. Both sexes are coloured alike, and are of a similar size; young animals are much the same as adults as far as their coats are concerned.

Monica Shorten remarks that very occasionally albino red squirrels are found. There is no black form in the British race, although on the continent such melanics do occur and may be more common than the normal red type in some reas.

The head and body length range is from 210 to 225 mm; tail length 170—195 mm; the hind foot 52—66 mm; and the weight range 260—345 g.

Habitat   Throughout its range the red squirrel is more closely associated with coniferous than with deciduous forest. Mixed woodlands which contain old trees and sheltered sites for nests may also suit red squirrels. Less tolerance is shown towards disturbance of habitat then perhaps anything else; although food, shelter and seclusion are also vital factors in a suitable habitat.

A mixture of tree species is necessary if enough food is to be found at all times of the year, every year. Pine trees have years of heavy crops and others when seed is very scarce. Though the red squirrel is often associated with the Scots pine, the introduced grey squirrel is linked with the oak, other pines, larches and spruces.

Behaviour   The squirrel is one of the few really wild species that the general observer may notice whilst walking in or near to woodlands. J. G. Millais wrote at the turn of the century: 'The red squirrel relieves the monotony of the pheasant cover, and, with the jay and the woodpecker, gives the townsman some cherished recollection of the silvan beauties of our country. The brilliant little eyes, the ease and rapidity of its movements, and the graceful wave of its "shadowy tail" all combine to render it an animal wholly fascinating and delightful to watch'.

The red squirrel is diurnal, with activity peaks in early morning and before dusk, and a minor peak at mid-day. It is a solitary species although little is known of its social organisation or behaviour on the ground. It is likely that, as in other squirrels, visual signals are important for communication; the flicking movement of its tail for example indicates some degree of apprehension.

Its voice is like a rasping chatter, sometimes followed by a hoarse call or whine; the young make a shrill piping cry. It has great agility and speed when climbing and jumping in trees; but it is more hesitant on the ground. Runways, like those made by rabbits, may be found where squirrels cross grassy space from one tree to another. Tree trunks may show roughened, chipped bark when regularly climbed; also sets of three parallel scratches from the claws. Normally, squirrels travel at a height where branches allow easy movement from tree to tree.

The male is very pugnacious in spring, when he drives off others of his own sex from the vicinity of his regular beat. It has been recorded that two red squirrels have been seen fighting on the ground like a couple of rats, locked in each other's embrace, biting, scratching and rolling over and over each other with all the zest and savagery of carnivorous animals!

Squirrels enter water voluntarily, and have been known to cross rivers and lakes; one such report states that a red squirrel swam across a loch in Scotland which was a mile wide. During swimming the hind legs provide the impetus, the forefeet being trailed for much of the time.

Most people think the red squirrel hibernates during the cold winter months and, prior to doing this, lays up large hoards of food to see it through its wakening stages. This is not the case: no squirrel truly hibernates during the cold winter months although the red squirrel's activity is greatly reduced during the colder weather when ice, deep snow and wind inhibit its movements. It buries its food when there is more than enough for immediate needs; but very often it buries items singly, and when it makes a concentrated hoard in a nest or hollow tree, the food often remains there, forgotten.

Diet   Most feeding goes on up in trees, the food collected from the ground usually being carried up before it is eaten. When feeding, squirrels sit up on their hindlegs and hold their food in their forepaws. They are considered to be the most wasteful of animals: whole trees full of nuts are attacked, and their fruit scattered on the ground, with only a few of the nuts eaten.

The most important foods of the red squirrel are seeds from the Scots pine, Corsican pine, European larch and various spruces. Other important food items are: acorns, beech mast, sweet chestnuts, hazel nuts and other tree seeds; buds, shoots, pollen, berries, fungi, bulbs, roots; insects and occasionally eggs and young birds. Although it is considered that the reports of carnivorous squirrels are merely instances of isolated individuals and not characteristic of the normal taste of the species, red squirrels have been observed leaping upon and catching numbers of chaffinches and stealing sparrow chicks from their nests, as well as seizing young pheasants from rearing coops and removing them to devour them up a fir tree.

Squirrels benefit from the presence of ponds, streams or waterlogged tree hollows in their habitat. During hot weather, a squirrel may come to drink every few hours at such a place. Chalk and bone are sometimes gnawed, and earth eaten. The scales from cones are gnawed in search of pine seeds and squirrels are reported to open hazel nuts by cutting a nick from the side of the point, then splitting them lengthwise into equal halves.

Breeding   Squirrels usually pair very early in the year, and generally construct fresh nests each year in which to place their young. The breeding 'dreys' are built by both the male and the female squirrel, and are generally composed of moss and sticks; sometimes they utilise old birds'-nest material for this purpose. The dreys are often lined with leaves, and sometimes a platform is built out from the main stem of the tree and on this the nest is placed. In general appearance, the breeding drey has been likened to the nest of a magpie; but it is more compact, possesses more moss and leaves and has fewer sticks. The opening is at the side, and it has been described as altogether the most comfortable home built by any British mammal!

The red squirrel has normally two breeding seasons in the year, which are often variable, depending on weather and food conditions. The first begins in January and lasts through to April. Mating is associated with much chasing and a chattering call, and after a gestation period of about 46 days most young are born in March, the size of the litter being usually 2–4, although from 1 to 6 young have been recorded. The young are weaned at about 8 weeks, and there is no post-partum oestrus. The female may resume oestrus in June, and the second litter will then be born in July or August, although pregnant females have been found as late as September.

At birth the new-born squirrel weighs 12 g (less than 0.5 oz) and is blind, toothless, with closed ears and no hair other than whiskers. Hair does not appear on its body until the youngster is a week old, and during the next two weeks the downy covering continues to develop; hairs appear on the tail 2 weeks after birth. At 3 weeks the lower incisors appear, followed during the next week by the upper pair. During the 4–5 week stage the eyes and ears open, when the youngster is at an approximate weight of 50 g. By the end of 7 weeks young squirrels have begun to explore outside the 'drey' and have started to sample buds, leaves, bark and other solid foods. The first dentition is almost complete at 10 weeks; milk premolars are cast at 16 weeks, soon after the moult of the juvenile coat, at an approximate weight of 200 g.

Old squirrels, in case of danger, have been observed to remove the young from the nest to some hole in a tree, carrying them one by one in the mouth, just as a cat carries her kitten. Millais records how he observed little ones sitting in a row outside their home just like a flock of young long-tailed tits, all snug and cosy together; and that one of the prettiest sights in the world is to see an old squirrel teaching a young one to jump. The mother is reported to pass the food to each of the infants with her mouth and not with her paws.

The coat of the spring nestling is equivalent to the winter coat of the adult and gets progressively paler until it is moulted out. The first moult is usually seen in June. Summer-born young are similar in coat colours to summer adults, but do not at first have pale tails; they moult into the adult winter coat. Sexual maturity is attained during the year after birth; it is considered that animals born in late summer do not breed until the second breeding period of the following year. A lifespan of up to 10½ years has been recorded.

Squirrels become tame in captivity, especially if taken young. Some authorities report that a group may have to be kept for several years before breeding starts and that their survival in zoo or laboratory conditions is not at all good. However, more recently the essential requirements for squirrels in captivity have been much better known. The breeding successes at the Jersey Wildlife Preservation Trust with the most delicate Sierra Leone Striped Squirrel *Funisciurus pyrrhopus leonis* well illustrate the squirrel's breeding potential, providing sufficient care is taken to satisfy its environmental requirements during a 5-year period: the progeny and descendants of a single original breeding pair came to number over 40 specimens, with at least third generation captive breeding having been recorded.

Population   The numerous records of the traffic in squirrel skins in days gone by at least shed some light on the numbers of the red squirrel: in 1642 a duty was charged per 1000 squirrel skins exported from England; in the mid-nineteenth century, one report recorded that no fewer than 14,123 red squirrels were killed during a 17-year period in one small area of Scotland alone.

In the British Isles, the population of the red squirrel has fluctuated: it approached extinction in Scotland during the late eighteenth and early nineteenth century, then was reintroduced, and spread. During the first decades of this century it suffered a severe decline which was mainly attributed to an epidemic disease, in particular coccidiosis. Now, red squirrels have disappeared in some parts of their former range, as well as becoming scarce in others.

There appears to be little information on densities in different environments, population turnover or factors of natural regulation. It has however been postulated that fluctuations follow a 7-year cycle; and that 1 squirrel in 5 acres is generally considered to be a fairly high density.

Distribution   The red squirrel is found throughout the wooded parts of Eurasia from the tree line south to the Mediterranean coast; it is absent from the Mediterranean islands. It occurs from Ireland in the west (it is uncertain if it was present in Ireland before the introductions of 1815—80) to Japan in the east, but not in the Caucasus, Syria, Persia or Asia Minor. It is present in Eire, Northern Ireland, Wales and Scotland, and absent from the Isle of Man. In England it is rare or absent in much of the midlands and south-eastern region, but present in East Anglia and in the northern and western counties. It occurs in Anglesey, the Isle of Arran, the Isle of Wight and in the Channel Island of Jersey. The British race, *Sciurus vulgaris leucourus*, is not found elsewhere.

Conservation   Although stoats, pine martens, wildcats, foxes, buzzards, goshawks, golden eagles, domestic cats and dogs are all known to prey on the red squirrel, they probably do not make any significant inroads into its population.

The almost complete disappearance of the red squirrel from Scotland during the first part of the nineteenth century was chiefly due to deforestation; and it was only the reintroduction of the species into developing plantations that enabled the red squirrel still to be present in Scotland today. After the first recorded introduction of the American grey squirrel into Britain in 1876, this rival species soon became established; subsequently the red squirrel has become scarce or has even disappeared in the areas fully colonised by the grey.

Throughout its range the red squirrel is closely associated with coniferous forest. In the British Isles, the American grey squirrel has now replaced the red in most of

36

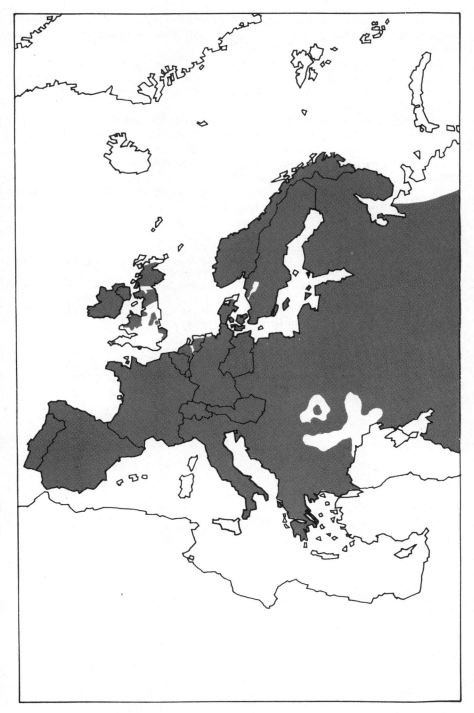

the lowland parts of the country; and in the north the isolation of many of the new coniferous forests may be the red squirrel's only defence against similar replacements.

In eastern Europe, the economic importance attached to the fur of the red squirrel results in its being trapped and exported in enormous numbers; should such trapping activities be increased, it could well result in a serious population reduction.

In 1973, it was reported that an official order permitting the use of 'warfarin' poison to control the grey squirrel, which has become a serious pest of young hardwood plantations in England and Wales, had come into force. Due to the factors of deforestation, trapping, competition from the American grey squirrel and the use of poison within the red squirrel's range, it is of the utmost importance that a close eye is kept on its population; for on the whole the red squirrel has had a history of instability, and over a long period its range has been progressively reduced.

Corbet, G. B. (1974): 'The distribution of mammals in historic times', in *Changing Flora and Fauna of Britain*, p. 195. Duplaix-Hall, N. (1975a): 'Species of wild animals bred in captivity during 1973'. Lydekker, R. (1915): *Wildlife of the World, Vol. 1*, pp. 34–7. Mallinson, J. J. C. (1975): 'Notes on a breeding group of Sierra Leone Striped Squirrels'. Millais, J. G. (1905): *The Mammals of Great Britain and Ireland, Vol. II*, pp. 142–58. Oryx (1973): *Vol. XII*. Shorten, M. (1962): 'Red squirrels', in *Animals of Britain, No. 6*. Southern, H. N. (1974): *Handbook of British Mammals*, pp. 268–75.

European Beaver

Castor fiber

Status: The re-introduction of the species into a number of regions within its former range has proved to be successful. Its population has increased from a few hundred in 1920 to some 50,000 at the present time

Description   The beavers, skilful architects and engineers of the northern forest waterways, make up a single recent genus with two species: the type species the European beaver *Castor fiber*, and the Canadian beaver *Castor canadensis* (although some taxonomists consider the two forms to be so similar that they recognise only one species). The several European sub-species differ from each other only very slightly.

The European beaver is the largest rodent in Europe and the second largest in the world (the largest is the South American capybara *Hydrochoerus hydrochaeris*). Beavers have a thick-set, heavy external form, and an unusually dense coat consisting of fine underfur overlaid with coarse guard hairs. The soft, short underfur usually has a slight tinge of lead colour; the long, coarse, shiny guard hairs mask and protect the underfur except on the lighter-coloured under parts where they are not so long or closely set. The upper parts are rich glossy brown or yellowish brown, and the under parts brown to tawny. The tail and feet are black.

The small eyes have nictitating membranes, the inner eyelid closing when the animal submerges; and both the short ears and the nostrils are valvular. The legs are short and each limb has five clawed digits. The broad, paddle-like tail is flattened horizontally, covered with large scales, and mostly naked.

E. P. Walker relates that paired scent glands known as 'castors' occur in both sexes, but they are largest in the male; these castors release a pleasant-smelling musk which is deposited on piles of stones or mud as a marker. The skull of the beaver is massive. The incisors are strongly developed and the high-crowned cheek teeth have flat grinding surfaces and numerous enamel folds, but these do not grow throughout life.

The head and body length is about 75—90 cm; the tail is 28—38 cm long and 10—14 cm wide, the hind foot 16—18 cm long, and the weight range is 14—38 kg.

Habitat   Beavers live beside waterways through heavily wooded regions or alongside old river beds and lakes. Woods of oak, ash, alder, elm, willow, poplar and birch with undergrowth are preferred.

Behaviour   Some of the habits of the beaver are well known, in particular their ability in tree-felling and dam-building. The great Swedish scientist Linnaeus wrote about the beaver that 'in the art of building he is surpassed by no living creature except man. With his admirable cleverness he regulates the level of the water outside his house, he digs channels and builds roads for the transport of his necessaries from the forest'.

Beavers build dams across the watercourse, upstream and downstream from the house. A dam is built higher than the water level and may be kept in repair for years, while the impounded waters may form ponds many acres in extent. It would seem that the purpose of these dams is to hold constant the water level of the pool on which the 'lodge' is built.

The Canadian beaver generally builds its lodge to serve as a permanent habitation, whereas the European beaver builds lodges like those of its North American relative only in certain remote parts of its range, particularly in Scandinavia and Russia; otherwise, where the bank of the river permits, it makes long burrows opening under water. It is reported that the beavers of the Rhone valley appear to have lost the habit of dam-building since the Middle Ages. However, it is considered probable that complete protection would cause the habit to re-appear, since rudimentary houses have been built by some individuals in semi-captivity.

The lodges, which are especially characteristic of the Canadian beaver, are generally surrounded by water and form islands made up of sticks and mud erected in much the same manner as the dam. The shelter has one or more underwater entrances below the ice level and a sleeping platform above the water level. The dome of the lodge is composed of boughs that always remain permeable to air, providing the chamber below with proper ventilation even in the depth of winter. The interior of the lodge consists usually of only a single chamber.

The whole business of cutting timber, hauling stones, building dams across running streams and small lakes, digging and transporting special mud to plaster them, excavating long canals to bring additional water, erecting houses, with complex entrances, internal flooring and other devices, and spending months of labour cutting special sticks and anchoring them in the mud at the bottom of the watercourse, is considered to be directed at but a single objective — namely to provide a safe winter home, with ample food supply under the winter ice, in which to raise young.

Beavers are often thought of as the 'engineers' of the animal kingdom. They work together in family communities with full co-operation and considerable discipline under the guidance of experienced individuals, thereby accomplishing engineering works of prodigious extent and great accuracy. But recent studies have shown that they appear to do the whole thing entirely mechanically. In many cases the dams are not in fact built where they would be the most efficient, and as Bourlière records 'the constant labour of reconstruction of the dams carried out by members of a colony seems to correspond with a deep physiological need. It seems that beavers have an inner need to obstruct all flowing water.'

Despite their lack of practical forethought on some fronts, beavers appear in other ways to draw upon sources of information that are difficult to comprehend. Consider their apparent ability to judge accurately the height of floods that are not going to materialise for several months: how do they know so exactly how far water is going to be backed up by a dam and just what pressures and stresses it will exert?

The members of a beaver colony — in Europe, a colony consists, almost without exception, of a single family, parents, young of the year and young of the preceding year — generally get on amiably together. They are mainly nocturnal, and on the whole shy, emerging just before sunset when they seek food and work on their dams and lodges. They walk on land rather slowly and clumsily, but swim and dive excellently. They have been recorded as remaining submerged for up to fifteen minutes, although a normal submersion lasts for about five to six minutes. They are thought to give warning of danger by slapping the water with their broad paddle-like tails as they dive. In addition to the warning dive, beavers have a 'quiet' dive which they use when undisturbed.

The beaver has the unusual distinction of being host in a commensal (food-sharing) arrangement to a beetle, *Platypsyllus castorsis*; this beetle is specific to the beaver, living in the coat and feeding on the mites which also live in the fur.

Diet In the autumn large quantities of trunks and big branches are felled by the beaver, using a gnawing action of the lower teeth, with the upper teeth acting as levers. The trees are then cut into sections which can be handled readily and dragged down a slope to the water, or in more level areas, floated to the pond through a number of beaver-made canals. The sticks and logs are then sunk in front of the entrance to the burrow or lodge to act as a store for winter food; for although beavers do not hibernate, their activity is greatly reduced during the colder months.

In summer, beavers eat a wide variety of green food: most aquatic plants along with thistles and meadow-sweet, and also leaves, twigs, seeds, and roots of deciduous trees and shrubs such as willow, alder and birch. But throughout the rest of the year the staple diet is bark. Conifers are eaten much less frequently than deciduous trees.

Breeding   Beavers normally pair for life, being one of the few species of mammals in which successive litters overlap in their period of dependence upon the parents. Mating takes place towards the end of the winter, usually in February, and 2–5 young are born in the burrow or lodge, after a gestation period of 9–12 weeks. The young or kits are born fully furred with their eyes open. During the initial rearing period the male occupies separate quarters.

The young remain with their parents throughout their first winter and sometimes throughout the second winter also, along with the younger litter. They are fully grown in 2 years, and are considered to reach sexual maturity at 2–2½ years. However, they probably do not normally breed until they are almost 3 years old when they leave their parents' home.

In captivity, when close approximation to natural conditions is attempted by supplying running water and an abundance of branches, the determined efforts of captive beavers to dam the running outlet of their pool presents a problem not easily solved; for means have to be arrived at to prevent the beavers from flooding the area by raising the dam level! Such a catastrophe can be avoided by regulating the water supply. However, exhibition difficulties arising from the nocturnal habits of beavers are not so easily overcome; but if they are maintained in natural areas, the structural results of their labours are always evident and popular, even if the beavers themselves are only about in the dark.

Beavers appear to breed quite readily in captivity, provided the basic accommodation and social requirements are given. In 1973, the Norfolk Wildlife Park reared the European race for the first time in the British Isles; during the same year eight international zoos recorded the successful breeding of the Canadian species. The lifespan of captive beavers has been recorded as 15–20 years.

Population   Due to unceasing persecution at the beginning of this century the beaver was on the very verge of extinction in Europe. However, more recently its numbers have increased from a few hundred in 1920 to some 50,000 at the present time. In Norway, the relatively small beaver population of 14,000 animals is so efficiently managed that a considerable number of beavers can be utilised yearly without adversely affecting the population. In Sweden, a few pairs were imported from Norway in 1922 and by the early 1960s the beaver population in the northern part of the country numbered a few hundred; at present there are estimated to be more than 7500. In Finland, the original beaver population disappeared at much the same time as it had done in Sweden. At present there are reported to be five new populations obtained by the introduction of the Norwegian beavers in the mid 1930s. In 1937, however, Canadian beavers were introduced and proved to have a higher rate of reproduction; large populations have since developed in three regions. There is now only one pure group of the European beaver in Finland, consisting of 40–50 specimens, for in other areas the European beavers have mated with the Canadian species. In 1974, the combined total population of beavers in Finland was estimated to comprise 1800–3000 animals.

In Poland there are reported to be fifteen beaver colonies and in 1960 the total population was put at 265. Unfortunately one third of the colonies are formed by the Canadian beaver. In the U.S.S.R., at the beginning of this century, all but a few small groups (comprising 1900 animals) had virtually disappeared, but since then beavers have been successfully introduced in many places. In 1964 the total number was put at 40,000. It is not clear from the literature available whether or not the introduced specimens included the Canadian species.

Distribution Formerly, beavers inhabited most of the forested regions of the Northern Hemisphere south to the Mediterranean and east through northern Asia to Siberia in the Old World.

G. B. Corbet records that literary references suggest the presence of the beaver in Wales in the tenth and twelfth centuries, but goes on to state that it is probable they were by then already rare and became extinct soon after. In Scotland, evidence suggests the possible survival of the beaver to a later date. As with the wolf, memory of the beaver is perpetuated in a number of place names in England, Scotland and Wales. Deforestation of the banks of lowland rivers must have played a part in the beaver's extinction in the U.K. but there can be little doubt that hunting for fur was the principal cause.

The beaver became extinct in Sweden in 1870 and in Finland by the end of the last century. At the beginning of this century, only a few small colonies survived in the Old World: in Germany (the Elbe River), in the Rhone Valley in France, and in Poland, Norway and Russia. More recently, beavers have been reintroduced into many areas. First, with great success in Norway, Sweden, Finland and the U.S.S.R., and after 1945 in Switzerland, Germany, Poland and France.

In North America, the Canadian beaver remains in most areas of its range from Alaska and Canada south to the Rio Grande, but in greatly reduced numbers.

Conservation During the Middle Ages the European beaver was persecuted because its body was believed to be endowed with various healing powers. As the animal spends much of its time in the water man hoped that its glandular secretion would provide a cure for rheumatic ailments. By the eighteenth century this unwarranted superstition, coupled with the beginning of hunting of beavers for their pelts and meat, had led to their extinction throughout most of central Europe. At the beginning of this century, due to the increasing persecution, they were on the verge of total extinction: only twelve residual populations were recorded in the whole Palaearctic Region.

When the value of the fur and the importance of the dams was recognised again, restoration programmes were started. The ecological value of the dams cannot be underestimated for they regulate floods in uninhabited areas, and aid in checking erosion and in maintaining a suitable water table. Furthermore the accumulation of sediment in a beaver pond, which eventually forces the family to leave, results in some of the pond sites becoming meadows which provide excellent land for grazing and cultivation.

During the last 35 years, great strides have been made in re-establishing this species securely throughout the distribution it enjoyed during the nineteenth century. First with great success in Norway, Sweden, Finland and the U.S.S.R., and after 1945 in Switzerland, Germany, Poland and France. As recently as 1969, a society to watch over the surviving European beaver colonies in the lower Rhone Valley was formed in Paris, 'La Société Nationale pour la Conservation du Castor'.

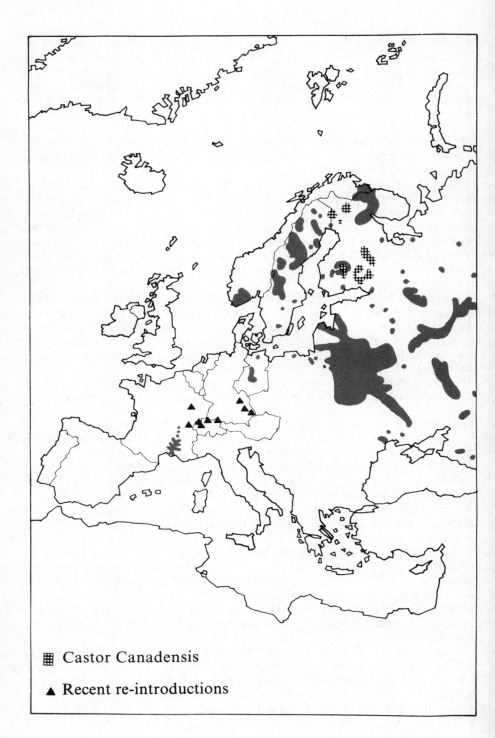

☷ Castor Canadensis

▲ Recent re-introductions

44

One of its activities has been to transfer animals in threatened areas to safer places.

Both Norway and the U.S.S.R. have instituted cropping schemes; as the species is scientifically managed as a renewable resource, no inroads are being made on the total population and in some areas the numbers are still increasing.

At present beavers are protected by law, wherever they occur, but it is important that this protection be maintained until optimal population densities are attained. Investigations should be carried out to establish whether the European beaver is managing to maintain its identity from the recently introduced Canadian species, in the regions where the two species have been introduced; and also whether it is holding its own in the areas at present being influenced by water pollution, the construction of hydro-electric plants and the reclamation of marshes.

Bourlière, F. (1967): *Natural History of Mammals*, pp. 94–5, 237–8. **Burton**, M. (1962): *Systematic Dictionary of Mammals of the World*, pp. 119–20. **Corbet**, G. B. (1974): 'The distribution of mammals in historic times', in *Changing Flora and Fauna of Britain*, pp. 179–202. **Crandall**, L. S. (1964): *The Management of Wild Mammals in Captivity*, pp. 225–8. **Duplaix-Hall**, N. (1975*a*): 'Species of wild animals bred in captivity during 1973'. **Hamilton**, B. Count (1962): 'Keeping beavers . . . in captivity'. **Oryx** (1969–74): *Vols X–XII*. **Sanderson**, I. T. (1955): *Living Mammals of the World*, pp. 117–18. **Smit**, C. J. and **Wijngaarden**, A. van (1976): 'Threatened mammals'. **Southern**, H. N. (1964): *Handbook of British Mammals*, p. 267. **van den Brink**, F. H. (1973): *A Field Guide to the Mammals of Britain and Europe*, p. 86. **Walker**, E. P. (1964): *Mammals of the World, Vol. II*, pp. 747–9. **Ziswiler**, V. (1967): *Extinct and Vanishing Animals*.

Common Hamster

Cricetus cricetus

Status: The introduction of modern agricultural methods has caused this once common species to decrease enormously, and even disappear entirely from many places

Description   The common hamster is the largest of the hamster species, of which there are about 14, belonging to five genera; three species, each representing a separate genus, are found in eastern Europe. The common hamster is stoutly built, with a thick neck, a rather pointed muzzle, medium-sized membranous ears, large and brilliant eyes, short legs, and small claws; it is equivalent in size to a guineapig and of similar proportions, except that it has a conspicuous although short tail. It frequently sits on its hind legs, giving the impression of a little bear doing likewise.

The pattern of the pelage is unique amongst European mammals in being darker below than above. The general colour of the upper parts is usually light brownish-yellow, but the upper surface of the snout and the region of the eyes, as well as a band round the throat, are reddish brown. There are big white patches on the cheeks and sides, while the underparts, the greater proportion of the legs, and a stripe on the forehead are deep black, but the feet are white. There is, however, great individual variation with regard to colour, with some almost black mutants occurring, while others are pied, and others again, almost wholly white. But usually the common hamster presents itself as one of the most richly coloured animals of Europe.

The body length range is 21.5—32.0 cm; tail length 2.8—6.0 cm (average 5.0 cm) and the hind foot 3.5—4.0 cm. The weight range is 150—385 g.

Habitat The common hamster is primarily a species of the steppe zone but leaning towards the wetter, wooded side rather than the drier, sub-desert zone. It has adapted itself to arable land, especially grain fields, and is found in field margins and river banks as well as on natural grassland. Especially on the western parts of its range, the hamster is strictly confined to loamy and loess soils.

Behaviour Hamsters are ground-dwelling burrowing rodents, with large cheek-pouches. They spend the majority of the winter in torpor, but not in true hibernation, for they are known to awake and feed from stored food at frequent intervals; the periods of low activity occur from October to March. Both sexes have a pair of glandular patches high on the flanks, which are considered to serve to set scent on the walls of their burrows. There is also a skin gland in the centre of the abdomen (as in the related gerbils).

The common hamster is essentially a solitary individual, but one that has always attracted a considerable amount of interest, from the elaborate structure of its burrows and the provident nature of its habits. It digs an extensive and very deep burrow system, up to a maximum of 2 metres in depth. The burrows contain several chambers, some of which are used for the storage of food. Bourlière makes reference to the fact that the hamster of central Europe is an example of a mammal that possesses two burrows of different types: the summer burrow with a single storage place for food, and the winter burrow which is dug very much deeper and comprises an entrance gallery, one or two chambers, and several storage places. In both cases, there is a nearly perpendicular entrance passage and an oblique exit.

It appears that the young, the females and the males generally occupy distinct burrows, which may be recognised by the size of their entrance passages, those of the males being the largest. When a burrow is tenanted, the passages are kept scrupulously clean, and the presence of any litter in them would at once proclaim that the habitation was deserted; chaff and straw, however, may be generally seen near the entrance of the burrow.

Although the entrance passage goes nearly straight down into the earth, it has a turn before opening into the dwelling chamber; and in old burrows the entrance and exit passages are polished smooth by the constant friction of the coats of the occupants. Activity on the surface is almost entirely nocturnal. When the weather becomes cold in October, the hamsters retire to their burrows' innermost recesses for their partial hibernation, the entrance and exit of each burrow being then closed with earth.

Diet   Hamsters feed predominantly on seeds, including cereal grain, but also upon leaves, bulbs, roots and even insects. Young hamsters have only a single granary in their burrows; but the old males, who spend the majority of the summer collecting and carrying surplus food in their cheek-pouches to their hoard, frequently have from three to five such chambers in which to store their foodstuff. These chambers are completely filled with corn, the passage communicating with the dwelling chamber frequently being stopped up with earth. All kinds of cereal are equally acceptable to these industrious little animals and it will often be found that, while one part of the store chamber is filled with grain of a particular kind, the other portion may contain a different sort. The establishment of such food reserves provides each hamster with storage chambers which may contain as much as 85 kg of cereal seeds, peas or potatoes. About the middle of March the adult males make their first appearance abroad; they are followed early in April by the females. At this time they are reported to devour ravenously almost anything that comes before them, not even refusing an occasional young bird, a mouse or a beetle.

On the completion of their summer burrows, the sexes pair up. Ventral-ventral copulation, in which the two sexes unite belly to belly, is known with the hamster. The breeding season extends from April to August, usually with two litters. The gestation period is 19—21 days and the litter size is very variable, usually 6—12, although a litter of 18 has been recorded: the hamster has 4 pairs of teats (mammae).

The nest chamber is furnished with a bed of soft hay. Towards the end of April the males visit the burrows of the females; if two males should meet in the same burrow, there is a fierce fight, the hamster, for its size, being an extremely ferocious and quarrelsome animal. When born, the young are naked and blind although furnished with teeth. The hair grows quickly, however, and by 8—9 days the eyes are opened; within a fortnight the young are able to burrow. At about 3 weeks they are weaned, soon after which they are driven away by their parents to feed for themselves. Hamsters are not fully grown until about a year old and they breed after their first winter. The lifespan is put at about 2½ years.

Although the common hamster has rapid powers of reproduction, and when conditions were right used to appear in countless swarms, under rainy conditions its reproductive capacity is very low.

Population   The wide distribution and nocturnal habits of the common hamster make it impossible to provide an accurate estimate of the species population. Early reports record that in the year 1888 no less than 97,519 hamsters were destroyed in the single district of Aschersleben — for which a reward of 1950 marks was paid. In the latter part of the nineteenth century some thousands of hamster skins were annually imported into England, and farmers attempted (unsuccessfully) to eradicate the species wherever it occurred. However, more recently, the introduction of modern agricultural methods has caused the species to decrease enormously, and its disappearance from many places has been recorded.

Distribution   Common hamsters are typical of the steppe zone over the whole of the Palaearctic region. Their range extends from Belgium and the southern part of the Netherlands in the west to Lake Baikal in the east, and from about 58°N in Russia, south to the Caucasus.

C. J. Smit and A. van Wijngaarden record that in Belgium the common hamster

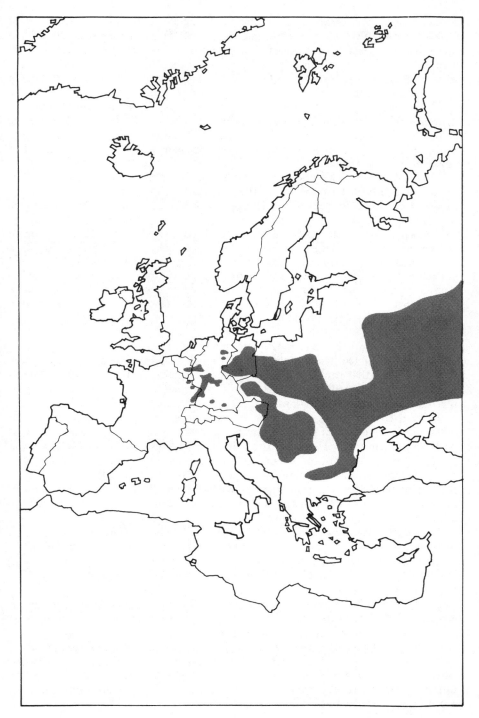

49

is found only in a narrow zone in the Loess region in the north eastern part of Belgium between Court St Etienne and Maastricht. In the Netherlands, the Belgian area continues east of the Maastricht—Roermond line. In the German Federal Republic, the species is found from the border to the Rhine; the animals live in the valleys of the Rhine, Main and Neckar. Small isolated colonies are still considered to occur along the Donau (Danube) near Ulm and near Augsburg. In France, the species is found on the Alsatian plain between the Rhine and the Vosges. In Lorraine it occurs near Sierk and Sarreguemines. In the German Democratic Republic, the species is reported to occur in a large part of the country from Pomerania to the Sudeten region. In Czechoslovakia, hamsters are considered to occur throughout the country.

There are conflicting reports as to whether the hamster exists in Switzerland, but in all probability it does not. In Austria, it occurs only on the Pannonian plain in Lower Austria and Burgenland. In Hungary, no data has been found concerning its distribution, but the species is undoubtedly present in a large part of the country. In Rumania, the hamster is found throughout Transylvania with the exception of the eastern part of Maramures, the northernmost part of Cluj, in the Reginnea Mures Autonoma Maghiara, and the eastern part of Brasov. In Moldavia and Walachia the species occurs everywhere except in the west. In Oltenia it is considered to be rare. In Bulgaria, it is considered to occur only along the Danube in the north. In the U.S.S.R., the species occurs throughout the steppe zone, within the boundaries described previously.

Conservation   Not so long ago the common hamster was considered a serious pest in areas where it had successfully adapted itself to arable lands. It was in these cultivated areas that it inflicted incalculable harm upon the harvest; and in spite of every attempt to eradicate it wherever it occurred, due to its rapid powers of reproduction it easily held its own.

Richard Lydekker recorded, in 1895: 'Fortunately, however, they [the common hamsters] have a host of enemies, and buzzards, owls, ravens and other predacious birds thin their ranks by hundreds; while among four-legged foes, polecats and stoats follow the track of the advancing legions, and kill them where and when they can. The polecat and stoat are, moreover, able to follow the hamsters into the recesses of their burrows, where they probably destroy them by hundreds. In many districts the flesh of the hamster is eaten, and is said to be not unlike that of the squirrel.'

During the last few decades, with the introduction of modern agricultural methods leading to the removal of the strips of grass and banks dividing small fields, harvesting with combines, deep ploughing right after the harvest, crop rotation, etc., the species has decreased enormously and even disappeared entirely from many places.

Some authorities consider that the only way to save the common hamster, at least at the fringes of its western European range, is the establishment of suitable reserves where old-fashioned agricultural methods are maintained. Such reserves, although on a small scale, are present in the Netherlands and also serve as a refuge for the weed flora of grain fields and old varieties of cultivated plants. It is also advocated that some breeding nuclei of this threatened species should be taken into various more controlled captive environments, so that a viable self-sustaining captive population can be established.

Bourlière, F. (1967): *Natural History of Mammals*. **Burton**, M. (1962): *Systematic Dictionary of Mammals of the World*, p. 132. **Corbet**, G. B. (1966): *Terrestrial Mammals of Western Europe*, pp. 226—9. **Lydekker**, R. (1894—5): *The Royal Natural History, Vol. III*, pp. 124—6. **Smit**, C. J. and **Wijngaarden**, A. van (1976): 'Threatened mammals'. **van den Brink**, F. H. (1973): *A Field Guide to the Mammals of Britain and Europe*, pp. 90—1.

Northern Vole or Tundra Vole

Microtus oeconomus

Status: Although this is a very common species throughout the majority of its range, there are a number of relict populations which are rapidly shrinking and could become extinct if conservation measures are not adopted and enforced

Description   The rodents of the sub-family Microtinae (family Cricetidae), which embraces the vole and the lemming, are a fairly clearly defined group. They are the dominant small herbivorous mammals of the Holarctic. Voles and lemmings are strictly ground-dwelling or semi-aquatic rodents. The cheek-teeth in most species remain rootless, and the cusps on the surface become worn immediately upon eruption, to form flat grinding surfaces. G. B. Corbet states that the total number of species in the Palaearctic region is probably about fifty, of which twenty, along with one introduced species, are found in western Europe.

Members of the genus *Microtus*, which embraces the field voles, are small with thick coats, usually greyish or yellowish brown, small ears that scarcely appear above the fur, and teeth which are rootless and sharply angular. There are six species in western Europe which can, with experience, be distinguished by their external features, although whenever possible it is best to check their identity by their dental pattern.

The northern vole is also referred to by some authorities as the 'tundra vole' as well as the 'Baikal rat-headed vole'. The use of the Latin name *oeconomus* for this species is somewhat controversial, for some authorities consider it may be that *Microtus ratticeps* is the correct one to use.

This species is one of the largest voles and can be recognised by its dark brown pelage, which often sports a buffy-brown line on the back, and its rather long tail. The underparts are greyish white, with a 'dirty straw' overcast visible at the tips of the hairs. Individuals with extremely dark backs and a generally mousy colour, tinged with rust, are occasionally encountered. The legs and ears are short, the inner sides of the latter being slightly hairy.

It has been reported that the northern vole can easily be distinguished from the similar *Microtus arvalis* (continental vole) by its much longer hind feet which vary from 1.8 to 2.2 cm, usually about 1.9 cm. The body length is 11.8–14.5 cm (usually about 13.0 cm); the tail length, which consists of about 40–45% of the total length of head and body, is 4.0–6.0 cm (usually about 4.6 or 4.7 cm). The weight range is 24–62 g.

Habitat   The northern vole is an especially characteristic species of wet grassy and marshy habitats, including very wet ground and reed beds; in this respect it resembles the field vole *Microtus agrestis*. This tendency to choose rather wet habitats is particularly apparent when there is competition pressure from other vole species. The northern vole occurs in a wide range of this type of habitat including salt marshes, fens, bogs, meadows, hay-fields, banks of small streams, taiga and even tundra (hence the alternative name).

Behaviour   It is reported that the northern vole burrows to a greater extent than the field vole, and is therefore less dependent upon thick ground cover. It makes underground holes with nest chambers and store-rooms and whilst digging it throws up little 'molehills'. The animal swims and dives well; its voice is subdued, like that of the field vole, but only repeated or chattering during encounters between breeding males. The species is active by day and night. It makes very prominent 'runs' in the vegetation, and builds nests in tussocks of grass and sedges.

Diet   In common with the other species of *Microtus*, the northern vole is almost entirely herbivorous, feeding on the leaves, stems and roots of a wide variety of grasses, rushes and sedges. Many other herbaceous plants are also eaten and, in winter especially, roots, rhizomes and bark. The field vole, in curious contrast with its staple vegetarian diet, occasionally eats carrion, including members of its own species; this habit has also been recorded for the equally herbivorous lemming.

Breeding   Regular cycles of population density, fluctuating with a three-year periodicity, are found in this species, and are indeed typical of the whole of the sub-family Microtinae.

The nest is usually constructed above ground, under a stone, log or clump of reeds, or slightly below ground-level, dug beneath a tussock of bush roots or other slight elevation. The burrows possess numerous apertures and branches; the individual holes are linked by passages which generally take the form of small underground runs. The nests are constructed of dry sedges, blades of grass, birch leaves and mosses, with a small amount of spruce and birch twigs up to approximately 10 cm in length. The nest normally takes the form of a flattened sphere about 20 cm in diameter and about 12–20 cm in height. A small almost hidden entrance hole opposite the run leads into the internal lair, which is kept meticulously lined with sedges and leaves; one report describes how the sedge blades are plaited in even rings around the walls. Several paths usually lead from the nest to join the subterranean burrows.

Breeding occurs between April and September, reproduction being most intense during May and June. Post-partum conception frequently occurs and therefore a succession of litters may be produced during the summer. The gestation period has been recorded as 21 days and the lactation period a little less. The litter size is most often 3–6, and provided the population density is not too great the young of the earlier litters usually mature quickly and may begin to breed at an age of 6 weeks. It is considered unlikely that many animals survive a second winter, and the average expectation of life, from weaning, has been put at less than a few months.

In 1973, *Microtus oeconomus* was recorded to have bred in two of the world's zoological parks: three animals were reared at Helsinki, Finland; and two at Posnan, Poland. As the life-cycle and ecology for this species become better known there appears to be every reason to hope that the northern vole will reproduce in laboratory-type conditions as readily as the lesser white-toothed shrew *Crocidura suaveolens* described previously (see page 3). If such a breeding programme could be started, further investigations on the biology and development of the species might be undertaken.

Population   Although the northern vole is in general the most numerous mammalian species in an enormous area of distribution, the numbers in the 'relict' populations are dwindling. The nature of the vole's behaviour and habitat prevents a real insight into the population size of the species. However, it is only in the isolated locations that population densities can properly be established.

Distribution   Throughout eastern Europe and Siberia it is a very widespread species, extending from the tundra zone south to the wooded steppes of northern China, Kazakhstan and the Ukraine. It also occurs in the tundra of Alaska and the adjacent parts of Canada. In western Europe it is found in many parts of Scandinavia and Finland, but south of the Baltic; its western limit runs from Rumania through Hungary and the centre of Germany as far west as the Elbe. Isolated populations occur in the Netherlands. Corbet states that this range is on the whole complementary to that of the closely related species, the alpine vole *Microtus nivalis*, which occurs throughout the principal mountain ranges of Europe south of the Baltic.

Although the northern vole is a very common species, it is nevertheless included among the threatened species because there are also a number of relict populations representing the distribution pattern in glacial periods. Many of these isolated groups are described as different sub-species.

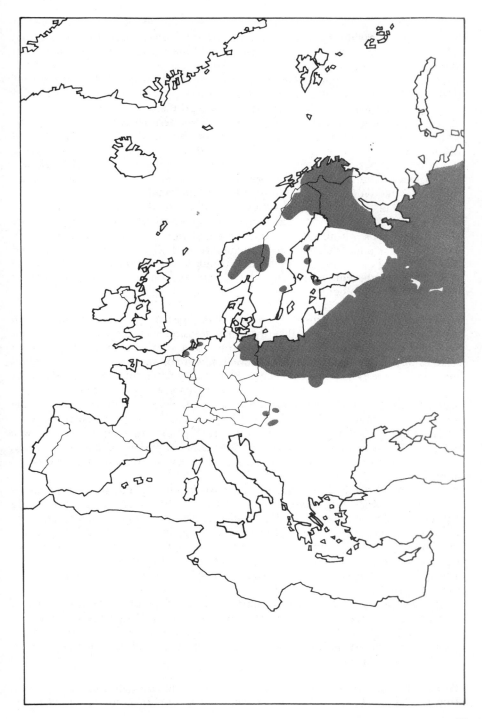

C. J. Smit and A. van Wijngaarden record that this species occurs in southern Norway in mountainous regions, while in northern Norway it is also found in the valleys. In Sweden, there are some populations in the central part of the country in Medelpad, Jamtland, the western part of Norrland, and near Stockholm. In Finland, a number of isolated populations still occur on some small islands in the gulf of Bothnia. Reichstein in 1972 states that the species no longer occurs in the Federal Republic of Germany. In the Netherlands, the northern vole still occurs in four places: (a) on some of the islands in the south-western parts of the country; (b) scattered populations in the western fens; (c) on the island of Texel; and (d) along the fens and lakes in the province of Friesland. In Austria, it is found along the shores of Lake Neusiedl in the upper stretches of the Phragmites belt. In Hungary, the species is found along the shores of Lake Balaton. In Czechoslovakia, the species is found on the island of Zitny Ostrov in the Danube.

At a great distance from the main area in central Asia there are relict populations along the rivers in the Ala Tau mountains in Kazakhstan (U.S.S.R.) and the Hangai-Mountains in China. Mountain vole populations even occur in some cases in Tsaidam and around the Nan Shan Mountains. S. I. Ognev gives the Baikal and Transbaikal regions as the geographical distribution for *Microtus oeconomus* in the U.S.S.R. and adjacent countries, although he goes on to say that the precise northern and eastern boundaries are still obscure.

Conservation   It is recognised that a great many species of voles can be harmful to agriculture and forestry, and that they may transmit endemic diseases; but voles also play a positive role in maintaining some of the balances of nature, for they serve as one of the main foods for economically important fur-bearing mammals in the more northerly parts of their range. Indeed they represent an important part of the diet of more species of predators than perhaps any other mammal. This is generally attributed to their numerical abundance, which in turn is made possible by their adaptation to utilise such abundant, varied and ubiquitous sources of food.

The most dangerous foes of the vole are the nocturnal raptors: barn owls, short-eared owls, eagle owls and snowy owls. Other important predators are stoats, weasels, ermines, polecats, martens, minks, cats, foxes, wolves, buzzards, eagles and harriers.

In the Netherlands, as a result of the construction of dams, the continental or common vole *Microtus arvalis* is reported to be penetrating into areas formerly occupied by *Microtus oeconomus*. In addition, the destruction of habitat resulting from recreation, reclamation, re-allotment of land, intensification of grazing and the dumping of refuse, represents a serious menance to the future of this species in the Netherlands as well as for the populations on the Pannonian plain. In an attempt to combat this, some small reserves have been established for this species in the Netherlands.

It is generally considered that the northern vole is as prolific as ever over most of its range; but in areas of the Netherlands, Austria and Czechoslovakia its population is rapidly shrinking. It is for this reason that the enlargement of the existing reserves, and the establishment of additional suitable reserves for relict populations should urgently be undertaken.

Corbet, G. B. (1966): *Terrestrial Mammals of Western Europe*, pp. 242—8.
Duplaix-Hall, N. (1975*a*): 'Species of wild animals bred in captivity during 1973'.

Ognev, S. I. (1964): *Mammals of U.S.S.R. and Adjacent Countries, Vol. VII*, pp. 206–36. Smit, C. J. and Wijngaarden, A. van (1976): 'Threatened mammals'. van den Brink, F. H. (1973): *A Field Guide to the Mammals of Britain and Europe*, pp. 101–5.

Dormouse

Muscardinus avellanarius

Status: Declining in numbers, mainly because of the disappearance of the type of woodland and rich shrub layer on which it depends so heavily

Description   The dormice, family Muscardinidae, are arboreal mouse-sized rodents, usually with a bushy tail giving them a resemblance to squirrels. The common dormouse (sometimes known as the hazel dormouse) is an attractive animal, much the same size as the somewhat leggy and athletic-looking long-tailed field mouse, but far more compact in shape. The presence of four pairs of cheek-teeth in both the upper and lower jaws distinguishes the European dormice from the members of the family Muridae which do not have more than three pairs in each jaw. The monospecific genus of the common dormouse is distinguished especially by the reduced size of the first cheek-tooth.

In general form the dormouse is stout and round. The dense fur on its upper parts and tail is a rich sandy to orange-brown in colour, with a fine sprinkling of darker hairs which are too sparse to affect the general impression of a light-coloured animal. It is much paler and sometimes even white on the under parts. Winter pelage differs little from summer pelage in colour, but the hair is thicker and denser, the underfur better developed. The tail is thickly furred on all sides, but not bushy, and may have longer and darker hairs at the tip; careful handling is essential to prevent the skin from stripping off the tail.

The eyes are large, prominent and black in colour; the small ears are rounded, smooth inside, covered with hairs externally, but show clearly above the fur. The fine black whiskers may be 28–32 mm long at each side of the nasal region and are a striking feature of the head – no doubt they are important as feelers during nocturnal activities. The young are at first brownish-grey and remain so until the first moult; in Britain, the moult into winter pelage occurs in October. A form with a white tip to the tail is not infrequent; and albinos, although rare, have been recorded. There are five sub-species described, southern European forms showing a tendency to be brighter in colour. The sub-species of common dormouse that occurs in Britain is the smallest representative of the European dormice, and is very easily distinguished by its orange-brown pelage and the absence of any facial pattern.

The forelimbs are short, and both front and hind feet are prehensile. There are four digits on the front feet, whereas the hind feet have four plus a vestigial stump for the first. The front feet are turned out laterally almost at right angles so that as the mouse climbs it grasps the twigs and branches easily and firmly. The remaining four digits on each foot are long and slender, covered on the upper surface in short, downy fur and with strong short claws at the end. When the animal is climbing, a gap is often seen between the fourth and fifth digit of the hind foot. The under surfaces show well-developed pads which assist in grasping and climbing.

The head and body length is 5.8–8.8 cm; the tail (without its terminal hair) 5.5–6.8 cm; the ear 1.0–1.4 cm; the hind foot (without claws) 15.3–16.4 mm. The weight is variable – 23–43 g – according to the time of year, being heaviest before hibernation.

Habitat   Most authorities agree that dormice prefer secondary growth of woodland and scrub, especially where there are trees with edible crops, e.g. beech, hazel, sweet chestnut. They prefer to live in places where there is plenty of undergrowth and thus favour thick brakes, copses and old hedges which have plenty of tangled vegetation. Woods where the trees are of mature growth and there is less undergrowth are not so suitable for them. A characteristic dormouse habitat found in the U.S.S.R. is described in detail by S. I. Ognev: 'The forests inhabited by *Muscardinus avellanarius* consist either of sparse oak plots 40–50 years old or of younger aspens. In both cases the understorey is very well developed and consists chiefly of hazel, linden, maple, ash, honeysuckle, spindle trees, bird cherry, rowan and viburnum. In some places these tree species form a dense, impenetrable and very shady thicket in the summer, entwined with papilionaceous plants and clinging hops. Nests are generally found in felled areas in young oak/hazelnut groves, or in old poorly shaded oak groves with an undercover of some of the above mentioned species. In all cases the animals preferred to nest in glades or along the edges of forest trails and paths.'

The summer and breeding nests are usually built 1–2 m above the ground, whereas the winter hibernation nests are more often at or below ground level. In one season, 3–5 of the summer nests may be built, and in Britain these nests are often betrayed by stripped stems of honeysuckle. Dormice generally select a fork in the vertical trunks of hazels, oaks, maples or apple trees. The nest is sometimes squeezed into a narrow space between thickset roots; in this case it is not rounded or slightly flattened, but elliptical, with a large perpendicular entrance hole. Even more rarely, nests hang in loops of trailing vines; these nests are irregular in outline, but the central part is usually globular. The entrance hole in a globular nest lies high up and slightly to one side: in an elliptical nest it is located midway up at the side. The shape and size of the entrance hole varies with the resilience of the leaves, which sometimes block the passage completely when the animal emerges.

In Britain, nests are often composed of shredded strips of honeysuckle bark, with the finest strands used in the centre of the nest. Other reports, from Europe, state that the external part of the nest is usually made of broad, flexible leaves (maple, hazel and oak) very skilfully interwoven to cling closely to the internal part of the nest; this consists of a thick layer of soft leaves, ferns, grasses, linden fibres, down, willow herb and wool. Often this warm, compact lining does not reach the top of the nest and the roof is made exclusively of a layer of tree leaves. The common dormouse is also known to inhabit the abandoned nests of birds (e.g. warblers and robins), reconstructing the roof in such a way that a side entrance leads into the nest. More rarely it inhabits hollow trees, and has been discovered in a woodpecker's hole in an oak.

Behaviour In Britain, the dormouse is the only native rodent that shows true hibernation. The onset of hibernation is indicated by the accumulation of fat; neither low temperatures nor the scarcity of food appear to be the primary cause. In hibernation, the whole metabolism of the dormouse slows down, its respiration and heart rate fall, and its muscles become so rigid that it can be rolled along any flat surface without uncurling. Just how the dormouse goes to sleep in its winter nest is well described by L. Harrison Mathews: 'There it rolls up into a ball, the head being bent down so that the chin rests on the belly. The hind feet are curled up forwards about level with the nose, and the hands, clenched into fists, are held either under the chin or alongside the nose. The eyes and mouth are tightly closed, the ears folded back downwards close to the surface of the head, and the tail is tucked forwards between the legs, its tip wrapping over the face and back.' The dormouse spends nearly six months of the year, usually from October until April, only just on the right side of the borderline between life and death. But its hibernation is not necessarily uninterrupted, for it may wake up occasionally and eat some of the store laid up in the nest.

As a species, it is a fairly quiet animal – the call is a thin, musical squeal – and a trustful one, usually becoming accustomed to man a few days after capture. It is sometimes slightly colonial, with a number of occupied nests being quite close together, although each nest rarely contains more than one individual. It is a strictly nocturnal species, spending most of its active life above ground level: its movements are agile, graceful and fluid, particularly when it runs along the thin twigs of bushes. When a number of dormice are frightened from their nests, they do not usually run far off, but scatter over the branches of the thicket and then stand stock-still. However, if pursued further, they will fling themselves to the ground and disappear in a flash. It is very easy to lose sight of them, as their camouflage is excellent.

Diet   The dormouse is largely vegetarian, living on nuts, seeds of conifers, fruits, berries, shoots and barks of trees; but it is also known to take birds' eggs, nestlings and insects. Prior to hibernation, it fattens itself on tree crops. In captivity, it will avidly devour all types of berries, apples and apple seeds, pears, grapes, cherries, acorns, chestnuts, hazel nuts, hips and haws, oats and bread. It is also known to suck the eggs of small birds, and eat various different types of insect. Its faeces are like those of mice, although often with a ridged, not a smooth, surface.

Sitting back on its haunches, the dormouse feeds in the same way as the squirrel; it can also suspend itself by its hind feet and feed quite comfortably from this apparently awkward position.

Breeding   Detailed information on the breeding habits of dormice in the wild state is very scant, and their reproductive cycle is not well known. There are probably at least two litters per summer, from May to September; nests with blind young in them have been recorded in Europe even as late as the middle of October. The earlier litters are reported to be larger than later ones.

After a gestation period of 22—24 days, litters ranging from 2 to 7, usually about 4, have been noted. The young are born blind, and develop rapidly. They are furred in 13 days, their eyes open at 17—18 days, they forage out of the nest at 30 days and are able to lead an independent existence after 5—6 weeks. The infants have a grey pelage; they moult at about 18 days into a paler pelage than the adult, which they keep until the following year. They do not become sexually mature in the year of birth, and during their first winter hibernation are still only a little over half of the adult weight. The hibernation nests are built any time from October onwards. Dormice mostly hibernate singly, but several of the young may sometimes hibernate together. Males are driven from the nursery nest by the female and occupy non-breeding nests near by.

The normal lifespan is probably about 3 years, by which age the teeth are heavily worn; however, a common dormouse has lived in captivity for a period of 6 years.

Population   In the British Isles, the population of the common dormouse is fairly sparsely distributed, and there appears to be a considerable decline in numbers. It is considered that the same holds for the majority of Europe; although a report in 1946 recorded that this species was very common after a good agricultural year in Czechoslovakia. However very little further information is available and, as with other small rodents and insectivores, we have to rely on field scientists, trapping for specific research projects, to provide us with any type of insight into the population and whereabouts of the species.

Distribution   With the exception of Asia Minor, the common dormouse is confined to Europe. Its range extends over the greater part of Central Europe, from northern Italy (although it may perhaps occur at high altitudes in southern Italy), not penetrating Jutland, to the south of Sweden. Eastwards it is found in western Russia, and the north-eastern boundary begins in the Baltic region below 57—59°N latitude. Island populations occur in Asia Minor, Sicily and southern England. It is absent from Scotland and Ireland.

In the United Kingdom, the common dormouse is found in suitable places throughout the southern and western counties, but becomes scarce and localised in

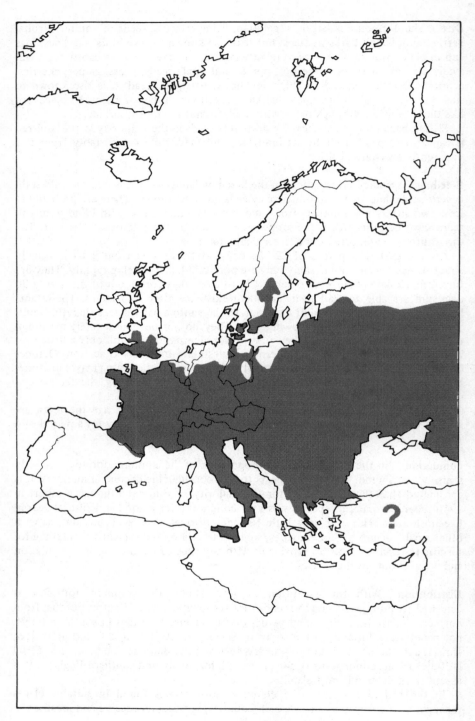

Wales; it is not found in the Isle of Man. It is distributed more thinly across the Midlands and is absent from most of East Anglia. Although nineteenth-century records show it once to have been distributed north at least to the river Tyne, the author has found no recent records north of the river Humber.

Conservation Little is known of the amount of damage predators inflict on the common dormouse, but owls are considered by some authorities to be about the most deadly. There are some reports of crows, magpies, etc. preying on dormice; but on the whole it is during hibernation that they are the most vulnerable, being preyed upon by stoats, weasels, badgers and foxes. One study has suggested a population loss of 80% during the winter.

In southern Sweden, the German Democratic Republic and the Netherlands, the common dormouse is considered to be rare, and in some of these regions protective legislation for the species has come into force. There are also similar hunting restrictions in some other member states of the Council of Europe: the German Federal Republic, Great Britain, Belgium, Luxemburg, Switzerland and Liechtenstein, where the species is reported not to be numerous.

In captivity, the dormouse has been found to be very placid and easily tamed, seldom, if ever, biting; and, if kept in good accommodation, it can live for considerable periods — although it has proved sometimes to be difficult to bring through hibernation, and care should be taken not to wake it up too suddenly.

In Britain the dormouse has certainly declined in numbers during the last 50 years, from being very common to being, in the majority of places, quite a rarity. The dormouse depends upon woodland with a rich shrub layer and it has almost certainly suffered a decline during the course of this century from the destruction of covert woodland. It is for this reason that the common dormouse was in 1975 one of the three mammals (dormouse, greater horseshoe and mouse-eared bats) considered to be included in the Wild Creatures and Wild Plants Protection Act, which aims to fill in several gaps in the existing legislation, and provide a means by which any animal or plant which becomes rare can be afforded protection. It is hoped that subsequent legal protective measures for the common dormouse will be able to stop its decline in Britain and help ensure that sufficient suitable habitat remains safeguarded throughout its European distribution.

In 1972, the Fauna Preservation Society, London, and European conservationists showed interest in the fate of a rare form of dormouse, *Eliomys quercinus*, found on Formentera in the Balearic Islands. This resulted in the Spanish Ministry of Agriculture halting an operation of exterminating 'rats' on the island. This intervention greatly helped this rare animal's chances of survival.

Corbet, G. B. (1966): *Terrestrial Mammals of Western Europe*, pp. 205–7; (1974): 'The distribution of mammals in historic times', in *Changing Flora and Fauna of Britain*, pp. 179–202. **Graf**, J. (1968): *Animal Life of Europe*, p. 60. **Harrison Mathews**, L. (1952): *British Mammals*, pp. 197–200. **Hurrell**, E. (1962): 'Dormice', in *Animals of Britain, No. 10*. **Millais**, J. G. (1905): *Mammals of Great Britain and Ireland, Vol. II*, pp. 164–71. **Ognev**, S. I. (1963): *Mammals of U.S.S.R. and Adjacent Countries, Vol. V*, pp. 466–75. **Oryx** (1972, 1975): *Vol. XI*, No. 6 and *Vol. XIII*, No. 1. **Smit**, C. J. and **Wijngaarden**, A. van (1976): 'Threatened mammals'. **Southern**, H. N. (1964): *Handbook of British Mammals*, pp. 310–15. **van den Brink**, F. H. (1973): *A Field Guide to the Mammals of Britain and Europe*, pp. 88–90.

Crested Porcupine

Hystrix cristata

Status: The species is still present in its former range but is considered to form a pest for agricultural crops, and hence is persecuted: its numbers appear to be decreasing, making it become rare in many regions

Description   The crested porcupine is the largest of the porcupine family, the heaviest rodent to be found in Africa and, after the beaver, the largest of the Old World rodents. With its stout body and long legs, it is easily recognisable by the upstanding crest of long, thin, backward-curved bristles along its nape and back, which are raised to give the crested appearance. The tail is short and hidden amongst the quills. The broad forefeet have four well-developed toes, each armed with a thick claw; the hind foot has five toes.

The most remarkable characteristic of the genus is the structure of the rattle quills on the tail. These are large hollow quills whose points break off as soon as they are fully grown; when the tail is shaken these quills strike against each other, producing a loud rattle.

The upperparts are covered by stout cylindrical black, dark-brown and white, or yellowish-banded quills, among which may be mixed longer, more slender and more flexible quills that are usually all white. The underparts are scantily covered with short, rather coarse, straight, usually black hairs.

The European members of this species are smaller than most of the African forms, but they have in common the crest predominantly white and the rump dark. The length of the head and body is 60–75 cm; the tail length 12–15 cm; and some larger spines are up to 30 or 40 cm long. The weight range is 15–20 kg.

Habitat   Crested porcupines live in rocky hills, open woodland and dry areas with vegetation cover; they live in pairs or in small groups in large burrows or in natural rocky dens. They are almost entirely nocturnal: during the daytime they remain under cover in their burrows or in natural cavities or crevices, whilst during the night they shuffle along in search of food.

Behaviour   If a crested porcupine senses danger, and is closely approached, it faces away from the enemy, stamps its feet, raises its quills, and vibrates them so that the long, large, almost hollow quills rattle together and produce a sound somewhat like that of a rattlesnake's rattle. Ivan Sanderson relates that crested porcupines are not aggressive but merely extremely arrogant, wandering about at night mumbling, grunting and rattling their quills. This part of their defensive mechanism is taken to be a proclamation to all and sundry that they are dangerous customers! However, these animals have extremely thin and delicate skins and they would be vulnerable to attack by any animal that really knew them, for their heads are almost entirely unprotected and they will succumb to a single light blow across the muzzle. They can be very quick moving animals, can spin around with remarkable speed and then suddenly rush backwards at an attacker, with quills and spines bristling: if they make contact, numbers of the spines lodge in the skin of their opponent and become detached from the porcupine. Meantime, they stamp with their back feet and growl, which can be most unnerving and distracting.

It has been recorded that men on foot chasing the crested porcupine in the so-called sport of 'pig-sticking' with a spear have had the porcupines reverse the game and drive their spines through a leg. Two further references by Bourlière record that in one case a panther was mortally wounded; and in another, an almost adult tiger, its liver and lungs perforated in many places, was found dead a few yards from its victim. From my own personal experience, I recall seeing a car that had collided with a crested porcupine whilst travelling at speed down a dirt road in Africa: some of the sharp tougher quills had actually perforated the front mudguard at the point of impact!

Diet   Crested porcupines eat all manner of roots, bark, fallen fruit, tubers, leaves and other succulent vegetation and they have been reported to eat carrion. They have most powerful incisors with which they gnaw. Their cheek teeth continue growing throughout life and are adapted for grinding. The jaws and the appropriate muscles to work them are claimed to surpass all but those of the carnivores in strength. Porcupines gnaw bones, which are frequently found in their burrows; in Africa they are reputed to gnaw on elephant ivory.

Breeding - In Europe breeding takes place in the spring. The offspring, usually 1–4, are born in a nest made up of leaves, grass and roots, after a gestation of about 3 months (up to 112 days). There are six mammae and it is not uncommon for females to have two litters a year. The young are born with their eyes open and their bodies covered with soft flexible spines which harden soon after exposure to the air. They only leave the burrows when the quills are strong and hard, which is usually after about 2 weeks.

The male parent confines himself to defending the offspring from intruders; otherwise he plays no part in rearing the young. The crested porcupine's activity is greatly reduced during the winter months, but hibernation does not take place.

Hybridisation in captivity has been recorded between the crested porcupine and the African crested porcupine *Hystrix africaeaustralis*; between the crested porcupine and the Indian crested porcupine *Hystrix indica*; and between the crested porcupine and the crestless porcupine *Hystrix javanicum*. Hybrids between *Hystrix cristata* and *Hystrix africaeaustralis* have not been recorded in the wild state, but there appears to be no valid reason why it should not actually take place, between the northern and southern species of this genus; there are no zoogeographical grounds to prevent it.

In 1973, world zoos recorded the successful rearing of 26 crested porcupines in 14 different collections. The lifespan of this species in captivity has been reported to be up to 20 years.

Population Although becoming increasingly restricted in Europe, this species occurs in considerable numbers throughout its extensive range in Africa, and it is doubtful that any serious inroads are being made into the species' overall population.

In captivity, the crested porcupine is the most frequently exhibited species of porcupine to be seen in the world's zoological gardens.

Distribution In Europe, the crested porcupine is confined to Italy, where it still occurs as far north as Pisa and Siena, and to two regions of Sicily: in both cases, most authorities consider that it was originally introduced by the Romans. There have been some reports that it has more recently been introduced into limited areas in the Balkans (Albania, southern Yugoslavia) but these reports have not been substantiated.

The range of *Hystrix cristata* outside Europe includes the savanna and steppe zones of the northern half of Africa, from central Tanzania to upper Egypt and along the south of the Sahara to Gambia; and again in north-western Africa from Morocco to Libya. Closely related species replace it in southern Africa and in south-western Asia.

Conservation The species is still present in its former range of Italy and Sicily, but its numbers appear to be decreasing, for it is already rare in some of the regions. As porcupines feed largely upon roots, but also on stems of herbaceous plants and on bark, they are unfortunately considered to be a serious pest to agriculture,

especially amongst root crops and in orchards. These animals are also known to injure crops of sweet potatoes, cassava and maize. Hence they are generally destroyed if found.

Due to the crested porcupine's armament, the species has no natural enemies except man. As it is considered in some places to be such a pest to agriculture, it is persecuted by hunters with dogs at night, as well as being destroyed by poisoned fruits. As the flesh of *Hystrix* is reputed to be excellent, it is also hunted for its meat.

In Italy, porcupines are protected to some extent, but it is felt important that a study should be performed to determine what amount of damage they actually cause. Even though the crested porcupine may not have been represented in Europe prior to its introduction by the Romans, it would be sad to allow it to become extinct. It is for this reason that it should be afforded total protection against any kind of persecution until its true status can be determined, and reserve areas be established.

Bourlière, F. (1967): *Natural History of Mammals*. **Burton**, M. (1962): *Systematic Dictionary of Mammals of the World*, pp. 102—3. **Corbet**, G. B. (1966): *Terrestrial Mammals of Western Europe*, p. 200. **Dorst**, J. and **Dandelot**, P. (1970): *A Field Guide to the Larger Mammals of Africa*, p. 34. **Duplaix-Hall**, N. (1975a): 'Species of wild animals bred in captivity during 1973'. **Gray**, A. P. (1971): *Mammalian Hybrids*, pp. 86—7. **Lydekker**, R. (1894—5): *The Royal Natural History, Vol. III*, pp. 162—7. **Sanderson**, I. T. (1955): *Living Mammals of the World*, pp. 146—7. **Smit**, C. J. and **Wijngaarden**, A. van (1976): 'Threatened mammals'. **van den Brink**, F. H. (1973): *A Field Guide to the Mammals of Britain and Europe*, pp. 118—19. **Walker**, E. P. (1964): *Mammals of the World, Vol. II*, p. 1007.

North Atlantic Right Whale

Eubalaena glacialis

Status: Although this species has been totally protected since 1936, there is no real indication of any notable population increase since the conservation measures came into force; the possibility exists that the species is still hunted

Description   All the representatives of the order Cetacea, which includes whales, dolphins and porpoises, are aquatic mammals and consequently breathe air, are warm blooded and bear live young which are suckled on milk. The whales now living form two distinct natural groups — Odontoceti and Mysticeti. Members of the first group have teeth, which can only be used for gripping food, whereas members of the second have no teeth at all. The North Atlantic right whale belongs to the latter group, which has, instead of teeth, an arrangement of heavy plates which are known as 'baleen' or 'whalebone'.

Following E. J. Slijper's classification of whales, the baleen/whalebone group comprises three families: the right whales, the grey whales and the rorqual whales; the last of these embraces the giant blue whale, which is not only the world's largest living animal but the largest that has ever existed. There are three species of right whales: the Greenland right whale, the Biscayan right whale (North Atlantic right whale; southern type = southern right whale) and the pigmy right whale.

The structure of a whale is well described by L. Harrison Mathews: 'The body of a whale is elongated but it is not strictly stream-lined although it is fusiform; the surface is smooth and hairless. There are no hind limbs although some small bones inside the body are the equivalent of the pelvis and leg bones of other mammals. The forelimbs are modified as flippers or paddles in which the length of the arm bones is reduced, as is the number of wrist bones, but the number of small bones in the five fingers is much increased. The nostrils are not at the end of the snout but on the top of the head where they form the "blowholes", and the eye lies rather far down near the corner of the mouth. The ear hole is minute but the internal ear, with which it does not communicate directly, is well developed. In all whales the long tail region, which is not sharply marked off from the rest of the body, ends in flattened flukes shaped much like a fish's tail-fin but set horizontally instead of vertically.'

The North Atlantic right whale is a large, slow moving whale (though smaller than the Greenland species); in common with other right whales, it has a completely smooth throat, no dorsal fin, broad and rounded flippers, large flukes, a narrow, greatly arched upper jaw, and a scoop-like lower jaw — with a large fleshy eminence on each side fitting into the arch of the upper jaw. The general body colour is black, sometimes with irregular white patches on the belly. The head is up to a quarter of the body length. On the tip of the snout there is a yellowish-white horny growth, called the bonnet, which is usually covered with parasites (especially goose-barnacles, worms and whale lice). The eyes are comparatively small.

Right whales and sperm whales have their bodies protected by an unusually thick layer of blubber, which in the case of the right whale can account for 36—45% of the animal's total weight. However, in spite of this amount of blubber, which helps to insulate the animal against the cold, it is remarkably mobile. Its short rigid neck adds to the streamlining effect of the rest of the body; since the motive force lies in the whale's tail, a less rigid head would flop in all directions and impede the animal's progress through the water.

As E. J. Slijper relates, the blow or 'blast', as it is called in whaling circles, is an important means of identifying the species, which the specialist can recognise by the type, shape and direction of the jet: 'the right whales have a double V-shaped blow, due to the division between the nostrils being so pronounced that two separate blows emerge; and these can therefore be easily distinguished from the closely related rorqual whale, which has a single blow due to the nostrils being both combined'.

The right whale's total length is 14—18.5 m; the weight is estimated at 40,000—72,000 kg. The upper jaw bears two rows of long, narrow and flexible baleen plates, which can measure up to 2.70 metres; each row contains 220—260 plates, hanging down from the upper jaw in a series of curtains at about 1.5 cm intervals.

Habitat   Right whales occur in temperate, plankton-rich waters. During the summer, North Atlantic right whales migrate northwards off the British Isles to colder regions; but according to Harrison Mathews, they do not come closer than the 100 fathom line, although they sometimes approach inshore waters. They return to temperate warm waters in the autumn and winter. In other parts of the world where there is less human traffic, right whales are reported to come close to the coast and often enter sheltered bays.

Behaviour   The right whales are very slow swimmers and rarely exceed 5 knots, their average speed being approximately 2 knots. They do not usually dive to depths greater than 25—50 fathoms, although it has been reported that if frightened they can dive much deeper, to 200 or even 250 fathoms. Most authorities agree that North Atlantic right whales are capable of remaining under the surface for 20 or 30 minutes at a time; the tail comes into view before such a dive. E. J. Slijper reports that the Greenland right whale is able to stay submerged for up to 60 minutes, and the rorqual whale for up to about 40 minutes. However, animals in this group usually only remain under water for 10—15 minutes, coming up for 5—10 minutes at a time; a deep dive is usually followed by 5—6 shallow dives.

Harrison Mathews gives several reasons why a whale can hold its breath for such a long time. First, it stores a comparatively large quantity of oxygen in its muscle as well as in its blood, in addition to that in the air in its lungs. Secondly, it uses the oxygen it takes down very sparingly, because it shuts off part of its blood circulation so that the oxygen is supplied chiefly to the brain and other vital parts. Thus a large 'oxygen-debt' is built up in the muscles and elsewhere, to be made good on surfacing. The blood vessels are highly modified to enable this to be done. De la Fuente relates that it has been calculated that every time a whale breathes in, it replenishes 80—90 per cent of the air in its lungs. This latter fact well illustrates how rapidly the oxygen can be replenished and re-stored.

Hearing is believed to be the sense on which whales rely the most, for water is an excellent medium for sound, which travels four and a half times as fast there as in air. Although the whaling industry has long been aware that whales have acute hearing, this feature was not studied scientifically until the 1950s, when dolphins were shown to have an acuteness of hearing second only to that of bats. Further investigations showed that the smaller toothed whales have the ability, along with bats and dolphins, to perceive objects by echo-location: that is, by emitting sound vibrations which are bounced off the objects and then picking up the returning sound waves, in the manner of sonar. More recently, there have been some observations which suggest that the baleen whales may also have this ability, using the echoes of ultra-sonic vibrations to build up a mental picture of their environment. There is still a lack of factual data concerning the larger baleen whales, which are considered to be much more difficult to study at close quarters, but there is no reason to suppose them dissimilar to the toothed whales in this matter.

Early literature reported that North Atlantic right whales once occurred in shoals of up to 100 individuals; but now they are mostly observed alone or in pairs, probably as a result of their extreme scarcity. The habits of this species are little known, but whales are generally sociable animals, often travelling in small close-knit groups within large 'schools'. Due to their curiosity, whales have been known to stick their heads out of the water in order to see people better on board ship or in an open boat. On one occasion, reported by Harrison Mathews, it was possible for people actually to pat living wild baleen whales on the snout; but this of course was very exceptional.

Diet   During the spring, the North Atlantic right whale migrates northwards to the Arctic regions where, during the summer months, it takes full advantage of the vast harvests of planktonic matter to be found there, and becomes extremely fat. Plankton is made up of a variety of small, drifting plants and minute animals, the most common of which is a tiny crustacean called krill; krill is the staple food of the baleen whales, and they devour it with consummate efficiency.

Faith McNulty points out that whereas the tropical land areas produce the most luxuriant plant life, matters are reversed in the sea, for cold waters are the richest. The following factors are given in order to qualify this reversal: first, cold waters hold more dissolved oxygen and carbonic acid than warm water; and secondly, the surface of the water near the poles contains an especially rich supply of plant nutrients, derived from the bodies of dead organisms and other waste products. In most ocean regions such debris sinks to the bottom, but in the polar regions there are vast areas of upwelling water — currents from the deep rising abruptly to the surface — which endlessly bring up supplies of food for the tiny plants floating in the sunlit surface layer. These sea plants, thriving in the almost endless sunshine of the polar summer, provide pasture for a host of small grazing organisms; one of the most abundant in the Arctic is the shrimp-like crustacean *Euphausia superba Dana* — otherwise, krill. In the high latitudes, krill can occur in fantastic concentrations, forming a rusty-red carpet up to 100 metres deep over several square kilometres of ocean.

Right whales are reported to swim through these thick masses of krill with almost constantly open mouths. The water streams into the mouth and out again through the openings between the baleen plates, while the krill is retained by the hairy fringe to the plates. A little later, the mouth is closed for a brief interval, and the tongue is brought up to push the krill towards the throat. In so doing, the tongue squashes the water out through the filter-bed formed by the hairy fringe and the spaces between the baleen plates, and so out between the lips and back into the sea. The krill can therefore be swallowed without the right whale drinking vast volumes of sea-water at the same time.

E. J. Slijper draws attention to the marked difference between the feeding method of a right whale, with its very long baleen and scoop-like action of the lower jaw, and that of a rorqual, with its very short baleen and a mouth that can be greatly distended from the bottom. The mouth of a rorqual whale can be greatly widened by virtue of a system of external folds and grooves. Consequently, it can take in large quantities of krill with one gulp, close the mouth, and contract the muscles of the tongue and the base of the mouth, thus squeezing the water between the baleen and expelling it over the edge of the lower jaw. Once the mouth has been closed, the krill is pushed towards the throat.

Although the echo-location system of whales can be used, amongst numerous other things, for the location of food, as far as is known the baleen whales eat little while in warmer seas during the winter, for plankton is never so abundant there as in the colder seas during the summer. The whales therefore have to survive on very meagre rations, relying on the fat accumulated in their blubber to keep them going – in the case of the right whales this may be up to 62 cm thick. The krill population dies down in the cold winter months, but when the brighter warmer weather arrives there is a great abundance of these planktonic crustacea; so when the whales travel to their lush spring pastures in the Arctic to replenish their survival reservoirs of blubber, this annual migration northwards aptly coincides with the weaning period for the young of that year.

Breeding   The young are born in the warmer waters during the winter, after an approximate gestation period of 12 months. The mating season for the closely related Greenland right whale is given by Slijper as February—March. The females come close to the shore to calf and to nurse their young, which are singletons.

Very little is known about the sexual behaviour of baleen whales, or indeed of whales in general. But the few observations that have been made suggest that the animals are monogamous and that a courtship and seduction ritual occurs prior to mating. One report is cited by Slijper of a pair of humpback whales: it relates that after some introductory love play, the whales dived, swam towards each other at great speed, then came to the surface vertically and copulated belly to belly. In so doing, their entire thorax, and often part of their abdomen, as well, protruded out of the water; after which they dropped back into the sea with a resounding slap. This action by the same pair was seen a number of times within the space of three hours.

No one has yet observed the birth of a baleen whale, and perhaps this possibility will only arise should a baleen whale be kept and a parturition occur in one of the scientifically operated marine aquariums. Similarly, the development of the foetus has only been traced through examination of the countless pregnant females that have been caught on whaling expeditions. However, thanks to the research carried out on a dolphin at the Marineland Aquarium, Florida, where they are able to film and record such events, we now know for certain that the cetacean calf is born tail first, under water.

The newly born baleen whale is reported to be approximately 30% of its mother's length. At first the baleen is rudimentary, and it does not grow large enough to be functional until the time of weaning, when a young whale is about six months old. The maternal ties are reported to be particularly close, the young ones always keeping extremely close to the mother. The female whale has two teats which are recessed in openings on either side of the genital slit, and are equipped with muscles that squirt the milk into the mouth of the calf; for the calf, which lacks soft lips, seizes the teat between tongue and palate in the corner of its mouth, and the milk is then squirted. The suckling always takes place under water. The mother is considered to keep in almost constant touch with her calf by sounds, and whenever she dozes off the calf may sleep on her tail.

Whale milk is reported to be three to four times as concentrated as the milk of cows, goats and also of human beings; it has the thick appearance of condensed milk with a water content of only 40—50%. E. J. Slijper reports that whales have a shorter period of lactation than many other large mammals; for whereas right whales suckle their young for about a year, undomesticated bovines such as the bison have a period of lactation of about two years.

73

Although a comprehensive study of the biology and behaviour of the blue whale has been carried out, which well illustrates the rapid growth rate of whales, no similar specific study has been done on the right whale. However, most specialists believe that the female baleen whale does not come into oestrus until after she has weaned her calf, and thus will only breed in alternate years. Furthermore, if one takes into account that the female attains sexual maturity between the ages of four and six years, and that she will not live for more than thirty to forty years, she is unlikely to bear more than about ten calves in a lifetime.

It is reported that nowadays very few whales in commercial catches are found to be more than thirty years old, and most of them are under ten years. However, let us hope that the conservation measures taken in 1936 for the North Atlantic right whale have been adhered to totally, so that the species' expected lifespan of up to forty years has now been restored.

Population   Right whales once swam by the thousand in the temperate waters of both the Atlantic and the Pacific oceans. Yet H. N. Southern reports that only 67 North Atlantic right whales were landed at Scottish whaling stations in the Outer Hebrides between 1908 and 1914, and no British strandings have been reported since 1913.

Although observations are on the increase, little is known about the number of right whales in the northern part of the Atlantic, apart from the fact that the species is extremely scarce there. According to estimates made by the Japanese in 1970–71, there were then about 400 specimens in the northern part of the Pacific. The number in the Antarctic region is put at between 1000 and 1500 individuals.

One report cited in *Oryx* magazine (October 1973), entitled 'Right whales not yet right', estimates numbers of the southern-type of the right whale at about 180 found off the South African coasts, and perhaps 1000 individuals in the whole southern hemisphere.

Distribution   The former and present European distribution of the right whale is given by Smit and Wijngaarden as follows. It was once common in the northern part of the Atlantic Ocean, from the north-west coast of Africa across to Bermuda and Florida in the south, up to as far as Newfoundland, Iceland, and Spitsbergen in the north. The species was often caught in the Bay of Biscay and west of the Hebrides in the Gulf Stream. Now it is very rare in the same area. It is seen in the summer around Iceland, the Hebrides, Newfoundland, and at the mouth of Davis Strait. In the autumn and winter it returns to temperate warm waters near Spain, north-west Africa, North and South Carolina, Florida, the Azores and Bermuda.

Conservation   The right whale is the rarest of all the great whales, driven as it was to near extinction in the late 1930s. Records show that the Basques inhabiting the coast of the Bay of Biscay began to hunt it in about the eleventh century; and they gradually turned whaling into a large-scale industry, extending it further and further across the Atlantic. As the right whale was massive and a slow swimmer, it was easy to catch from an open boat, and hence it was the earliest to be attacked by primitive hunters. Also, when it is dead, its carcass floats, and for this reason, as well as its high oil content, it became known as the 'right' whale to catch — hence its name.

E. J. Slijper relates that as long as the whalers restricted their activities to the

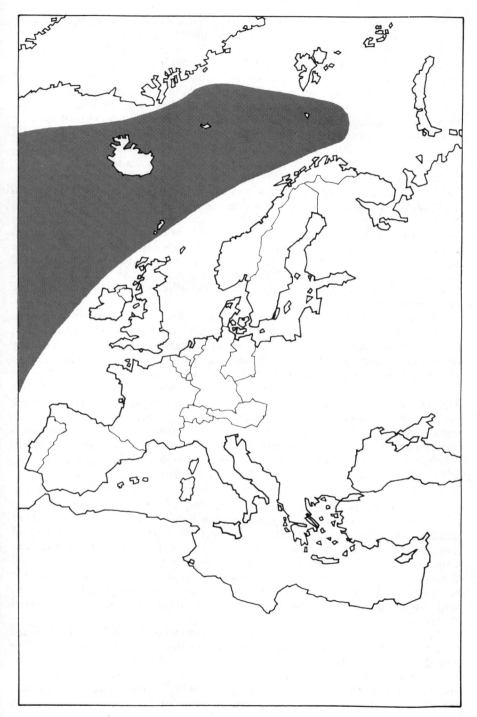

coast alone they could use the flesh of the animals, but as the hunt took them to distant parts their interest centred more and more exclusively on only two whale products: lamp oil and whalebone. At a time when steel and elastic were unknown, whalebone was the ideal material for whips, umbrellas, stays, crinolines, and countless other articles. With the increasing prosperity of Western Europe, whale oil and whalebone came into ever greater demand. As houses required better lighting and women better clothes, and as the local stock decreased, the whalers became more ambitious in extending their voyages in pursuit of the right whale. One historical note records that in England, after the Norman conquest, the whale was proclaimed a royal fish, and the king was made an Honorary Harpooner, entitled to the head of all captured whales, while the Queen was given the baleen.

Although the Basques were the first whalers, other Europeans soon joined in, and by the sixteenth century they had destroyed the stock on their Atlantic coasts. Faith McNutty reports that a couple of hundred years later, American whalers did the same on their coasts. In the nineteenth century, a great fleet of whaling ships from many different nations swept the Pacific, both north and south, almost completely polishing off the right whales there. McNutty points out that, as the right whale is so rare and yet still exists, it poses an interesting dilemma for biologists: 'Why is it', she asks, 'that, although it has not been hunted for such a long time, it has multiplied so little? Or, on the other hand, why has it not gone under entirely?'

The North Atlantic right whale and the Greenland right whale have been protected since 1936: could it be that their numbers were so severely reduced, their distribution so fragmented, and the population spread out over so comparatively large an area, that the danger has been realised that individuals are simply unable to find each other and subsequently reproduction cannot take place?

The advent of steam vessels, the invention in 1864 of a cannon-fired grenade harpoon and the arrival of the factory ships at the beginning of the twentieth century, where whales could be flensed and dismembered on the spot, made catastrophic inroads on the world's whale populations. In 1932 the first international attempts to limit whaling activities were made. In 1946 the International Whaling Commission (I.W.C.) was set up, to which eighteen nations are now affiliated. The Commission was empowered to regulate the whale catch, and by so doing, it was hoped, ensure the effective conservation of the world's whale stocks.

Richard Fitter reports that since the founding of the Commission, the Commission and its scientific advisers have striven hard to impress the short-sighted whaling companies with the self-evident fact that they were overhunting and destroying their own industry. In the end, most of the former whaling nations dropped out of the industry by 1967, leaving the field to Japan, Norway and Russia. Not until this year was a sensible whaling quota agreed, and by that time two more species, the hump-back and the giant blue whale, had been hunted to the verge of extinction; the taking of both is now prohibited throughout the oceans of the world.

The twenty-fourth meeting of the I.W.C., held in London in June 1972, failed to accept fully the proposal for a ten year moratorium on commercial whaling passed with an overwhelming vote (51—3) at the May Stockholm United Nations Conference. However, as Fitter reports in *Oryx*, 'the entrenched tradition of commercial whaling in Russia and Japan was evidently once more too powerful'. For although the I.W.C. confirmed a complete ban on hunting of five threatened species and the implementation of the independent observer scheme, as well as the setting and agreeing of actual quotas for certain whale species, the chance of building up stocks was missed.

In November 1974, it was reported in *Oryx* that I.U.C.N. made a forthright statement at the recent I.W.C. meeting, reaffirming its support for the Stockholm whaling resolution, deploring the repudiation by Japan and Russia of three major conservation agreements made at the 1973 meeting, and calling for a comprehensive world programme of research on living as well as dead whales. At the June 1976 London meeting of the I.W.C., amongst other matters, the Fauna Preservation Society urged that the Commission should accept without serious amendment the advice of its scientists and should not raise quotas for extraneous considerations. For the previous year's Antarctic catches had suggested a shortage of whales; for instance, only 80% of the Sei/Bryde's whale quota was taken.

The unrestricted slaughter that resulted in the near-extermination of whales in the Northern Hemisphere during the last century could be in part excused on grounds of ignorance; but since the foundation of the I.W.C. in 1946, this excuse is no longer valid. In February 1977, Richard Fitter condemned the bad management of the I.W.C., stating that: 'Had the commission listened to its scientists twenty years ago, there could have been a flourishing whaling industry today, instead of a dying one'. In a table given by Fitter on the Quotas and Catches for 1975/6 and 1976/7, it can be seen that all the nils, coupled with the continued downward spiral of both quotas and catches, underline this short-term policy of failing to conserve the whale stocks of the world.

As the I.U.C.N. point out, the seas cover 70% of the earth's surface, governing its climate and sustaining much of its life. It is in connection with this factor that I.U.C.N. have prepared for the World Wildlife Fund their 'The Seas Must Live' campaign, 1977/8, which aims at raising $10 million for such a programme. Should this target be realised, $2 million is to be earmarked for a global action plan for the conservation of cetaceans, for as this plan for the conservation of cetaceans states: 'The breeding and feeding areas of whales, dolphins and porpoises need to be identified and protected, for so little is known about even the most threatened species that investigations of their behaviour and requirements are needed first.'

With so much attention now being focused on the severe plight of the whale family, let us hope that such conservation plans can be put into effect before it is too late; and that good sense can be brought to bear on those who appear to be wanting to achieve deliberately, even at the cost of their own whaling industries' self-destruction, the ultimate extinction of one of the world's most magnificent groups of animals.

Burton, M. (1962): *Systematic Dictionary of Mammals of the World*, p. 267. **Fisher**, J., **Simon**, N. and **Vincent**, J. (1972): *The Red Book: Wildlife in Danger*, pp. 60–9. **Fitter**, R. (1968): *Vanishing Wild Animals of the World*, pp. 85–7; (1972): 'Whales: the next step?'; (1974): 'Future for whales'; (1975): 'Whales and whaling: a dance of death'; (1977): 'International whaling: eating the seed corn'; **Fuente de la**, F. R. (1974): *World of Wildlife*, *Vol. 10*, pp. 279–300. **Harrison Mathews**, L. (1963): 'Baleen whales', in *Animals of Britain*, 24. **I.U.C.N.** (1976): *Monthly Bulletin, Vol. 7*, No. 12. **McNutty**, F. (1974): *The Great Whales.* **Oryx** (1969–73): *Vols X–XII*. **Simon**, N. (1966): *Red Data Book: Mammalia, Vol. 1*. **Slijper**, E. J. (1962): *Whales.* **Smit**, C. J. and **Wijngaarden**, A. van (1975): 'Threatened mammals'.

Southern, H. N. (1964): *Handbook of British Mammals*, p. 322. **van den Brink**, F. H. (1973): *A Field Guide to the Mammals of Britain and Europe*, pp. 183—4. **Walker**, E. P. (1964): *Mammals of the World, Vol. II*, pp. 1140—1. **W.W.F.** (1976): *World Wildlife Fund, New Feature*.

Wolf

Canis lupus

Status: Although three European countries still have low but viable populations, international co-operation will be needed if wolves are to be preserved at all in Western Europe

Description   Not so very long ago the wolf was the most dreaded of carnivores. Its ferocity and frequent ravages of domestic stock were matters of common notoriety, so that even naturalists described it as untameable, and incapable of true attachment. This, like so many other early descriptions of mammals, much maligned the real integrity and potential friendliness of this fascinating species.

The wolf bears a considerable resemblance to an Alsatian dog: but it has a stronger build, with a wider head, slanting eyes and stouter eye-teeth, the profile of the head showing a marked step between the muzzle and the crown. The length of body is 110–140 cm; the height at the shoulder 70–80 cm; the tail length 45 cm; the hind foot length over 20 cm; and the weight 25–50 kg. The coat is yellowy-browny-grey mixed with black on top, the neck usually a greyish brown, and the underside yellow grey-white: the colour of the coat varies with age, territory and the season of the year. The ears are erect and black at the edges, while the tail is long, bushy and drooping. The wolf has five toes on its fore feet (the first being placed high up), and four on its hind feet. Much like the jackal, the wolf has a scent gland situated on the back and at the base of the tail.

Habitat   Wolves frequent wooded plains and mountains, and also open country with adequate cover.

Behaviour   Farley Mowat's adventures with a family of wolves in the Canadian wilderness demonstrated that wolves are not always nomadic, as was until then almost universally believed, but are usually settled beasts and possessors of a large permanent estate with very definite boundaries. Once a week, more or less, the wolf family that Mowat was studying would do the rounds of their territory, leaving their personal marks by urinating on each convenient site. This careful attention to property rights was perhaps made necessary by the presence of two other wolf families whose lands abutted on theirs. To test the validity of such marking, Farley Mowat staked out a property claim of his own, embracing approximately three acres with his tent in the middle. After drinking copious quantities of tea, he spent the majority of a night making property marks of his own on stones, clumps of moss and patches of vegetation at intervals of not more than fifteen feet around the circumference of his claim. He had not long to wait before the leading male of the clan appeared over the ridge, padding homeward with his usual air of preoccupation. As usual the wolf did not deign to glance at the tent; but when he reached the point where a property mark was in existence, he stopped abruptly, his attitude of fatigue vanished, and a look of bewilderment replaced it. Cautiously the wolf extended his nose and sniffed at one of the human-marked bushes; after a minute of complete indecision, he backed away a few yards and sat down; and finally, he looked thoughtfully and directly at Farley Mowat and his tent. After some time, the male wolf got again to his feet and had another sniff at the offending human marker. Then with an air of decision he made a systematic tour of the whole area that had been marked, carefully placing one of his marks on the outside of each clump of grass, or stone. Once this task was complete, he retired to his home territory apparently well satisfied. Wolves have more recently been extensively studied and filmed following the migrating caribou to and from their breeding grounds in Alaska.

It is well known that wolves are social animals, hunting in packs. This applies mainly to the winter when the pack usually has a definite composition, consisting of the male wolf and his mate, who normally remain paired for life, and their young of the previous year and perhaps also of the year before that. Such a pack may travel extensively: there is one report of a pack that was tracked in Alaska, within an area of about 100 by 50 miles — it travelled 700 miles in 6 weeks. On the whole the wolf is now mainly nocturnal, although in areas where it is not persecuted it will still hunt mainly by day. The technique of hunting varies greatly according to the prey, but normally involves an initial stealthy approach followed by a rapid short chase. In hunting, hearing and sight are just as important to a wolf as scent: and although able to yelp, growl, occasionally bark and sometimes utter a doleful howl, it remains silent while hunting.

Diet   In the absence of any competitors, wolves will prey especially upon the larger ungulates, which they bring down by hunting in packs: their chief victims in the north are reindeer and elk, but they will also hunt horses, cattle, sheep and goats. They are known to feed on dogs, hares, birds, carrion, mice, frogs or almost any small animal. In extremity they will eat even potatoes and fruit, and are said to seek nourishment from buds and lichens. The damage to cattle in Russia in 1873 was estimated to value seven and a half million roubles. In 1875, it was reported that 161 persons fell victim to wolves in Russia, although in more recent years there are no authentic records of wolves killing men.

Breeding   Wolves make their dens in bushes, between the roots of trees or under rocks; either digging the holes themselves, or utilising and expanding those of other animals. There is a single period of oestrus lasting about 5 days, which according to the latitude occurs between January and March. The gestation period is 7 weeks, with the litter size usually 5 or 6.

The young are born in the den, and during the early days of lactation the father hunts for his family. The young begin to leave the den at about 3 weeks. At first they feed on the mother's milk, later on regurgitated food, and they are finally weaned at about 5–6 weeks. The den is abandoned after about 3 months but the family stays together, and may be joined in the autumn by the young of the previous year. Wolves do not breed until they are 2 years old. As puppies they are tameable, and become accustomed to associate with man like dogs. The maximum longevity recorded for a wolf is 16½ years.

Wolves breed readily in captivity, but every effort must be made to ensure that the various races are not intermingled. On 24 May 1974 the Abruzzo National Park announced the birth in the Pescasseroli Zoo of 1–3 wolves of the pure Apennine wolf stock. As this Italian sub-species of the wolf is very rare and endangered such captive breeding projects could be essential for this race's survival.

Canis lupus has been recorded to have hybridised with the domestic dog *Canis familiaris* on numerous occasions, with reciprocal crosses occurring. The hybrids are said to be fully viable and fertile in both sexes. Wolf crosses have also been recorded with the dingo *Canis familiaris dingo*, and the coyote *Canis latrans*. Although often referred to, there are no reliable records of the wolf hybridising with the European red fox *Vulpes vulpes*.

Population   In Great Britain and Ireland the wolf was numerous in the Pleistocene age, its earliest known remains having been found in the Norfolk 'forest bed', which belongs to the first portion of this period. Early remains of the wolf also occur in nearly all the caverns and brick earths of England, and have been found in Scotland (the Pentland Hills) and in Ireland (Shandon).

Wolves were abundant when the Romans arrived in Britain and, according to the earliest chronicle, in the Anglo-Saxon period they were so numerous that the month of January was set apart especially for hunting them. King Edgar is said to have made an attempt to stamp out wolves in Wales by imposing an annual fine of three hundred wolf skins on the Welsh King Ludwall, which caused great destruction. In 1066, at the Norman conquest, the dead bodies of the English were said to have been left on the battlefield to be eaten by 'worms, wolves, birds and dogs'. There are constant references to wolves in the reigns of Richard I, of King John (1209) and of Henry III (1216–72). Thereafter the wolf seems gradually to have become scarce, though records of wolf hunting occur in England as late as 1486.

In Scotland in 1427, during the reign of James I, a law was passed in an attempt to combat the 'wolf plague' which then existed. The wolf plague in Scotland is said to have reached its height in the reign of Mary, Queen of Scots, and to have spread unprecedented devastation in the country. In 1563, five wolves were killed as the result of a great drive in the forest of Athol. Further wolf killings were recorded between the years 1690 and 1700, until the wolf finally succumbed to the pressures of persecution as recently as 1743.

In Ireland wolves were reported to be in abundance in the wilder parts up to the latter part of the sixteenth century. In 1669 they were still common, but the beginning of the eighteenth century seems to have heralded the doom of the species.

In the U.S.S.R. there was a rapid increase in wolves during the Second World War (1939—45), at the end of which the population was estimated at 150,000—200,000 animals. In 1946, 62,700 were killed and 40,000—50,000 animals were killed each year thereafter for the next fifteen years. A marked reduction of wolves became apparent in the late 1950s, and during the past decade the kill has been approximately 15,000 a year.

In 1970, the wolf population in Finland was estimated at no more than 10 animals. In 1973, no more than about 15 animals were said to exist in Finland, and the total number of wolves in Norway and Sweden was estimated hardly to exceed half a dozen. In Italy in the early 1970s, wolves were believed to number about 100; in January 1977 it was reported that 100—150 wolves remain in the Apennines, occurring in scattered packs.

In 1974, there were approximately 200 wolves of the *Canis lupus* species held in world zoos. Although the majority of these were the Canadian timber wolf, there are some cases of zoological parks making an effort to look after the threatened sub-species of the common wolf.

Distribution   Originally the range of the wolf was very large, from the steppe and Mediterranean zones in the south well into the tundra in the north. It is now extinct over most of western Europe, though still present in parts of Finland, Norway, Sweden, Spain, Portugal and Italy, and reported to be present in central France. The last native wolf in Germany was killed in 1841 but 6 wolves were released into the wild in 1975. In eastern Europe it is present in Bulgaria, Czechoslovakia, Greece, Poland, Rumania and Yugoslavia; but in the U.S.S.R. it is still found in great numbers. From Russia its range extends eastwards right across Siberia to India and China. It is widely distributed in North America. The wolf was supposed to have become extinct in England between the years 1485 and 1509, but survived in Scotland until about 1743, and in Ireland until the years 1770—1821.

The present distribution in western Europe has been largely determined by persecution and is therefore difficult to define, because individuals may wander far beyond the normal range.

Conservation   In Europe the wolf is extinct in eleven countries. In 1970, in spite of extinction being in sight for wolves in Finland, bounties were still paid for them due to the damage they were said to do to reindeer. In 1974, wolves were still completely unprotected in Finland and could be shot anywhere in the country, even in National Parks. In 1976 it was reported (in *Oryx*) that the Finnish Parliament had passed a law to discontinue the official bounty of $130 for killing a wolf, and that the Ministry of Agriculture will in future issue permits for reindeer breeders to shoot not more than 10 wolves in the worst-hit cattle and reindeer areas.

A major effort to change the image of the wolf and save it from extinction was discussed by international experts of I.U.C.N.'s Wolf Specialist Group of the Survival Service Commission, at the group's first major meeting, held in Stockholm in September 1973, in conjunction with the Eleventh Congress of the International Union of Game Biologists.

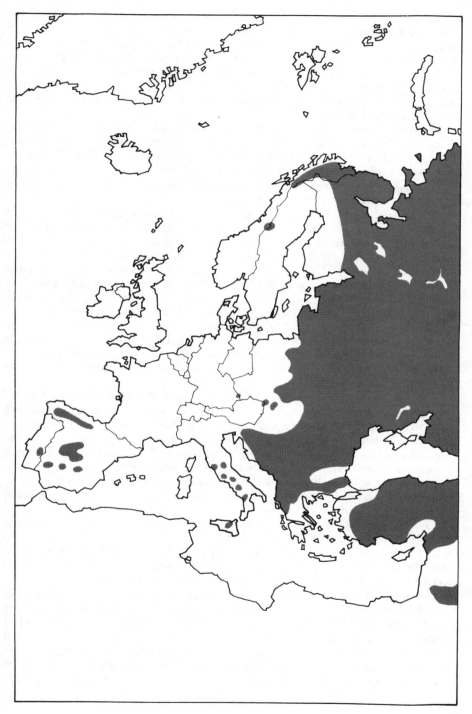

Representatives from many European countries, including the U.S.S.R., heard from Canadian and United States specialists how, in their countries, the public image of the wolf had changed from that of a blood-thirsty killer to that of a highly developed social animal which was no threat to man. Dr Douglas Pimlott of Toronto University, Chairman of the I.U.C.N. Wolf Specialist Group, who had spent three months of the summer of 1973 touring European countries where wolves survive, expressed optimism that a similar revolution in attitudes to the wolf could be achieved in Europe.

Dr Pimlott suggested that in terms of the present status of the wolf, the countries of Europe could be divided into four categories: extinct; virtually extinct; endangered; and viable populations still existing. The wolves in Finland, Norway and Sweden are in the virtually extinct category. Those in Bulgaria, Czechoslovakia, Italy, Poland, Portugal and Spain are endangered; Greece, Rumania and Yugoslavia appear still to have viable low populations.

The remaining wolves are protected in Norway, Sweden and Italy and partly in Poland and South Finland. In 1975, bounties were still paid for the killing of wolves in Czechoslovakia, Bulgaria and parts of Poland; although in 1977 it was reported (*Oryx*) that the Czechoslovakian Government will no longer pay bounties for wolves, and will no longer allow people either to catch or to kill them for any reason between 1 March and 15 September. They are classified as game animals in Spain, and can be killed at any time by any method in Portugal. In the U.S.S.R., the wolf populations in the Baltic, Byelorussia, Ukraine and the central region of Russia are considered to be optimum; and there is no threat from extinction to any sub-species in the U.S.S.R. in the near future. The European tundra species *Canis lupus albus* is closest to being in the endangered category; however, it was the Russian delegates' belief that the republics would not allow elimination of wolf populations to take place.

This first international meeting on the conservation of the wolf concluded with a manifesto comprising a declaration of principles and some recommended guidelines on wolf conservation. The manifesto stated that it was evident that international co-operation would be needed if wolves were to be preserved because many of the remaining wolves exist in border areas. This is true of Bulgaria, on its borders with Yugoslavia, Greece and possibly Rumania; of Czechoslovakia and Poland which share borders with each other and each separately with the U.S.S.R., and of Portugal and Spain. Only Italy is in a position to deal with wolves as a national conservation problem.

Investigations into the behaviour and status of wolves in the Abruzzo National Park, Italy, carried out by Drs Luigi Boitari (Italy) and Erik Zurien (Sweden), had been in progress for some three years when in April 1974 these studies were extended by a successful operation involving the capture of three wolves and the attachment to them of VHF locating transmitters. Valuable information on the range of movement and composition of contacts made by these animals was collected for conservation purposes. In January 1975, it was reported that the scientists, who had been puzzled because radio contacts showed one of the wolves as almost stationary, finally found its body in a stream. It was presumed that it had been shot by a poacher, thus indicating the hazards to which the handful of wolves and other wildlife remaining in Italy are exposed, even in protected areas. Two other wolves were shot in the Abruzzo area outside the Park, and another near Lake

Bracciano during a boar hunt, although the species has been a protected animal in Italy since 1972.

In 1976, sixty-four more red deer were released in the Abruzzo National Park, to provide a stock of wild prey for the wolves. The latest batch came from the Bayerische Wald in south Germany. There are now believed to be 130 red deer in the park, although roe deer have been less successful, their numbers being only 22. In January 1977, it was reported (W.W.F.) that Italy's surviving wolves have a more secure future following a country-wide ban on killing them, the government having decreed complete protection for the wolf for an indefinite length of time.

In the Wolf Specialist Group's declaration of principles it is recognised that world populations have differentiated into numerous sub-species which are genetically adapted to particular environments. It should be every government's objective to maintain these local populations in their natural environments in a wild state; and at the same time zoological gardens should accept the responsibility of maintaining a gene pool of locally adapted races, and so provide a source for possible reintroduction into the wild.

Mr Mats Segnestam of Sweden, on the Nordic Wolf Project, seeks to develop co-operation between Sweden, Norway and Finland to maintain northern wolves in captivity in order to convince people and governments that they should be reintroduced into wild areas. More recently a three-way agreement has been made between the U.S. Department of the Interior, the Tacoma Zoological Society and the Point Defiance Zoo in Texas with the aim of saving the highly endangered red wolf by setting up a captive breeding unit at the zoo. It is now believed that the wolves of the Danube delta were ecotypically distinct; unfortunately this can never be proved, because this population became extinct in 1960. As wolves breed readily in captivity, it is of the utmost importance for 'reservoirs' of the endangered races to be established, so that other sub-species are not thus irretrievably lost through extinction.

The case for the wolf is finely expressed by Dr Pimlott. 'The wolf is one of the most interesting and adaptable mammals that has ever existed. It is true that they may take domestic stock and some of the sport hunter's game, but there can be no pretence that killing of wolves is justified because of danger to human lives. Wolves, like all other wildlife, have a right to exist in a wild state. This right is in no way related to their known value to mankind. Instead it derives from the right of all living creatures to co-exist in a manner unhampered by man as part of natural ecosystems.'

A.A.Z.P.A. (1975): *Vol. XVI*, Newsletter No. 4, p. 13. **Corbet**, G. B. (1966): *Terrestrial Mammals of Western Europe*, pp. 123—5. **Graf, J.** (1968): *Animal Life of Europe*, p. 22. **Gray**, A. P. (1971): *Mammalian Hybrids*, p. 50. **I.U.C.N.** (1973, 1974): *Monthly Bulletins.* **I.Z.Yb.** (1974): *Vol. 14.* **Millais**, J. G. (1904): *Mammals of Great Britain and Ireland, Vol. 1*, pp. 185—99. **Mivart**, St G. (1890): *Monograph of the Canidae: Dogs, Jackals, Wolves, and Foxes*, pp. 3—7. **Mowat**, F. (1963): *Never Cry Wolf.* **Oryx** (1970—7): *Vols X—XIII.* **Southern**, H. N. (1964): *Handbook of British Mammals*, p. 351. **Valverde**, J. A. (1971): *El Lobo Espanol*, pp. 229—41, 4 figs. **van den Brink**, F. H. (1973): *A Field Guide to the Mammals of Britain and Europe*, p. 120. **W.W.F.** (1973—4): *World Wildlife Yearbook*, pp. 295—7. **W.W.F.** (1972—7): *Press Releases*, No. 3/1976 and No. 3/1977.

Brown Bear

Ursus arctos

Status: Protected by law in some restricted areas, but owing to persecution its survival is no longer guaranteed

Description   In all bears the female is smaller than the male, less heavily built, with the features less coarse and the forequarters less powerfully developed; the ears are small and the tail is very short. The colour of the brown bear is greatly variable, ranging from very dark brown to a pale creamy fawn, although usually a rather light yellowish brown. The coat in winter is long, close and soft; in summer shorter, thinner and darker; and on the lower part of the body generally woolly at all seasons, but never without some brown. Most young bears have a white or at least light-coloured band round the neck, which runs along the anterior part of the back, and on the top of the neck is forked, the first branch extending to half an inch behind the ear, while the other runs along the back and curves at the end towards the front. This marking is also subject to variation; the collar round the neck is seldom closed, some young animals do not possess it at all, while some of the fully grown retain it till death.

The size of the brown bear also varies considerably, with a length of up to 210 cm in male specimens and a weight of up to about 200 kg, which is nevertheless small in comparison with some Asiatic and American races, the record being held by the animals on Kodiak Island in Alaska which can reach as much as 1000 kg (1 ton).

Habitat   Mixed woods, nowadays mainly restricted to woodland in the mountains.

Behaviour   In spite of their clumsy-looking heavy build, bears are very active, leaping well and climbing with ease. Old bears only climb trees with strong branches, but can negotiate smooth trunks that offer difficulties to younger animals; trees with rough bark are very easily ascended. In climbing slender trunks bears embrace them with the forelegs, pressing their breasts hard to the stem, and planting the naked soles of the hind paws firmly on the bark. Should the trunk be thick they can support themselves by their claws, and on horizontal branches are able to walk to and fro with perfect ease, or even to stand upright. When turning round on a branch, in the upright posture, they grip a higher one with the forelegs, or even hang their whole weight on this support. If there is no higher branch within reach, they lie down full-length and swing the body round. On the ground bears move the two legs of the same side simultaneously – it is this that causes their ungainly walk; nevertheless, their long legs enable them to progress rapidly. In deep snow they lift the forelegs very high, and put them down quite together, one almost above the other. When the snow is so deep that they cannot withdraw their legs, they push through with their chest as if swimming, at the same time throwing up the snow with their paws.

When walking slowly, the bears hold their non-retractile claws close together, but when walking through swamps or when attacked they spread them out. The strong and muscular fore paws are the parts of the body most used – both as tools, to climb, dig, and drag or carry heavy carcases, and as weapons to maul their foes or their prey. With one strike of these powerful paws they are able to knock down an animal as large as a cow, while the short neck and broad chest possess such power that they can carry as great a weight by their teeth as with their paws; it is said that while walking erect they can carry the carcase of a cow through water.

Brown bears are solitary, territorial animals, active mainly at night, especially in inhabited country. The males are entirely solitary and always hibernate alone in a den excavated in rocks or under a tree. Hibernation begins any time from September in the north of the species' range to December in the south. The bears are particularly voracious in autumn, when they build up a thick layer of subcutaneous fat to tide them over hibernation. No food is taken during the period of hibernation itself, although there is little reduction in temperature and the sleep is very light; some individuals, especially males, may not hibernate at all.

The mental faculty of a bear appears as well developed as that of any other beast of prey in the wild state; and although sometimes its intellect seems limited, many of its actions display calculation and reflection. A bear's eyesight is by no means good, and it has been frequently asserted that the sense of hearing in this species is far from being acute. The latter seems unlikely, however, since it is stated by R. Lydekker that in still weather a bear will hear the cocking of a rifle at a distance of 70 paces, the snapping of a twig as thick as a finger at 135 paces, and a low whistle at 60 paces. In all such cases a bear immediately raises its head, and moves its ears rapidly and continuously in different directions so as to locate the noise. The bear's excellent sense of smell enables it to detect food or foes at considerable distances.

Diet   Brown bears are quite omnivorous. Their diet is largely vegetable, including roots, tubers, bulbs, berries, fruit, nuts, fungi and grain. When feeding on the latter they glide along on their haunches, drawing the plants towards them from right and left with their fore paws, and forming regular lanes through the crop, which they often completely ruin. Other foods include domestic animals, especially sheep, carrion, insects, honey, frogs, small mammals, birds' eggs, fish and occasionally larger wild animals including deer and boars. Bears rarely secure the chamois, which is much too active and quick-sighted to be caught.

Breeding   Mating takes place in July, the females being monoestrous. The father leaves the female after mating and takes no part in rearing the cubs. On the approach of winter, the female bear retires earlier than the male and devotes more care to preparing her lair, which is lined with a soft warm bed of twigs, leaves, moss, grass and other dry materials. She builds up a thick layer of subcutaneous fat to tide her over hibernation, and in mid-winter, after a period of gestation of about 7 months, the young, usually 2 cubs, are born. Litters of 1—4 cubs have been recorded.

At birth the young of all bears are extremely small, only about 350 g in the case of the brown bear. They leave the den with the mother in the spring and are weaned by about 4 months. The mother bear only leaves the winter quarters when the cubs are able to follow her; and even then undertakes no distant expeditions, but remains for weeks or months in the neighbourhood diligently teaching the cubs to climb and search for food. When the cubs can stand hardship, the family begins to wander, and then the mother suspiciously scrutinises every object, and is specially anxious about indications of the presence of man.

The female hibernates one year in the company of her grown young, then the following year alone, giving birth to the next litter during hibernation. The sub-adults reach sexual maturity at 2 years, and the bear's lifespan is recorded at 20—30 years.

The brown bear has probably suffered more than any other species of animal from excessive taxonomic hair-splitting, no fewer than 150 specific and sub-specific names having been applied. In captivity, the vast majority of the races are accounted for under one species, and the records show that in world zoos well over 100 cubs are born each year. These captive breeding successes chiefly reflect a growing understanding of the requirements of pregnant animals. For since all bears give birth in a concealed place, zoos have to provide suitable facilities for them. What is accepted by a particular female depends to some extent upon the species concerned, but individual characteristics are also important. A tame female is easier to accommodate than a shy, fearful female, and an animal who has had a normal upbringing with her mother and other young is better prepared than a bottle-fed, isolated female. Food must of course, contain adequate nutrients, vitamins and minerals.

Population   Only about 20 brown bears survived in Czechoslovakia when they were first protected in 1932. In 1969 between 300 and 330 were reported in northern and central Slovakia.

In Finland, 52 brown bears were killed in 1969 and in the dozen years up to 1971 it was estimated that 536 bears had been shot there. In September 1970, it was reported that the brown bear population was somewhere between 100 and 200, but decreasing in number. However, in May 1971, it was recorded that the downward trend of the brown bear population had stopped, mainly due to the extension of the close season, and their number was established at about 150 animals. In June 1974, the number was estimated to have increased to 150–200 individuals.

In 1969, it was estimated that the last European brown bears in the Alps numbered 8–10 animals. In 1973, a maximum of 10 specimens were recorded as surviving over the entire Alpine range. During the 6 years from 1966 to 1971, 6 bears were reported to have been killed there.

In September 1969, there were about 60 brown bears in the Abruzzo National Park, Italy. In January 1972, the total number of this population may have been not less than 100 animals. In February 1977, *Oryx* magazine reported that only 80–100 are believed to remain in Abruzzo.

In 1972 the Barcelona Zoo, Spain, was recorded as having 2 males and 1 female of the Pyrenean race of the Brown bear *Ursus arctos pyrenaicus*.

Distribution The brown bear used to occur throughout the whole of Europe ranging over a large portion of the Northern Hemisphere. Apart from the Balkan countries the range in western Europe is fragmented into four small southern groups – Cantabria, Pyrenees, Italian Alps, Abruzzo – and a Scandinavian group. The bear is more abundant in the U.S.S.R.

The date of extinction of the brown bear in Britain is conjectural, being confused by the practice of bear baiting and undoubted importation of captive bears for that purpose. It is considered that it was probably extinct by the tenth century, but it is possible that it survived in the wilder parts of the country to a later date. The brown bear was last seen in the French Alps in 1937. Bears were hunted for sport, for food and for fur, and were caught alive for baiting.

The present range of the brown bear in Finland covers a narrow zone on the eastern frontier in North Kardia and Kainuu, together with eastern and central Lapland. The last European brown bears in the Alps are in the Italian province of Trento. The Abruzzo race *Ursus arctos marsicanus* is found in and around the Abruzzo National Park. In 1975, it was reported that brown bears had recently returned to the Sonfjallet forests in Sweden, whence they were driven in the 1950s and 1960s. Their numbers are considered to be increasing.

Conservation Brown bears are generally considered to be a danger to livestock and are hunted for sport; so they are persecuted throughout the majority of their remaining range. The strictest protection of the territory where they are still to be found must be enforced if the diminishing populations are to survive.

The Italian National Appeal of the World Wildlife Fund has a project on bear protection in Italy – the organisation of research into bear population status and living requirements. Whilst the Abruzzo brown bear is protected in the Abruzzo National Park, the safety of the Alpine brown bear, even though it is protected by law, is not guaranteed. The Italian National Appeal is doing all it can to save the specimens of the latter race that remain – only 10 at the maximum. During 1973 they continued to employ a guard to supervise and protect this population. An expert was also employed to locate the exact areas frequented by the bears; he succeeded in covering the south-east Trentino area, but this research only provided vague information and nothing concrete, although in places he was able to localise

some specimens. Bears were observed to take most of their food from abandoned orchards. The bears often visited rubbish-dumps looking for waste meat and other trash. Observing this acquired habit led to consideration of the provision of a meat store for the animals, who would return regularly to this supply. The study is still to be completed, but some useful proposals have been made to the authorities:

1 Increase protection and take action against poaching, employing at least one guard for each of the three areas frequented by the bears.
2 Forbid use of poison at least in the areas frequented by the bears.
3 Forbid hunting of hares and roe deer with dogs.

The vital importance of expanding the park's boundaries has been urged – it should include most of the area that the bears use intensively, for bears do not recognise park boundaries that are only lines on a map, and some of the habitat that is vital to them lies outside the boundaries and is threatened by human activities.

The brown bear is protected by hunting laws in Scandinavia, Switzerland, Spain, Italy and all the eastern European countries. As reported in *Oryx* in 1976 there was heartening evidence that the Italian judiciary is at least beginning to take wildlife conservation seriously, for fines and costs totalling 275,000 lire plus an indemnity for damages to the Abruzzo National Park were imposed on a man who killed a brown bear in the park. Special protection is given in France (the animals are totally protected in the Pyrenees National Park). In the eastern European countries an excellent management policy is followed and hunting is permitted by special licence only.

Numerically, some of the races of brown bear have reached such a low level that they urgently need every form of assistance they can get if they are going to survive at all. So it is important not only that their habitat should be protected, but that as a safeguard, what have been called 'Zoo Banks' should be created. This means that a sufficient number of the threatened species should be given sanctuary in zoological gardens or, preferably, in a specially established breeding centre where, free from all the natural and unnatural hazards of existence, they can live and breed successfully – for it has already been seen that brown bears readily accept the standard modern zoo accommodation for the breeding of their species and reproduce liberally.

Once endangered races are safely established in a number of zoos and breeding centres, reintroduction into areas from which they have already vanished, such as the Haut-Vercors area in France, should be undertaken in order to increase and strengthen wild populations. Until really effective protection can be afforded to wild populations, it is hoped that the various races of the European brown bear already in captivity, such as the Pyrenean form, will become self-sustaining and so provide much-needed reservoirs for the threatened races concerned.

Ariagno, D. and Delage, R. (1970): 'Oiseaux et mammifères du Haut-Vercors'. Corbet, G. B. (1966): *Terrestrial Mammals of Western Europe*, pp. 131–3; Corbet, G. B. (1974): *Changing Flora and Fauna of Britain*, pp. 179–202. Graf, J. (1968): *Animal Life in Europe*, pp. 24–5. I.Z. Yb. (1974): *Vol. 14*. Jacobi, E. F. (1975): 'Breeding of sloth bears in Amsterdam Zoo', in *Breeding Endangered Species in Captivity*, pp. 351–6. Lydekker, R. (1915): *Wildlife of the World, Vol 1*, pp. 437–43. Oryx (1971–7): *Vols XI–XIII*. Simon, N. (1969): *Red Data Book: Mammalia, Vol. 1*. W.W.F. (1973–4): *World Wildlife Yearbook*, pp. 106–7.

Polar Bear

Thalarctos maritimus

Status: Now considered to be holding its own. The five circumpolar nations recently signed a treaty providing almost complete protection for the polar bear. However, renewed hunting by trappers and sportsmen could easily cause the species' extinction

Description   Polar bears, skilful and solitary hunters of the North, are probably the best-known members of the bear family. Their fur is uniformly white or creamy throughout the year, although yellow tingeing may be more marked in the summer months. The long neck, relatively small and flat head, the 'roman nose', very short ears and small, dark brown eyes all contribute to their characteristic appearance.

These bears are well adapted to an arctic environment. Their thick winter coat of white guard hairs and dense, cottony underfur, and their often thick subcutaneous fat layers, provide protection against both cold air and water. Moreover, the fat layers, sometimes three inches thick on the haunches, help to increase the animal's buoyancy in water. The hair's whiteness not only decreases heat loss, but also serves as camouflage, resulting in more efficient hunting. The feet are very large, with the soles densely hairy; the fur on the feet probably is of greatest assistance in maintaining a footing on ice, as well as being a valuable insulation against the cold.

The canines are larger and the molars smaller than those of the brown bear; the polar bear's teeth illustrate a most interesting and important adaptation to its environment: it has specialised from an omnivorous diet, typical of bears, back to a carnivorous one. Head and body length is usually 2.2–2.5 m; tail length up to 1.6 m. The maximum weight of the males goes up to 720 kg, with an average of 410 kg, and with females weighing about 320 kg. Polar bears from Svalbard (Spitzbergen) and east Greenland are somewhat smaller: a male rarely weighs more than 500 kg.

Habitat   Smit and Wijngaarden relate that the polar bear's habitat is the drift-ice zone of the Arctic Ocean up to the zone of permanent pack ice, and the Arctic islands and shore. In the Hudson Bay region the animals penetrate sometimes as far as 150–200 km into the coniferous forest.

Behaviour   Polar bears are normally solitary, nomadic animals and are the greatest wanderers of all their family, sometimes travelling great distances. They are swifter than most people think, as they can outrun a reindeer over short distances on land. They also have great strength and endurance. Their ability to scale very rough pressure ridges and steep slopes with apparent ease, and to make clever use of cover, promotes their survival by improving their hunting or hastening their escape from man. Their swimming ability also helps them to escape from hunters as well as to approach their major prey, the seals. Using their large paws as powerful oars, they can sometimes reach a speed of about 8–9 km per hour at the surface. Under water they normally keep their eyes open, their nostrils closed, and their ears flattened back, and it is claimed that they can remain submerged for up to two minutes. Their pelts are well adapted to shedding water, because of the slipperiness of the guard hairs, and after a swim they usually shake themselves like dogs, thereby decreasing any chill effects.

The bear is a master in the art of killing seals. He uses the most astute methods to glide up towards them and then suddenly bound forward and deliver the mortal blow; for it is only on land that he kills them. As silent as a cat he creeps towards the seal, hiding behind irregularities on the ice. If the seal lifts its head, the bear will immediately flatten himself out and become motionless. It has been said that he uses one paw to hide the black tip of his muzzle so that it will not betray him! As soon as the seal has assured itself that all is well the bear advances again until he can jump on to it and kill it with a blow on the head. When the ice is flat and lacking in hiding-places the bear moves along on his belly and, according to the Greenlanders, has been seen to push a piece of ice in front of him as cover!

Diet   Seals and fish are the principal prey of the species. Polar bears are almost entirely carnivorous, their other food including seabirds (e.g. eider) and their young or eggs, and such land mammals as reindeer, musk-ox and arctic hares. From autumn until early spring they feed mainly on several species of seal, particularly bearded seals (*Erignathus barbatus*), ringed seals (*Pusa hispida*) and harp seals (*Pagophilus greenlandicus*). But during the summer break-up of the ice the bears have to leave the ocean and move on to land, where suitable food is frequently scarce. During this lean period they will eat berries and leaves and various types of tundra vegetation, as well as carrion or almost anything edible that happens to come their way.

Breeding   Mating takes place in mid-summer and the male takes no part in rearing the young. Usually only the female hibernates, in a short burrow excavated in the snow; although occasionally young animals and old males will do so for a few days or weeks during bad weather. The young, which number from 1 to 4, although twins in most cases, are born between late December and April after a gestation period of 230—250 days. At birth the cubs are remarkably small, measuring about 25.4 cm in length and weighing little more than 0.68 kg. They are hairless, blind and deaf, and cannot see or hear well until a month or more after birth.

The cubs (or cub) emerge from the den with the mother when they are about 3 months old and they remain with her for about a year, hibernating with the mother during the winter following their birth. Females reach sexual maturity in their fifth year and males in their sixth; adult females breed only every third year. The maximum lifespan has been recorded at about 40 years. It has been reported that polar bears remain fertile until they reach 25 years of age.

In 1973, approximately 25% of the polar bears in world zoos had been bred in captivity. But it was only as recently as 1968 that specific guidelines for the successful breeding of this species had been established. Up to then the breeding results of polar bears in captivity had been generally very disappointing. Unsuitable maternity dens were found to be the main cause. These should be completely enclosed and kept very quiet, without outside disturbances. The female should be isolated to this den and have a separate run, at least a month before the birth is expected, and heavy bedding should be provided. She must not be disturbed until she comes out with the cubs in the early spring.

Generally speaking, all animals that bring forth helpless young care for them for a prolonged period in a concealed place. They come out of their den at an age of weeks or even months. In nature the pregnant female chooses the place to give birth. Its type and location depend on the kind of animal and the available possibilities. In all cases, however, the mother feels completely safe and undisturbed in the chosen place and moves out with the young when she thinks fit.

This same feeling of complete safety is necessary in captivity, so it is imperative for zoological parks to be aware of these requirements — for if the mother does not feel safe, fear will suppress her normal inborn nursing behaviour and the young will die.

Population   When the sealing industry began to replace the impoverished whaling industry, the pressures on the polar bear increased too. In 1942, Norwegian seal hunters alone killed 714 bears. The late-developing fur trade was an additional stimulus to hunters, and the polar bear's range has shown signs of significant contraction since the 1930s at least.

In 1959, it was estimated that the world population of polar bears was between 17,000 and 19,000 animals. In 1965, the annual Alaskan polar bear kill was put at about 200. The Canadian kill approached about 600, and minimum annual kills for Greenland and the Norwegian Arctic were about 150 and 300 respectively. In 1965, when severe restrictions were imposed on hunting the species in the Soviet Arctic, at least 120 polars bears were killed in Svalbard (Spitzbergen).

As recently as 1970, over 500 bears were killed in Svalbard. In 1972, the

Norwegian Government reduced the polar bear harvest quota from a previous 170 to a total of 85 bears in Svalbard; in the season 1972–3 they announced a ban on killing thereafter.

In 1973, 518 polar bears were recorded to be in world zoos, and 127 of these had been bred in captivity. Today, it is estimated that the world population is somewhere between 10,000 and 20,000 bears.

Distribution   The polar bear is almost entirely a marine species. It has circumpolar distribution, living on the drift ice and the shores of the Arctic sea and seldom penetrating far from the coast. Its distribution is governed by its need for land during part of each year, particularly when seals are scarce and alternate sources of food must be found, as well as during the denning period. These ecological requirements mean that the actual land area used by the bear is a relatively small portion of the vast Arctic regions. It normally travels as far north as the sea is open, and individuals have been seen as far as 88°N, but such reports are exceptional, and only seldom are bears sighted in the zone of permanent polar ice.

In the European sectors of the Arctic, polar bears are resident only in Svalbard and Norway's Zemblyn, but they also occasionally reach Iceland on floes. Generally, it seems that Alaska, Canada and perhaps Norway possess the healthiest bear populations.

Conservation   Following the recommendation of the 1955 I.U.C.N. General Assembly that the Arctic countries should take measures to protect the polar bear, a law was passed in 1956 in the U.S.S.R. banning all polar bear hunting and improving the protection of the denning areas. In 1960, a reserve was established on Wrangel Island, the most important breeding area.

Canada gave total protection for the polar bear in Newfoundland and Labrador; in Alaska, hunting quotas were introduced and the use of aircraft banned. The Canadian Wildlife Service initiated in 1961 a five-year investigation on the ecology and population density of the polar bear.

In September 1965, the first international meeting on the polar bear was held in Alaska: this resulted in a circumpolar research programme for the years 1968–9. The general consensus of opinion was that progressive improvement in the global status and management of the polar bear depended on starting and developing a careful, well co-ordinated circumpolar research programme, designed to obtain the fundamental data on which an internationally acceptable management programme could be based. Until recently, each of the five nations concerned had been conducting its own independent research with little understanding of the requirements of the others or knowledge of what they were doing. In order to achieve more effective and continuing collaboration, the I.U.C.N. invited leading polar bear specialists to participate in a working meeting at its headquarters in Switzerland in January 1968.

In 1972, the Norwegian Government's announcement, banning the killing of polar bears in Svalbard after the 1972/3 season, was a major step forward in the conservation of the great white bears. In the same year, a draft protocol banning polar bear hunting on the high seas from 1973 onwards was being studied by the circumpolar nations – the Soviet Union, Norway, Denmark (for Greenland), Canada and the United States (Alaska).

An agreement on the conservation of polar bears was concluded at Oslo on 15

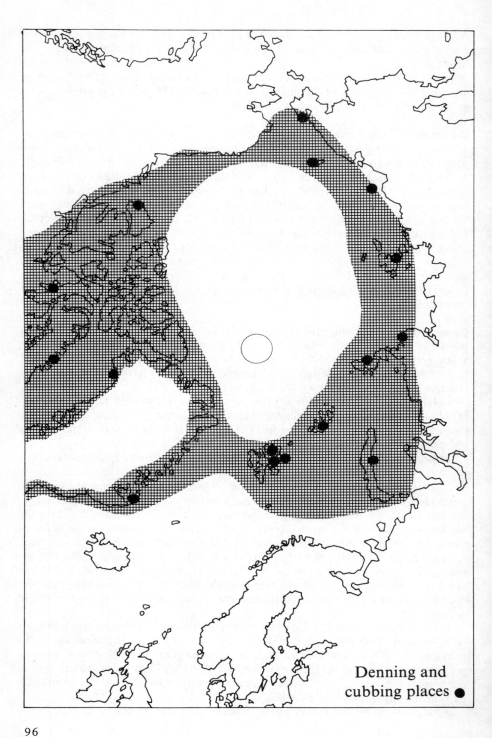

Denning and
cubbing places ●

November 1973. The new accord gave almost complete protection for polar bears in the Arctic. The taking of polar bears was banned, although some defined exceptions were allowed, most importantly traditional hunting by Eskimos and all local people using traditional methods. The ban might also be lifted for scientific and conservation reasons, but in these cases the skins might not be sold. Hunting by aircraft was prohibited. The agreement called for each of the five Arctic states to carry out research on polar bears and to co-ordinate research and exchange information with other parties. A resolution of the conference called for a ban on the taking of females with cubs and their cubs, and also for the protection of denning sites. This treaty recorded the first international agreement by Arctic nations to protect and conserve a common resource.

The I.U.C.N. Polar Bear Specialist Group of the Survival Service Commission held its fifth meeting in December 1974. One topic of major concern was the difficulty of establishing movement patterns and locating denning areas. Concern was also expressed that the rapidly increasing prices for skins were becoming a big incentive, and poachers had been identified from nine countries outside the five that comprise the polar bear's range. The situation had been brought to the notice of the poachers' governments. However, all members of the group reported encouraging progress in the application of conservation measures. A comprehensive system of national parks and reserves was being developed in Greenland. In addition to protecting polar bear populations, these areas would serve as reservoirs of bears to ensure their availability in sufficient numbers to those people traditionally dependent on them.

Because of mining, oil-drilling and military activities, the Arctic regions have become more densely populated than ever before. Modern guns, outboard motors, motorised snow-vehicles and light aircraft are at the disposal of the hunter. Polar bear skins are becoming increasingly commercially valuable, and as so much of the life-cycle of the polar bear takes place in the Arctic non-man's-land beyond territorial boundaries, it is clear that only international co-operation and agreement can ensure the species' survival.

The I.U.C.N. Polar Bear Group, with its December 1973 agreement on Conservation of Polar Bears, has proved to be most valuable and a highly successful experiment in international co-operation. For on 26 February 1976 the U.S.S.R. deposited its instrument of approval of the Agreement on Conservation of Polar Bears, bringing the number of governments to have ratified the agreement up to three, the minimum necessary to bring it into force on 26 May the same year. The two other countries were Norway (the depository government) and Canada. Denmark and the United States signed the agreement but had not yet formally approved it. Let us hope that this type of agreement will become one of many, so that fauna, environment and ecological situations elsewhere in the world can be satisfactorily resolved at the same international level.

Corbet, G. B. (1966): *Terrestrial Mammals of Western Europe*, pp. 130–1. Fisher, J., Simon, N. and Vincent, J. (1972): *The Red Book: Wildlife in Danger*, pp. 68–73. Harrington, C. R. (1965): 'The life and status of the polar bear'. Holloway, C. W. (1971): 'I.U.C.N.'s second working meeting of polar bear specialists'. I.U.C.N. (1973–6): *Monthly Bulletins.* I.Z.Yb. (1975): *Vol. 15.* Jacobi, E. F. (1968): 'Breeding facilities for polar bears'. Larsen, T. (1970): 'Polar bear research in Spitzbergen'. Larsen, T. (1971): 'Polar bear: lonely nomad of the north'. Oryx

(1969–75): *Vols X–XIII*. **Pedersen**, A. (1962): *Polar Animals*, pp. 85–107. **Simon**, N. (1966): *Red Data Book; Mammalia, Vol. 1*. **Smit**, C. J. and **Wijngaarden**, A. van (1976): 'Threatened mammals'. **Walker**, E. P. (1964): *Mammals of the World, Vol. II*, p. 1176. **W.W.F.** (1973–4): *World Wildlife Yearbook*, pp. 205–7.

Pine Marten

Martes martes

Status: Until comparatively recently, heavily persecuted and restricted by destruction of suitable woodland habitat; in more recent years, expanding its range in some areas chiefly due to expansion of state forests and relaxation of direct persecution

Description The pine marten is a member of the amazingly successful weasel family (Mustelidae). The martens represent the arboreal branch of this family of small to medium-sized carnivores, all of which have five toes on both hind and fore feet, short rounded ears, and scent glands near the anus. The martens are clearly characterised by their long slim bodies, long tails and long muzzles.

H. G. Hurrell (1963) states that fossil remains on the Continent show that the pine marten of forty million years ago appears to have been identical with the present-day animal. This suggests a remarkably efficient and versatile creature able to cope with wide variations in its environment.

The pine marten's nearest relative in Europe is the beech marten *Martes foina*;

although they are very similar in size, they are specifically distinct. Perhaps the best guide as to their difference is the colour of the throat, for almost without exception the pine marten has an undivided bib which varies considerably from distinct orange to a pale cream, in contrast to the white bib of the beech marten which is usually divided into right and left parts. The pine marten is also slenderer and higher on the legs than the beech marten; the ears are longer and broader, while the eyes are slightly smaller, and the skulls of the two species have distinct differences.

Although some authorities have named up to seven sub-species, showing a tendency for pine martens to increase in size in northern Europe but decline in size eastwards to Russia, other authorities consider that the pine marten of the Continent is racially indistinguishable from the British pine marten. The American marten is substantially smaller and usually darker than the European pine marten, and has paler markings on the face which are absent in the latter. Females of all these species – American, Continental and British – are only between two-thirds and three-quarters of the size of males, and they also have slightly finer lines to the shape of the face.

The colour varies from a rich chestnut-brown to almost black on both upper and under sides. In some individuals the body is paler than the bushy tail, legs and face, which are dark. The outer fur is darker and coarser than the reddish-grey underfur. The ears have pale edges, and although as previously described there is a yellowish-cream throat patch, the size and shape of this patch is highly individualistic, and Hurrell makes reference to a marten without any patch at all that was caught in Ireland many years ago. The soles of the feet are densely haired, so that the pads are mostly hidden in the fur; the muzzle is dark. In the late spring the coat starts to moult, commencing with head and legs, and by June the pine marten appears in a short, dark summer coat, having a thinner tail; the long winter coat is grown in October.

The length range of head and body is 42–53 cm; length of tail 22–28 cm; shoulder height 15 cm; hind foot 8.5–9.5 cm; weight 1–2 kg. 100 specimens examined in Germany by F. Schmidt (1943) were specified as follows: length of head and body ♂.♂. 48–53 cm, ♀.♀. 40–45 cm; length of tail ♂.♂. 25–28 cm, ♀.♀. 23–26 cm; weights between 900 and 1500 g according to sex and age.

Habitat   The pine marten is predominantly a woodland animal of coniferous and mixed woods, and is especially characteristic of northern conifer belts up to the tree line; it is however also found less frequently in mature deciduous woods.

In some parts of its range it is known to inhabit open rocky hillsides and sea-cliffs; but Corbet (1966) points out that in colonising such habitats, the pine marten is perhaps simply occupying a niche left vacant by the polecat (which, as far as the north-west of Scotland is concerned, is probably extinct and which appears never to have been in Ireland). In this type of habitat, the pine marten is known to resort to mountain 'screes' and cairns in which it makes its summer home. It is also known to utilise the deserted nests of some bird species, including those of buzzard and magpie, as well as occupying squirrels' 'dreys'.

Behaviour   Pine martens are generally solitary animals, mainly nocturnal, and especially active at dusk. Field scientists who have followed their tracks in the snow have recorded that pine martens move around the circumference of their range,

100

travelling around in a circle of from 5 to 30 miles. J. D. Lockie (1966) makes reference to the fact that most small or medium-sized carnivores have scent glands, and that these are presumably used to mark territory; for it has been well established that pine martens set scent. In addition to this scent marking, Lockie's field investigations have recorded how the pine martens in the Beinn Eighe National Nature Reserve in west Scotland use the partly overgrown timber extraction roads and deer tracks to move about the countryside. They deposit their dropping and urine along these tracks at varying intervals with one to three droppings at each point. The droppings are often found to be of different ages, suggesting a repeated use of the track and a renewal of scent. So a scenting expedition of even up to 30 miles, which may take no more than 3 days, may well be feasible.

H. G. Hurrell (1963) refers to one trail that was followed which showed the complete nocturnal activities of a pine marten in a single night: 'This marten went straight from its den to a clump of rhododendron bushes and back the same way, a total distance of 5 miles'. A further reference is made to one record of a distance of 15 miles being covered in one night.

Although the British Isles foraging takes place mainly on the ground, the pine marten climbs with great agility. J. G. Millais (1905) relates that the pine marten is the shyest of all creatures that dwells 'amidst the untrodden ways', and due to this it lives a life of more complete seclusion than any other British mammal except the hill badger.

The activity and grace with which a marten runs and leaps along and over branches through the forest are delightful to behold. It is not unusual for it to jump from tree to tree, and Hurrell has described a pet one of his that frequently did a downward jump of 12 feet (3½ metres) or more. It is not unusual for a marten to fall, sometimes through a branch breaking; in this event it has the ability to land on its feet. On one occasion, one of Hurrell's martens, high up in the woodland canopy, reached one of the unclimbable smooth ash trees in their wood. The marten had no difficulty in going from branch to branch at the top where the foliage of adjacent trees was touching; but while trying to negotiate the smooth and slippery branches of the ash, it fell some 60 feet to the ground where it made a successful four-point landing.

Martens are active throughout the year, although in the winter, in some parts of their range, they may stay in their dens for a day or two in unfavourable weather, or descend to lower elevations in mountainous regions. They burrow rarely or not at all, and seldom swim. They usually sleep in a hollow tree, in a squirrel's nest or a rocky den; but they are not considered to occupy any single nest except when they are breeding. Although usually silent, Southern (1964) records that they make a deep 'huffy' noise, emphatically repeated with a long drawn-out moan, when slightly alarmed or annoyed. A high-pitched chattering squeal when angry or fighting is the noise most often heard from a wild marten.

F. R. de la Fuente (1972) relates that squirrels are hardly a match for their two principal forest predators, the pine marten and the beech marten, for the slender marten is just as agile as its squirrel prey, leaping audaciously from branch to branch, even though the boughs bend precariously under its weight, and making use of its tail as a rudder in mid-air. Ognev (1962) refers to a very interesting phenomenon among martens in Russia: in the late Fall period when the snow has already fallen, the martens often migrate. This occurs in years of extensive squirrel migrations, when numerous martens have been recorded to trail the squirrel packs.

Diet   The food of the pine marten consists mostly of small mammals, birds and invertebrates, although the latter are of secondary importance. J. D. Lockie's investigations in the Scottish Highlands showed that the food taken varied greatly in size and composition, but rodents and small birds formed the bulk of the diet throughout the year. The bird prey contained a high proportion of tits, wrens and treecreepers. Of small rodents 90% were short-tailed voles; beetles, caterpillars, carrion, fish and berries were found to be eaten seasonally.

Southern (1964) quotes reports from Sweden where, in a predominantly woodland environment, the winter diet was found to consist of 51% squirrels, 21% small mammals, 13% game birds, 5% other birds, 2% bilberries, and various minor items. There were big differences in diet from one winter to another, according to the abundance of squirrels and small rodents. Reports from northern British Columbia indicate similar variations for the American marten: small mammals and varying hares predominated in the diet one winter, whereas voles and birds did in another. It is reported from study of captive animals that the daily food intake is approximately 10% of the marten's body weight.

H. G. Hurrell (1963) records that wild rabbits and rats have been killed by his own ranch-bred pine martens when taken out for a walk. Some of them, however, showed a strange reluctance to enter rabbit burrows, there being no inner predilection for making use of such burrows such as is shown by every ferret. Hurrell has also observed his tame martens, when at liberty, killing frogs and small mammals, as well as bumblebees and cockchafers. They usually avoided slugs, although on occasions these were eaten after being dragged about with the fore paws in order to remove the slime. Hurrell watched one of his martens in a nearby bluebell wood capturing one bumblebee after another by knocking them down with a fore paw and then quickly eating them. Although martens drink, they appear to be satisfied with a small quantity of water.

In the British Isles, the majority of the marten's food is obtained on the ground, but in other regions it seeks arboreal prey — birds with their eggs and young are a source of food, and squirrels in particular are the dominant prey, which the marten is well equipped to exploit. The pine marten's technique as a squirrel hunter is well described by F. R. de la Fuente: 'Once the pine marten has located its victim the ensuing chase will be fast and furious. The squirrel skims like a tightrope-walker along the thinnest branches in the hope that in this way it will throw off its pursuer. The marten's answer to this manoeuvre is to take an outflanking path to cut off the squirrel's escape and thus force it down to a lower level in the tree. As the trapped squirrel makes a desperate leap to safety the marten lunges upwards to intercept the victim in mid-air, seizing the smaller animal with its sharp claws, dragging it to the ground and rolling over and over until it finds an opportunity to sink its canines in the squirrel's throat. The marten can tackle larger animals equally effectively by implanting its long teeth in the neck of the prey and breaking the spinal column.'

Another interesting account of martens hunting squirrels is given by S. I. Ognev in Russia: 'There are numerous old frozen squirrel nests in the forest and fewer inhabited ones. After long runs, the marten finally comes to a halt near a nest which exudes a fresh squirrel scent. It carefully determines the point of entry, which is plugged from the inside with moss or linden basts, bursts ferociously into the nest and seizes the sleeping occupant. The squirrel attempts to struggle free with a cry. Nesting material flies from the nest on to the snow. Only rarely does the marten succeed in strangling the squirrel inside the nest. More often both cling to the twigs and fall onto the snow where the terrible nocturnal incident comes to a close.'

Whilst hunting terrestrial prey such as hares and rabbits the marten hunts by sight, but when view of the game is lost it will follow the trail by scent, frequently stopping to gaze in all directions, after the manner of the stoat. J. G. Millais relates that the final onslaught is delivered with a rush which the terrified victim feebly tries to avoid.

Breeding   A female has only one litter a year and comes into oestrus after the young are weaned in July—August. H. N. Southern records that, when in oestrus, the marten makes a clucking noise as she goes about frequently depositing scent and urine. During copulation, both sexes are said to purr and growl, the male dragging the female round by the scruff of her neck; such matings can last up to an hour, and have been observed in a tree.

After fertilisation, the blastocysts remain unimplanted until mid-January; this phenomenon is known as delayed implantation. A litter of 2—6 young (average 3) are born in late March to April, after a total gestation period of about 270 days. The sex ratio is considered to be about equal. The young at birth weigh around 30 g, and are blind for the first 12—14 days. They are born with a thin covering of white or yellowish hair. At 8 days distinct grey stripes appear, reaching greatest development at 16 days, but disappearing at 20 days. The general colour up to 3 weeks is grey, after which it changes to brown. The tails have only short hairs at first, but begin to bush out at about 3 months. The young emerge from the breeding den at about 2 months, being weaned at 6—7 weeks. Both sexes reach adult weight at about 3 months in the first summer and become solitary; they show no signs of sexual activity until the second summer. In October, they acquire the full winter coat which is appreciably longer than their earlier pelage.

H. G. Hurrell states that the cubs are very playful 'but at first they seem terrified of heights, clinging anxiously to a trunk as though they must hang on at all costs. Perhaps it is an instinct to obviate premature climbing, just as an otter cub is restrained from making too early an entry into water by an innate fear of this element when it is very young.'

In the wild state, a marten is not ready to mate until it is about 15 months old, and is therefore two years old before it is able to have young. The first recorded captive breeding of the pine marten was reported by Millais to have occurred in 1882. Since that time, all the fertile matings that have been known to occur in both zoological parks and laboratory-type environments have happened only when the marten concerned has attained its third or even fourth summer.

The beech marten does not occur in the British Isles, but in those parts of the pine marten's European range where the two species do overlap, they do not interbreed. However, A. P. Gray (1971) reports that in captivity there is one incidence of a breeder succeeding in obtaining hybrids, after many unsuccessful attempts, between a male beech marten and a female pine marten, but the mother failed to rear them. Hybridisation has been reported in the Soviet Union between a pine marten and a sable; as well as an alleged hybridisation between the pine marten and a European polecat. The lifespan of the pine marten is 14—16 years.

Population   G. B. Corbet (1974) states that in the British Isles the pine marten probably reached its lowest ebb, along with the polecat and the wildcat, some time between 1910 and 1940; since that time the population has expanded, especially in the Scottish Highlands. Reference is also made to a number of isolated individuals and even breeding populations at widely separated locations in Yorkshire and elsewhere; these have been either overlooked survivors, long-distance immigrants, introductions or escaped pets.

Due to the extreme shyness and secretive nature of the pine marten, information on population densities is almost non-existent, although evidence from field work in the winter on the American marten gives an overall density for the latter species of 1 marten to approximately 3 square miles.

Distribution   The ranges of the pine marten and the beech marten overlap throughout central Europe, although the former species is the more northern of the two. The pine marten occurs northwards up to the tree line at approximately 70°N; further eastwards its northern boundary descends following the forests. It occurs southwards to northern Spain, Italy, and Jugoslavia, where it hardly penetrates the Mediterranean zone; east to the Urals in the north, and to the Caucasus and western Siberia up to 1,700 metres. As Corbet points out, the pine marten extends eastwards as far as the Yenesei, beyond which it is replaced by the sable throughout the Siberian taiga (sub-arctic coniferous forest).

Until the destruction of the forests in the British Isles, the marten was widely distributed. Having been greatly reduced during the nineteenth century, it is now restricted to the north-west Scottish Highlands, to the Lake District, to Wales and to Ireland, apart from a few isolated populations.

Conservation   During the last few centuries, deforestation with the subsequent lack of suitable habitat has been the chief reason for the pine marten's decline in the British Isles. Suggestions have been recorded by Millais that, in the reign of Elizabeth the First, the marten was considered by the chroniclers to be getting scarce, due to its fur being so much sought after, as well as to its being killed as vermin. In the following years, it was increasingly sought after due to the value of its pelt, which was worth far more than that of the Continental beech marten, and almost as much as the sable.

In the nineteenth century the marten was heavily persecuted, especially in the interests of game preservation and its supposed threat to poultry. Apart from man being the marten's main predator, foxes have sometimes been reported to kill them; also, the marten is not infrequently caught in traps set for foxes. In more recent years, especially since 1940, the marten has expanded its range in some areas chiefly due to the expansion of state forests, and the relaxation of direct persecution.

Seventy years after J. G. Millais wrote: 'Personally I despair of seeing intelligent legislation for the protection of creatures that ought to be protected, such as the otter, the wild cat, the marten, and the weasel, when destroyers of such pestilential rascals as certain gulls and other really destructive vermin are threatened "with the utmost rigour of the law"', the British Wild Creatures and Wild Plants Protection Act 1975 was passed. Perhaps now, with the greater awareness of threatened wildlife brought by the new Act and the expansion of a suitable habitat for it to live in, the pine marten can justifiably feel more secure.

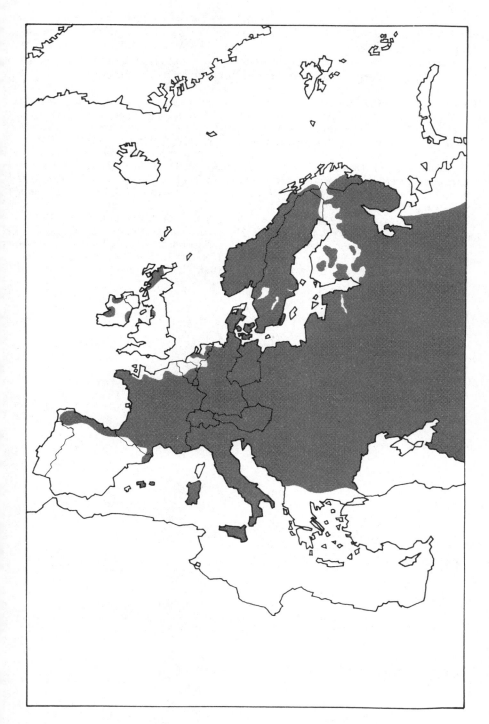

It will undoubtedly delight many people if the pine marten continues to repopulate certain areas, for it should be admired not only for the tenacious way it has managed to hang on in remote areas and survive, but also because it is an animal which has aptly been described as the most beautiful of all the fur bearers.

Burton, M. (1962): *Systematic Dictionary of Mammals of the World*, pp. 161–2. **Corbet**, G. B. (1966): *Terrestrial Mammals of Western Europe*, pp. 134–6; (1974): 'The distribution of mammals in historic times', in *Changing Flora and Fauna of Britain, Vol. 6*, pp. 179–202. **Fuente de la**, F. R. (1972): *World of Wildlife, Vol. 5*, pp. 195–6. **Gray**, A. P. (1972): *Mammalian Hybrids*, p. 53. **Hurrell**, H. G. (1963): 'Pine martens', in *Animals of Britain, 22*. **Lockie**, J. D. (1966): 'Territory in small carnivores', in *Play, Exploration and Territory in Mammals*, pp. 143–65. **Lydekker**, R. (1915): *Wildlife of the World, Vol. 1*, pp. 49–51. **Millais**, J. G. (1905): *Mammals of Great Britain and Ireland, Vol. II*, pp. 71–93. **Ognev**, S. I. (1962): *Mammals of Eastern Europe and Northern Asia, Vol. II*, pp. 446–60. **Schmidt**, F. (1943): 'Naturgeschichte des Baum- und des Steinmarders'. **Southern**, H. N. (1964): *Handbook of British Mammals*, pp. 358–64. **Thorburn**, A. (1920): *British Mammals, Vol. 1*, pp. 70–1. **van den Brink**, F. H. (1973): *A Field Guide to the Mammals of Britain and Europe*, p. 135. **Walker**, E. P. (1964): *Mammals of the World, Vol. II*, p. 1197.

European Mink

Mustela lutreola

Status: Numbers are decreasing in Europe due to human persecution, for its valuable fur and its predatory habits, and to the serious menace of water pollution

Description   Mink are medium-sized species of the genus *Mustela*, which is one of the more primitive (i.e. least specialised) genera among the Carnivores. They are close relatives of the polecat, but of slightly shorter and more compact form, and with even thicker and more lustrous fur. They have short legs with slightly webbed feet.

The semi-aquatic minks of Eurasia and North America belong to several species. The European species *Mustela lutreola* is very similar to the North American mink *Mustela vison*, though *lutreola* differs in usually having a white throat, chin and upper lip. The American mink is usually bigger and its coat thicker and softer, and is therefore regarded as the more important species for the fur trade.

The dense fur is uniformly deep-brown. In America, it has been reported that as a general rule the mink inhabiting northern regions are dark, whereas the further south one goes, the lighter and redder they become. In captivity, new colours have been produced through taking advantage of rare mutations; these colour varieties range from white through trade-favoured mutants like 'sapphire' and 'silverblue' to almost black. Like the martens, the minks have a long and somewhat bushy tail; the ears are smaller than in any of the allied forms, and scarcely appear above the general level of the fur.

The body length of the European mink is 30–40 cm (the American mink 30–43 cm), the tail length 13–14 cm (12.7–22.9 cm) and the hind foot 5–6 cm. It can attain a weight of 500–800 g (565–1000 g).

Habitat   The European mink lives closely associated with fresh water. It frequents reed beds along slowly running rivers or pools, especially in the region of woods and marshes, where there is adequate ground cover.

Behaviour   The mink is a solitary, nocturnal animal and an excellent swimmer; its habits closely resemble those of the otter. Sliding is a favourite game of the otter, and it is the same with the mink, for observers have described how it lets itself slither on its belly down a wet river bank or a snowy slope.

In its general habits the mink is thoroughly amphibious. Its home is usually a hole in the bank of a stream or lake, a rocky cleft or hollow tree, and a well-trodden path always leads from the entrance of the den down to the water. From such dens it appears that the animal will not only make daily excursions for the sake of procuring food, but also wander into neighbouring districts, from which it may not return for a week or two. One field observer reported that the mink not only swims and dives with facility, but can remain for a long time under water, and pursues and captures fish by following them under logs or other places whence there is no escape. In winter it moves to streams that are too fast-flowing to freeze. In summer, it lives in areas not larger than 15–20 hectares.

Richard Lydekker wrote in 1894 that all who have hunted the mink bear witness to its extraordinary tenacity of life; there were several instances of mink being found alive after having lain for fully 24 hours with their bodies crushed flat beneath a heavy log. The countenance of a mink is described as far from prepossessing at any time; but when caught alive in a steel-trap these animals are said to have an almost diabolical expression!

The mink is remarkably strong for so small an animal, and a single one has been observed to drag a mallard duck more than a mile in order to get to its hole. The unpleasant scent characteristic of all members of the Mustelidae is extraordinarily well developed in the mink which, with the exception of the skunk, possesses the most offensive of these penetrating odours as its method of defence. Although the mink is normally silent, it will shriek when alarmed, and both sexes make purring and piping noises during the mating season.

Diet   The mink catches the majority of its food in water and is known to feed particularly on small rodents, especially water voles; but many other aquatic species such as frogs, newts, ducks, crayfish and molluscs are also taken — as well as snakes, insects and birds' eggs.

Breeding   As in the marten and the fox, the lengthening days of spring are responsible for increased sexual activity in both male and female mink, and day length also controls termination of the delay in implantation of the fertilised ovum. Delayed implantation in turn is responsible for the variation in the gestation period, which can run from 39 to 76 days. On fur farms, it has been established that this sensitivity to light, or 'photo-periodicity', greatly influences not only the reproductive cycle of the mink, by the day length to which it is subjected, but also the fur growth, fur primeness and moulting.

Mating takes places from late February to the end of March; the female has up to four oestrous cycles, each lasting 7—10 days. In the mink, ovulation is not spontaneous, but follows copulation or a similar stimulus by approximately 48 hours. While the litter usually contains only young (kits) produced from the last mating, young from each of these ovulations may be born, or all the kits may be from any one or two of the matings. The young are born from April to June, according to the latitude, in a nest which is generally well lined with feathers and other soft substances.

A single normal litter consists of 5—6 young; but in captivity a larger number of up to 17 has been recorded. The young are naked at birth, blind, about 3.8 cm long and 1.3 cm in diameter. Development is very rapid, for the young will start sucking at food brought into the den by the dam at 10—12 days old, and at approximately 25 days the eyes are opened and the young are looking around for solid nourishment. If adequate food is available the young are quiet, seldom making sounds other than a subdued cheeping. However, if they are cold and hungry, their cheeps are loud and insistent and continue so until the condition is remedied.

The sire assists with the care and feeding of the young, and if the food supply is good and satisfactory growth has occurred, they can be weaned at 5—6 weeks. They are reported to leave their parents at the end of the second month, and normally mate during the spring following birth, when they are 10—12 months old.

No hybridising has been attained with the mink, in spite of attempts with the ferret and the European polecat. Although the distribution of the European mink overlaps with that of the introduced American mink, the two species have not been recorded to have hybridised — a situation somewhat similar to that of the American lynx and the bobcat.

The American mink was first raised in captivity in the United States for the production of fur in 1866, although it was not until the early 1930s that the trade really expanded. After World War II mink ranches proliferated in such a way that the trade soon represented a lusty industry. The lifespan of a mink is given as about 10—12 years.

Population   It is reported that for two decades in the latter part of the nineteenth century, the total number of European mink skins marketed averaged 55,000, whereas the exports of American mink from the New World reached 160,000; but in the year 1888, the number of American mink skins was upwards of 370,000. In Rumania, it was reported around 1960 that 1000—10,000 European mink were shot each year. Further estimations as to the numbers killed are not available. However, with the introduced American mink expanding its range in Europe and Iceland, it is important to refer to the 1200 specimens of American mink shot in Iceland in 1948; 324 caught in Scotland in 1965; 3850 killed in Norway during the 1959—60 hunting season; and 20,000 killed in Sweden during the 1963—4 hunting season.

Thus in trying to establish the European species' distribution, any estimate on present status is difficult to obtain because of its confusion with the American mink.

109

Distribution   The European mink has apparently never occurred in Britain, but was distributed throughout the northern parts of Europe and Asia, and in north-western Europe as far as the south-west of France.

In Czechoslovakia, the last European mink had already disappeared from Bohemia in the nineteenth century; it was considered to have disappeared from the other parts of the country around 1900. In Germany, it is reported that the species has disappeared during the last few decades, with a last sighting in the Aller river near Wolfsburg in 1948. In Austria, the species occurred in Burgenland in 1933, but it has not been reported since.

To define the European minks' precise present distribution is difficult, owing to the likelihood of its being confused with the introduced American species. However it is considered probably to be still present in several parts of eastern Europe west of Russia, confined to the central and southern parts of Finland, as well as perhaps in western France.

The western limits of distribution at the moment lie approximately along a line from Finland southwards through Lithuania, Poland in the Bieszczady mountains, Rumania especially in the Danube delta, Yugoslavia in the Republic of Servia, to the marshes along the Danube in Bulgaria.

Conservation   Because of its valuable fur and its predatory habits, the European mink is hunted intensively, and has therefore been exterminated throughout the majority of its former range in western Europe. In regions of industrial expansion, water pollution from industrial waste and high levels of pesticides are destroying fish stocks and have undoubtedly damaged the mink's chances of survival.

In some areas the European mink occurs together with the American mink. Since the two species choose the same habitat and take similar kinds of food, they enter into competition; and in some regions the European mink – like the European red squirrel to the American grey squirrel – comes off second best.

As the American mink is now firmly established in the wild in parts of the continent of Europe as well as in Britain, it is thought important to provide some information about this rapid colonisation.

The American mink is the most recent introduction into Britain that can be considered to be well established. Mink farms increased greatly in Britain after 1945 and by 1956 escaped mink were breeding in the wild. Feral animals at first spread widely in Devon, but the very rapid colonisation of a large part of the country from Cornwall to Inverness and Ireland has been due to expansion from a considerable number of separate centres. Some authorities consider that the mink has spread so rapidly because it is in a niche that is doubly vacant: the European mink has apparently never occurred in Britain, and the alternative competitor, the polecat, has been exterminated from all but Wales.

In North America, the Canadian otter and the mink live in harmony together, although the numbers of each may not attain the same height as they would in the absence of the other; perhaps the British species might similarly coexist.

In 1973, a survey of otter hunts in Britain recorded that mink were found in seven of the otter hunt areas and have become fairly to very common, increasing markedly over the years; six of the seven hunts in these areas kill mink whenever possible and by various means, a policy that is welcomed particularly by fishing interests in five of the six areas. In the seventh the reaction is varied.

In 1971, it was reported that the Russians had introduced American mink on the

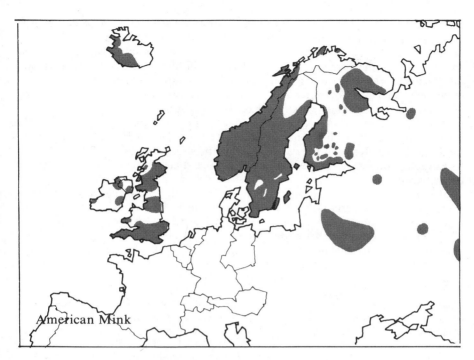

American Mink

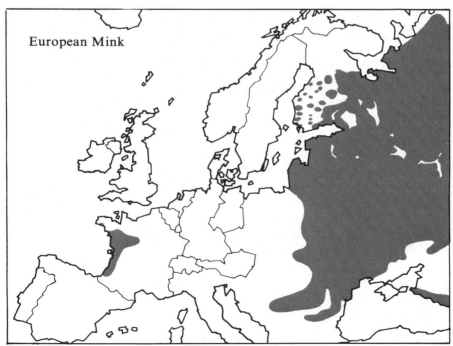

European Mink

east slopes of the Ural mountains, in an area of wooded river banks and ice-free pools, and all hunting, fishing and wood-cutting had been banned in the area until the mink had settled. In some of this region the American mink has adapted well, and perhaps in the vastness of the U.S.S.R. it will be possible to contain it; most other countries to which it has been introduced are now engaged in battle with this determined destroyer of other species of wildlife. In Iceland, for example, mink decimated the wildfowl on Myvatn, a large lake in the north of the country.

Although there were no recordings of the European mink having been bred in captivity during 1973, there is every reason to suppose that if it were ranched in a similar way to its New World relative, it would be equally prolific.

European minks are totally protected in Poland and Czechoslovakia, as well as partially protected in Finland.

Measures are needed to protect the European mink by law in areas of Rumania, Yugoslavia, and Bulgaria where numbers are found to be dwindling. In France, the mink should be totally protected, not only by law but also by the establishment of suitable reserves free from water pollution.

It is a sad reflection on mankind, that on the one hand we allow a species to become threatened in some parts of its range, whilst on the other hand facilitate the introduction and colonisation of its closest relation.

Bassett, C. F. (1957): 'The mink', in *UFAW Handbook*, pp. 568–74. **Bourlière**, F. (1967): *Natural History of Mammals*, p. 184. **Burton**, M. (1962): *Systematic Dictionary of Mammals of the World*, p. 160. **Corbet**, G. B. (1966): *Terrestrial Mammals of Western Europe*, pp. 144–5; (1974): 'The distribution of mammals in historic times', in *Changing Flora and Fauna of Britain*, pp. 179–202. **Graf**, J. (1968): *Animal Life of Europe*, pp. 28–9. **Gray**, A. P. (1971): *Mammalian Hybrids*, pp. 54–5. **Larousse** (1972): *Encyclopedia of Animal Life*, pp. 560–1. **Lydekker**, R. (1894): *The Royal Natural History, Vol. II*, pp. 68–9; (1915): *Wildlife of the World, Vol. I*, pp. 393–5. **Oryx** (1971–4): *Vols XI–XII*. **Sanderson**, I. T. (1955): *Living Mammals of the World*, pp. 203–4. **Smit**, C. J. and **Wijngaarden**, A. van (1976): 'Threatened mammals'. **Southern**, H. N. (1964): *Handbook of British Mammals*, pp. 372–3. **van den Brink**, F. H. (1973): *A Field Guide to the Mammals of Britain and Europe*, p. 130.

Wolverine or Glutton

Gulo gulo

Status: Numbers reduced throughout its range but still not uncommon in some areas

Description   The wolverine or 'glutton' is the only representative of its genus and is the largest member of the weasel family (Mustelidae) which also embraces such animals as skunks, badgers, otters, minks and martens.

It is rather bear-like in stance and movements – a fair picture of its general appearance is 'somewhat between a marten and a bear'. The whole animal is heavily and rather clumsily built and walks with the greater part of the soles of the feet applied to the ground. The limbs are thick and rather short; the feet are provided with long, curved, semi-retractile claws, and have their soles thickly haired. The back is much arched and both the head and short bushy tail are carried low. The head is broad and rounded, with a rather short and pointed muzzle, small and widely separated eyes, and small rounded ears projecting only a little above the general level of the fur.

The fur of the body and limbs is rather coarse, long and thick: and there is also a thick woolly underfur. The general colour is dusky or blackish-brown; but there is a distinct band of light brown which extends from the shoulder to the rump along each side of the body, joining its fellow over and across the base of the tail. The front and sides of the head are light grey, while upon the throat and chest there may be one or more light spots.

The female is smaller and lighter than the male, and there is considerable individual variation in size. The length of the head and body is 62–87 cm; the tail 15–26 cm; the height of the shoulder is about 40–45 cm; and the weight is usually 9–30 kg.

Habitat   The species frequents mountain woodland with rocky slopes, often near marshes. Although capable of climbing trees, the wolverine is primarily ground-living, and in summer the northernmost animals leave the shelter of the forests and scrub and wander extensively on the tundra.

Behaviour   The wolverine is active by day as well as by night, although in the summer it is mostly nocturnal. Its lair is mostly a shallow scrape on a rocky slope in thick bushes or between rocks. The animal growls and hisses when angry or threatened, and grunts and squeals when playing. It is an excellent swimmer, and will not hesitate to swim rivers in pursuit of its prey.

Wolverines are usually solitary and are active all the year. They tend to have a cycle of activity for three or four hours and then rest for about the same length of time. They are not nomadic, for each animal inhabits a definite area. A male may share his realm, which can be about 300,000 hectares, with two or three females. They love to play and they can climb trees with considerable speed. Their ability to learn and their strength are important factors in survival. Wolverines soon learn what to avoid, and they seem to be unexcelled in strength among mammals of their size. There are many species that prefer to hunt from cover, along a path or near a water-hole. The wolverine is known to hide behind a rock or on a branch of a tree, whence it drops on to its victim's back, often clinging there for a hundred yards or more. It is reported to drive bears and mountain lions from their kills, and is powerful enough to kill elk and moose that are hampered by snow. So this aggressive creature, though slow and clumsy, wins its prey by patience and cunning. Indeed it is reputed to inspect the snares set by hunters and to remove the bait or snared animal for itself.

All sorts of lurid tales are current about the physical powers, cunning and appetite of the wolverine: it is left alone even by the large cats and bears. The Latin name *Gulo gulo*, translated directly, means 'the swallowing thing who has gone blind', or as we might say 'The Blind Glutton'.

Diet   When it gets the chance, a wolverine will attack almost anything it meets, ranging from prey as large as the moose, reindeer and snow bighorns to foxes, lemmings, rabbits, hares, mice, birds, frogs, fishes, as well as birds' eggs, fruit and berries. However, its speciality is carrion, and it has a reputation for destructiveness to hunters' food caches, as well as to animals caught in traps. It is credited with eating more than any other carnivore, but also may fast for a week or two. It has been known to drag a carcase three times its own weight over rough ground.

Breeding   Mating occurs in the autumn and it seems likely that delayed implantation occurs, since the young are not born until February through to May. Usually

2–3 young are born, but litters of as many as 5 have been recorded. They are born with thick woolly fur in a den either in a hollow tree or among rocks. They are nursed for 8–10 weeks and remain with the mother for about 2 years, when they are driven from the territory. Wolverines are sexually mature at 4 years and have lived up to 16 years in captivity. It is reported that the mother is exceedingly fierce when defending her offspring, and at such times will not hesitate to attack human beings.

Wolverines are seldom exhibited in world zoos, and during a 10-year period (1964–73) only three zoos — Boras, Sweden; Helsinki, Finland; and Colorado, U.S.A. — were reported to have bred the wolverine in captivity. Three out of the four litters recorded consisted of brother and sister twins. At the Colorado Zoo, the young were born on 16 February 1965 and first emerged from their den during the latter part of April but only at night when they could not be readily observed. They first came out during daylight in the middle of May. The young were pure white at birth, but by 3 months their colour pattern resembled that of the adult animals. Although births and subsequent maturation of wolverines in captivity are still uncommon, if properly accommodated and maintained there is no reason why they should not breed as readily as other Mustelidae.

Population   Numbers are reduced everywhere, especially where a bounty system for them is in operation. However, in some sparsely populated and isolated areas, they are still not uncommon in parts of the range.

In 1970, it was reported that no more than 40–60 wolverines were left in Finland, and as bounties were still being paid by the Finnish Parliament, extinction is in sight for them. In 1973, it was recorded that only 40 wolverines survived in the wild in Finland. A census taken in northern Sweden in spring 1972 found only 75 wolverines.

Distribution   The wolverine is found in both the Old World, from Scandinavia to Kamchatka, and the New World, from the Arctic to the north-western parts of the United States. It is a circumpolar species of the taiga and (in summer) the tundra zones. In Europe it is therefore confined to the northern and montane parts of Scandinavia, Finland and Russia.

It was common in France and England during the Ice Age, but retreated northwards as the climate grew warmer. In the British Isles, its fossilised remains have been discovered in the caverns of Derbyshire, Glamorganshire and the Vale of Clwyd, while they also occur in the older 'forest-bed' of the Norfolk coast. Evidence of the former existence of the wolverine on the Continent has also been obtained in the caves of Dordogne in the south of France.

Conservation   Wolverines are remorselessly hunted, for in territory where one of the principal human occupations is fur-trapping the wolverine's habit of inspecting the snare lines and removing the carrion for itself makes it a very unpopular animal. Also, apart from its gross destructiveness, its own fur is in demand, for it has extra protective qualities in that it will not freeze. When the fur is not being utilised as a complete coat, Eskimos like to have wolverine fur as a trimming about the hoods of parkas, as the moisture from the human's breath will not freeze as with other furs.

The wolverine has been fully protected in Sweden since 1968, and now partially in Norway. In Finland, up to 1976, parliament retained the bounties for both the

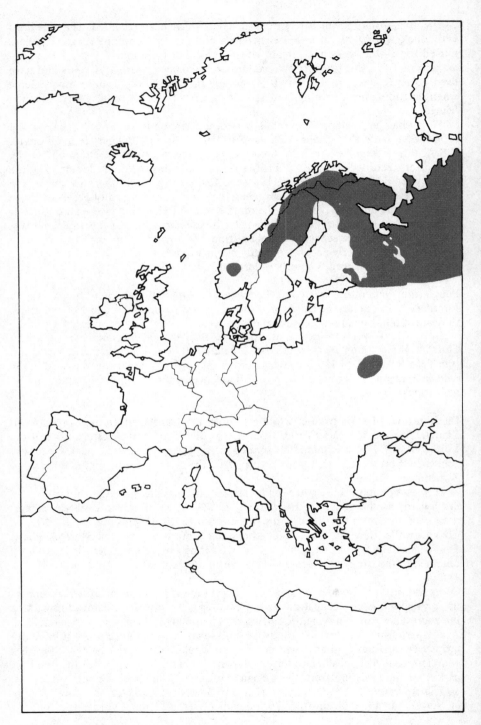

116

wolf and the wolverine throughout the country, including the Lemmenjoki National Park where they are the most numerous. In 1976, the Finnish Parliament passed a law to discontinue the official bounty of $130 for killing a wolf or wolverine; and the Ministry of Agriculture will in future issue permits for reindeer breeders to shoot not more than ten wolves and ten wolverines in the worst-hit cattle and reindeer areas. However, until really effective protection can be afforded to the remaining wild populations in Scandinavia and Finland, European zoos such as Boras, Sweden, and Helsinki, Finland, which have already had success with breeding this species, should make every effort to establish self-sustaining populations so that reintroduction into National Park areas could be possible once the opportunity arises.

Bourlière, F. (1967): *Natural History of Mammals*, p. 59. Burton, M. (1962): *Systematic Dictionary of Mammals of the World*, pp. 162–3. Chernyavsky, F. B. (1970): 'The snow bighorn . . . of Chukotka, USSR'. Corbet, G. B. (1966): *Terrestrial Mammals of Europe*, pp. 137–8. Davis, D. G. (1967): 'A brief note on the birth of wolverines . . . at Colorado Zoo'. Larousse (1972): *Encyclopedia of Animal Life*, p. 562. Lydekker, R. (1894): *The Royal Natural History, Vol. II*, pp. 71–4. Oryx (1970–6): *Vols X–XIII*. Sanderson, I. T. (1955): *Living Mammals of the World*, p. 205. van den Brink, F. H. (1973): *A Field Guide to the Mammals of Britain and Europe*, p. 138. Walker, E. P. (1964): *Mammals of the World, Vol. II*, p. 1204.

Badger

Meles meles

Status: Although comparatively common throughout its range and at present protected in some countries, there has been widespread concern in Britain at the Government's recent decision to eleminate all badgers in areas where they have been proved to be carrying bovine T.B.

Description   The weasel family (Mustelidae) is represented in western and central Europe by the martens, weasels, badgers and otters. The badgers are distinguished from the other members of the family by their greater size, and their powerful legs and strong claws; they have five toes on each foot with larger claws on the front feet which they use for digging. They are compact, heavy, somewhat bear-like creatures with a pointed nose and short ears and tail. The skull has a particularly prominent sagittal crest; the lower jaw is articulated in such a way that dislocation is impossible without fracturing the skull. In common with other members of the family they have scent glands, which in badgers are situated beneath the tail.

    The badger's coat is long and coarse, the hair colour showing a good deal of variation; although appearing grey from a distance owing to the colour of individual hairs, it is usually marked with a dark stripe on each side of the head, running from the muzzle across the eyes and on to the ears, which are otherwise white; the rest of the head is also white. The back is whitish-grey mixed with black; on the sides of the body and on the tail the coat is reddish-brown while the underparts and feet are blackish-brown. Albinos are known to occur, and a single prolonged moult lasting most of the summer takes place.

Neal (1962) remarks that it is difficult at first to distinguish males (boars) from females (sows), as the general colouration is the same. However, when seen head on, the adult boar has a much broader head, and when seen from the side his neck usually seems much thicker and the head more blunt. The sow by contrast appears to have a smaller head, and a slender appearance generally. The badger is commonly called 'Brock' in Britain (from the Gaelic 'Broc'), a title which has been included in many place names such as Brockenhurst, Brockworth, etc. The name 'badger' is considered probably to be derived from the French word *bêcheur* – a digger.

In Britain, Southern (1964) records the average adult badger as 915 mm (3 ft) in length, which includes 100 mm (4 in) for the tail. The average adult weights (taken from 50 recordings) are: boar, 12.3 kg, sow 10.9 kg. Weights of over 18 kg are not unusual, with three of over 27 kg recorded; badgers are at their heaviest during December and January, and at their lightest in the early spring. Van den Brink (1973) gives the range of the body length as 610–720 mm (2–2⅓ ft); tail length 150–190 mm (6–7½ in); hind foot 90–110 mm (3½–4½ in); height at shoulder 300 mm (12 in); weight 10–22 kg. It is interesting to note that Ognev (1962) also gives a much longer tail measurement for the badger than Southern recorded: length of tail without distal hair 160 mm (6½ in); same with distal hair 210 mm (8½ in). The maximum weight of a Caucasian badger is up to 24 kg.

Habitat   Badgers are primarily animals of open woodland, but they occur commonly in open country provided there are banks in which they can burrow or rocks to provide a den. They make their setts in a wide variety of places, such as in woods or copses especially when these border pastureland; slopes are preferred and old rabbit warrens are often taken over. They are also found on cliffs by the sea, in quarries, on mountain sides and in hedgerows, but low-lying marsh areas are avoided.

Ognev (1962) reports that in the central regions of the U.S.S.R. badgers chiefly select dry parts of the forests cleft by ravines. They are also known to frequent semi-desert and desert zones, making their burrows in sand dunes. In the mountain regions they are more or less associated with forests, although sometimes they are encountered in the plateau between bare stones and rocks. Some reports about badgers found at heights of 1500–2100 m in fir forests have inferred that they may inhabit hollows of large trees, e.g. ancient firs.

Behaviour   Badgers are more social than most other Mustelidae. Neal (1962) states that although badgers are social animals each individual behaves independently, and they are also known to live alone sometimes. They spend the majority of the day under ground in their sett; these vary greatly in size according to the age and type of soil, but may be very extensive. The sett consists of a labyrinth of tunnels connecting up the various chambers. A typical sett will penetrate 10 or 15 metres into the hillside. Tunnels of over 100 metres in length are known, and there may be as many as three different levels. The number of exit holes varies from 1 to 40 or 50 – although in these large setts many of the holes are no longer used by the badgers.

The sett is usually dug in sand due to the comparative ease of such an excavation. The chambers are usually lined with heaps of bedding which the badgers laboriously collect together on dry nights. The nesting material may consist of bracken, grass, moss, leaves, bluebell leaves, ferns and a variety of other plants according to their availability. The living quarters are kept quite clean; occasionally the bedding is brought up and strewn around the entrance of the sett to air for an hour or so before being returned to the chambers.

The badgers are known to collect the material into bundles, and then shuffle backwards towards the sett, keeping the bundle in position with the snout and forelegs. One report cited by Millais (1905) relates how all the old winter bedding thrown out during a regular spring-cleaning can amount to as much as three or four cartloads of material: 'The badger will come out, take a look round and sit awhile close to the mouth of the hole. He will then shuffle about and get further from the hole. You will watch him descend into some bracken-covered hollow, and will see nothing more of him for a while. Then you will hear him gently pushing and shoving and grunting, and know that he is very busy over something. He will reappear bumping along backwards, a heap of bracken and of grass or old straw under his belly and encircled by his arms and fore-feet. He will continue this most undignified and curious mode of retrogression to the sett, and will disappear, tail first, down his hole, still hugging and tugging at his burden.'

Badgers become very fat in the autumn and are capable of remaining below ground without food for many days. In Scandinavia, Poland and northern Russia, badgers pass most of the severe winter in prolonged inaction; they begin to show indications of renewed activity with the onset of the warm weather, even if the warm days are brief and temporary and only just rise above zero. In western Europe badgers remain active throughout the year, although in winter their activity is reduced (especially in December), but no true hibernation occurs.

Badgers usually emerge very cautiously from their dens at dusk, although this varies according to sex, age, season and environmental conditions such as the nearness to human habitation or the intensity of light. They glance around, at the same time sniffing the air, and if they find nothing suspicious, they go off to their hunting grounds. As Neal (1962) points out, a badger's life is spent almost wholly in darkness or poor light, and its reactions to light are interesting, for if you shine a weak torch on it, it will probably take no notice whatever. If it is a strong light the badger will become uneasy and probably bolt, but a strong torch with a red filter will not alarm it at all — a fact that greatly facilitates field studies of the badger.

Around the sett there are dung pits, sunning grounds and areas for play, as badgers play all sorts of games, including leapfrog; they are also fond of bathing. Both the hearing and the sense of smell of badgers are extremely acute. Adults utter growls of warning followed by a staccato bark should other animals approach too close. The sow's single note of warning has been likened to that of a moorhen (Southern, 1964). At the mating season the boar makes a deep purring noise and when excited this becomes prolonged and is higher pitched. The sow is also known to use purring noises in order to encourage her cubs.

The badger has often been described as an extremely lazy, cautious creature preferring seclusion and indolence, but as with the majority of animals its timidity and caution develop in direct proportion to hunting. Ognev (1962) sums up the badger by relating that it is a perpetual malcontent, constantly grumbling and angry, as demonstrated by its constant huffing and puffing. He also states that it is a most harmless predator which never needlessly molests anyone and only wishes to be left in peace. However, when attacked and in danger, the badger will defend itself actively against all comers, not even fearing man, and it will attack dogs with ferocity. When surrounded, it usually seats itself on its rump, defending itself with its paws and flailing out against its attackers with heavy blows. There have been several reports of a badger seizing a dog so firmly in such a skirmish that it becomes incapable of reopening its jaws; it will also utter blood-curdling screams which may be repeated many times during the course of the fight. The badger is not considered to be a highly intelligent animal. If handled from an early age it can become remarkably tame.

The musk glands are situated in the anal regions and are well developed; they are able to secrete a yellowish oily liquid which has a strong musky smell. The scent is emitted as a result of fear or excitement, as well as being deliberately set by the badger by squatting: by setting a scent trail in unfamiliar country, a badger is able to find its way back. The smell stimuli is therefore considered to be an important factor in providing a general guide to the objects in the vicinity of the sett and aiding the marking out of the badger's territory, different plants and animals being recognised by their scents. Scent setting is also used in the mating season for soliciting potential mates.

Diet   The badger is the most omnivorous of the mustelids. Southern (1964) states that the diet is largely dependent on food availability. Animal matter includes rabbits, mice, rats, voles, moles, hedgehogs, amphibians, slugs, snails, earthworms, wasp grubs, beetles and other large insects. In the British Isles, poultry is taken occasionally. Lamb killing is extremely rare, although still-born lambs are occasionally taken. Carrion is also sometimes taken.

Stomachs of badgers killed in Russia have shown remnants of coarsely masticated fledglings, grass frogs, some terrestrial snails, several beetles, and a certain amount of grass and earth. In one animal there was found a great amount of wasps which the animal had swallowed together with the clay soil; the stomach had become distended to the size of a medium-sized watermelon. Also, remains of dung beetles have been found, as well as numerous snakes, including vipers (Ognev, 1962).

Vegetable food includes tubers, bulbs, fruits of all kinds from windfall apples, pears and plums to acorns, blackberries and other succulent berries. Green food including grass is taken; in the British Isles, this is especially eaten during the winter. Oats are occasionally eaten, as well as mushrooms and other fungi. In other parts of their range, badgers are known to eat cherries, cedar nuts, chestnuts, hazel nuts and walnuts, and they have a great love for grapes which they usually locate just as the vines are ripening when the grapes become both sweet and succulent.

In their search for food, badgers are described in reports from Russia as attacking calves and foals, and inflicting wounds, chiefly in the hindquarters and flanks; in this respect the Transbaikal badger is even more audacious and bloodthirsty than the European variety. It is considered that a badger is only driven to this type of predation when the variety of foodstuffs is severely limited, for, as has been remarked previously, badgers in western Europe have only very occasionally been known to attack lambs, and their most important single item of diet is earthworms; young rabbits are also important, although these have been severely curtailed in areas where myxomatosis is rife.

Breeding The breeding pairs of badgers usually remain together throughout the year and the cubs are born in a nesting chamber which is not very far away from the entrance of the sett.

Neal (1962) states that at the mating season the boar makes a vibrant deep throaty noise which may continue on and off for long periods. The sow shows oestrus behaviour immediately after giving birth, and is inseminated. Copulation stimulates ovulation; the eggs pass into the uterus where they attain the blastocyst stage, and then remain in this stage and free in the uterus for a considerable time. Some implantation generally takes place in the first fortnight in December; in France, Canivenc (1966) reports that the period of implantation coincides with the time when the nights are longest, the young being born around 1 February. The period from implantation to birth is in the region of 40—50 days. Neal records that in England the normal time of birth is January to April, with the peak period occurring during the first three weeks in February in the south and south-west. In Russia, the young generally make their appearance at the end of March or the beginning of April (Ognev, 1962).

The most usual litter sizes are 2 and 3; but single cubs are occasionally born and 4 cubs are not uncommon, and there are some reports of litters of 5. Reports of a higher number of cubs are considered to be due to two families living together. The cubs' survival rate during the first year is often low. When born the cubs are blind and about 12 cm in length, and they are covered with a rather dirty white fur; the facial stripes can usually be seen after a few days. The eyes are open by about the tenth day, but some authorities consider that it is unlikely that they can use their eyes effectively for some weeks. The cubs first come above ground at 6—8 weeks, and weaning starts at about 12 weeks when the sow is known to regurgitate semi-digested food. At 12—14 weeks the cubs search for food independently of the sow. Cubs make high-pitched whickering noises when tiny, and loud squeals if danger threatens; when older they make 'puppy' noises when playing. It has been recorded that a badger cub made its first attempt to dig a burrow at 101 days and undertook its first olfactory marking of its territory on the 118th day, when its first wrestling play was also observed (Bourlière, 1967).

The young grow very rapidly and have been recorded to attain the weight of 8.8—9.2 kg by the beginning of September, and 10.4—11.2 kg by the end of the same month. The cubs live with the sow at least until the autumn when they are about three-quarters grown, and sometimes over the first winter. The female cubs usually become sexually mature when 12—15 months old, whereas the male cubs take up to 2 years. Females will usually reproduce each year.

Millais (1905) describes a litter of tame badgers that he had had the pleasure of observing: 'The mother would every evening take each cub in turn and thoroughly overhaul its coat for parasites; grooming each in turn, with champing jaws, she turned them over and over with her nose till every part of the offspring had been successfully explored and thus relieved them of the annoying pests which at that age they seemed unable to destroy.' One further report from the same source relates how one observer had seen the female badger turn back and shake severely a cub that would insist on following its dam away from home, 'the poor little chap hobbling a retreat, very injured at heart, stopping to perch on its haunches and gaze wistfully in the direction its mother had gone'.

Badgers have been bred in captivity on numerous occasions. In 1974 three zoos in Great Britain were successful in breeding them, and the Norfolk Wildlife Park at

122

Great Witchingham reared three males from parents both of which were themselves captive bred. It is interesting to note that the Edinburgh Zoo has a wild badger 'sett' within the zoo grounds, where a family of 5–6 wild badgers have firmly established residence and breed each year. The lifespan of the badger is between 12 and 15 years.

Population   In many parts of the Continent the badger is still common and it appears to remain ubiquitous in both Britain and Ireland; at present there is no real indication of any marked reduction in overall numbers. However, whereas Southern (1964) reported that there appeared to have been a marked increase in the badger population in the British Isles over the previous 60 years, 9 years later members of the British Mammal Society representing 30 counties reported that in 13 of these badgers were believed to be decreasing, and in 10 others badger populations were considered to be static. During 1975/76, the Ministry of Agriculture decided to eliminate all badger setts where badgers have been proved to be carrying bovine T.B., although fortunately at present the infected zone has been confined to four small areas in the West Country.

There appears to be little information on densities in different environments, but Southern suggests that a population density of 3 adults per square mile is possible in typical badger country; the peak number of resident badgers to be found in any colony in the British Isles will occur between May and September. The total at this time of the year may be as many as 12.

Oryx magazine (July 1976) quoted Dr Ernest Neal's estimates of the number of badgers in Britain. The winter population of badgers in England, Scotland and Wales was put at between 75,000 and 90,000. Dr Neal emphasises that it is impossible to make any accurate assessment because of insufficient data; his estimate is based on the 8000 setts surveyed by members of the Mammal Society. He puts the number of setts in England at 18,000–20,000, of which 6000 would be in the six south-west counties; in Wales, 4000–5000, and in Scotland, 3000–5000, giving a total of 25,000–30,000 setts, for which he thinks a winter average of 3 badgers per sett would be reasonable. Numbers would be boosted in the early months of the year by cub births but adjusted again by the late autumn by adult deaths and cub mortality.

Distribution   The badger is found throughout practically all the countries of Europe, from the Mediterranean coast, including some of the Mediterranean islands, north to southern Scandinavia, and including Britain and Ireland. In Eurasia it occurs as far north as 65°N and throughout the Asiatic steppes south to the Himalayas, to northern India and Nepal, and still further east to Burma, i.e. approximately 15°N.

The badger is widely distributed in the British Isles: it is found in every county of England, Wales and Ireland, and in most of the counties of Scotland. It is absent from the islands round Britain except for Anglesey. Neal (1962) states that in England it is rarest in the flat lands of East Anglia and most common in parts of Cornwall, Devon, Somerset, Gloucestershire and the New Forest area, Monmouthshire, Herefordshire, Yorkshire, Cumberland and Durham. In Wales it is most numerous in the south and west, and most scarce in Caernarvon. In Scotland it is widely distributed but nowhere really common, the more favoured areas being East Lothian, Perthshire and the Spey Valley. In Ireland the badger is common in most parts.

123

Conservation   The hairs of badgers are still used to make a variety of different kinds of brushes, in particular the badger-hair shaving brush. Due to the very strong waterproof qualities of their skins, the hides are utilised for making goods ranging from pistol holsters in the Caucasus and Siberia to rugs in various parts of Asia, and sporrans in Scotland. The badger's fat is also quite highly valued, since it makes a good lubricator and is in some demand in folk medicine; and sometimes badger hams are even eaten. As recently as January 1972, it was reported that the latest threat to badgers in Britain was the demand for pelts from fashion houses for use in trimming hats (*Oryx*).

In 1965, Ernest Neal reported that badgers were decreasing in Britain, in some areas seriously, for reasons varying from death on the roads and electrification on the railways to effective keepering and the destruction of habitat. *Oryx* magazine (September 1969) made reference to a fifth factor − death by organochlorine poisoning from seed dressings, which according to D. J. Jefferies of the Nature Conservancy's Monks Wood Experimental Station accounted for up to 12 deaths out of 17 badgers examined. It was noticeable that all the poisoned badgers were found in March and April, the time of the spring cereal sowing, while the other 5 of the 17 corpses examined, which had been killed on the roads, were spread over the year.

A report in *Oryx* (May 1973) considered that the main threats to the badger were road killings and the gassing and digging out of setts. However, thanks partly to public revulsion at the latter and a general upwelling of feeling in favour of the badger, two badger protective bills went before Parliament. One was aimed to provide a blanket protection for badgers, and the other was directed solely against trespass for the purpose of badger digging. So people's awareness of the dangers threatening the badger were gathering force.

The Badger Bill, privately introduced by Lord Arran, received the Royal Assent in July 1973 and came into force in January 1974. The new Act makes it illegal to kill or take a badger except when damage to property or crops can be proved, or under licence − from the Natural Environment Research Council (N.E.R.C.) for scientific or educational reasons, or from the Ministry of Agriculture (in Scotland, the Secretary of State) in cases of disease. Moreover, on the recommendation of the Nature Conservancy, any area may be declared 'an area of special protection for badgers'. The badger was therefore the first land mammal, apart from 'game' animals, to gain legal protection in Britain. In November 1974, it was reported in *Oryx* that four men had been recently fined at Winsford, Cheshire, magistrates' court, for badger digging.

In 1972, a disturbing discovery was recorded, for a population of badgers in the Cotswolds was found to be infected with bovine tuberculosis. This came to light because the incidence of the disease in the local cattle was well above the national average. In the spring of 1973 the Ministry of Agriculture's Pest Infestation Control Service surveyed an area that included 1038 badger setts and found the tuberculosis in seven of 152 faeces samples. An area in Cornwall also revealed that the badgers were similarly infected.

In 1976, the problem of tuberculosis in British badgers still appears to be a local one, confined to the south-west; the number of infected animals is small, and no other wild mammal or bird appears to be affected. Such are the findings of the Ministry of Agriculture after a careful study and the examination of 700 badger carcases. More than one fifth were infected, but all came from small areas in

Cornwall, Avon and Gloucestershire and one from Wiltshire (*Oryx*, 1975–76). A later Ministry of Agriculture's report of bovine T.B. in badgers relates that out of some 2500 badgers examined, about 450 were infected, just over 17%. However, some other species, which included the fox, the mole and the rat, also failed to have a clean bill of health.

Brian Jackman's report in the *Sunday Times* (1977) deals very fairly with the pros and cons of the Ministry of Agriculture's decision to eliminate all badgers in setts where T.B. has been proved. And Eunice Overend (1976) explains why this drastic step is considered necessary and why many conservationists have regretfully agreed to support it. However, both underline the illegality for anyone except Ministry officials to kill a badger, and then only in an area where bovine T.B. has been found. (Sympathetic people who attempt to save a badger's life by moving it to another area, only do harm by spreading the infection.)

Within the Badger Act, 1973, and the British Wild Creatures and Wild Plants Protection Act, 1975, it is considered that, provided bovine T.B. in badgers is confined and eventually eliminated in the south-west, the badger's future in Britain will be secured. Certainly these two conservation Acts provide a certain degree of security for the badgers in the long term, and other undertakings such as the construction of a badger underpass under the M5 near Wellington, Somerset, which followed the example set when a culvert under the M53 in Cheshire was modified to allow the passage of badgers, foxes and other animals, well illustrate the public's enthusiasm for one of the most interesting animals we possess.

Victorian naturalists described the badger as an animal of considerable strength of character and individual charm, and though its little peccadilloes may bring it into conflict with either the farmer or the game preserver, few animals of its size can boast so blameless a life. Today, the badger is considered by most authorities to do little harm and indeed a great deal of good; let us hope that we can learn to live in better harmony with each other.

Bourlière, F. (1967): *Natural History of Mammals.* **Burton**, M. (1962): *Systematic Dictionary of Mammals of the World*, pp. 165–6. **Canivenc**, R. (1966): 'A study of progestation in the European badger'. **Corbet**, G. B. (1966): *Terrestrial Mammals of Western Europe*, pp. 147–8. **Jackman**, B. (1977): 'Why persecute the badger?'. **Lydekker**, R. (1915): *Wild Life of the World, Vol. 1*, pp. 48–9. **Millais**, J. G. (1905): *The Mammals of Great Britain and Ireland, Vol. II*, pp. 36–70. **Neal**, E. G. (1962): 'Badgers', in *Animals of Britain, 1*. **Ognev**, S. I. (1962): *Mammals of Eastern Europe and Northern Asia, Vol. II*, pp. 320–42. **Olney**, P. J. S. (1976): 'Species of wild animals bred in captivity during 1974' and 'Multiple generation captive births'. **Oryx** (1965–76): *Vols VIII–XIII.* **Overend**, E. D. (1976): 'TB in British badgers'. **Southern**, H. N. (1964): *Handbook of British Mammals*, pp. 376–81. **van den Brink**, F. H. (1973): *A Field Guide to the Mammals of Britain and Europe*, p. 126. **Walker**, E. P. (1964): *Mammals of the World, Vol. II*, p. 1206.

Otter

Lutra lutra

Status: Although the otter occurs throughout the majority of its former distribution, it is on the decline. It remains to be seen whether measures being taken to reduce water pollution and other pressures will be sufficient to guarantee its survival in any but the remotest areas

Description   Otters share the same family as stoats, weasels, polecats, mink, martens and tayras, all of which show a considerable family resemblance. Other members of the same family, the wolverines, skunks and badgers, are superficially much less otter-like. The otters, of which *Lutra* is one of the six currently recognised genera in the sub-family Lutrinae, are by far the most aquatic of the Mustelidae, all having a long thick muscular tail, very small ears, and webbed toes.

As might be expected of a group of animals whose habitats range from the Himalayas to the Amazonian jungles, otters show a considerable diversity of size, ranging from the little clawless otter of the East Indies to the giant Brazilian otter. Similarly, the general appearance varies a good deal from one form to another. In size, the European otter occupies a central position in the group, and is perhaps the best known.

The most distinctive features are its flat head, well-whiskered muzzle, long, thick tapering tail and webbed feet. Its neck is no smaller than its broad, flattened head and leads into a muscular body which reaches its greatest breadth at the hips, the whole being very 'streamlined'. The strong tapering tail is fully haired like the body; it not only serves as a rudder when in the water, but is relatively flexible and is used by the animal in other ways. Otters frequently stand up on their hindlegs to see over obstructions and on such occasions the tail acts as a brace or third leg to balance them.

The otter has dense brownish fur, with glossy underparts somewhat lighter; the front of the neck and sides of head are whitish or grey-brown; the lips and edges of ears are light. The tone of the fur is variable, with occasional specimens of cream or even white recorded. The colour also varies with the season, being richer and darker brown in winter after the moult. This water-resistant pelt provides warmth, insulation and buoyancy, and when the otter emerges from the water the guard hairs mat into a spiky appearance. Females look more compact than males, which tend to be 'lankier', but thicker about the neck.

When an otter dives, the graceful undulations of its long slim body leave hardly a ripple. The rather small eyes are situated at the top of the head, enabling the animal when almost submerged in the water to see what is happening above and around it. This is a useful aquatic adaptation found in many other animals that spend much of their time largely submerged, such as the frog, crocodile and hippopotamus. When on land, however, the position of the eyes has disadvantages, as an otter is unable to see directly in front of its nose. Otherwise, its eyesight is fairly good, especially at night.

The nostrils are situated at the top of the muzzle, so that when swimming with most of the head and body submerged the otter is still able to breathe. A valve closes each nostril automatically when it dives and enables the animal to drink with its head right under water. This it prefers to do, instead of lapping like a dog or cat. It surfaces every few minutes to breathe. The otter's sense of smell is well developed.

The very small ears provide little resistance to the water when swimming. They are also closed by hairs and valves when the animal submerges. The otter's hearing is very good and is one of its most important senses.

The whiskers or 'vibrissae' that are prominent on an otter's head are long and rigid and are mainly situated on either side of the nose in two patches, but there are others further up the face and several on the throat. They are highly important sense organs of touch. With them an otter can judge its distance from boulders or

128

the bed of the stream, even if the water is turbulent. It is also possible that the vibrissae help to detect the position of prey in the water by the currents set up. Some of these bristles also occur on the elbows, serving in the same way as organs of touch.

The head and body length range is 62—83 cm; tail length 36—55 cm; hind feet 11—13.5 cm; and shoulder height 30 cm. The weight range is from 12 to 15 kg.

Habitat   Otters live beside lakes, rivers, streams, canals and marshes as well as in coastal waters where they have been caught in crab and lobster pots. They try to avoid polluted rivers and prefer stretches where there is plenty of cover on the banks. They are sometimes found far from water, but usually only when crossing a watershed from one river system to another. In more mountainous areas they have been observed up to 2800 m; it has been suggested that they move up to the headwaters when fish migrate there to spawn, then come down to the lower reaches and the coast in the spring.

Behaviour   The otter is an expert swimmer and diver, but while on land its action is a fast waddle. The legs are rather short, so the body is kept near the ground. As the hindlegs are longer, the hind part of the back appears curiously arched; nevertheless otters can run quite fast, but not nearly so fast as a dog or a fox.

Otters can be active day and night, although they are usually nocturnal for they are very shy and cautious. During the daytime they lie up in burrows or 'holts'. The holt is a natural hole, or one the otter has dug for itself, in the bank of a river, stream or lake. It has several passages and a roomy living chamber above the level of the water, lined with dry grass and the like, and provided with a ventilation shaft to ground level. One entrance is always under water. Other entrances and exits are recognisable by tracks and remains of food. With the possible exception of the badger, river otters are probably the most playful of the Mustelidae. They live solitarily or in families, but when together their acrobatics are wonderful to watch as they wrestle and chase each other in the water. They will use any convenient object as a toy — a log, for instance, as it rotates in the water will keep them amused for a long time — and they will constantly dive for pebbles and try to bring them up to the surface. Some species engage in the year-round activity of sliding down mud and snow banks, and individuals of all ages participate.

Although often silent for long periods, otters can make a variety of sounds, the best known being the shrill whistle which appears to serve as a means of communicating location. A long drawn out moan probably denotes apprehension, while a rather low-pitched chortle is commonly used when pleased, and a hiss or high-pitched chatter when annoyed.

Diet   Fish forms the basic diet of European otters. But their food is very variable, depending on locality and the abundance of the prey at any one time, so many other kinds of animals are eaten and crustaceans generally form an important part of their diet. Amongst the food items that they have been recorded to eat are eels, trout, salmon, minnows, crayfish, crabs, newts, tadpoles, frogs, snails, earthworms, beetles, fresh-water shrimps and even aquatic birds. Various mammals are also eaten occasionally, especially rabbits and small rodents such as rats and water voles; carrion is also taken.

129

Breeding   In this otter, breeding seems to be less seasonal than in any other species of European mammal, and the young have been recorded in every month of the year. But the normal mating season has been put at the end of February or early March, with the female whelping in May.

Oestrus takes place every 24—28 days and copulation takes place in the water. As pregnancy develops the female becomes particularly belligerent and the male is usually rejected prior to parturition; unlike some of the other otter species *Lutra lutra* males take no part in rearing the young.

After a gestation period of 60—62 days, 1—5 cubs are born, although usually 2 or 3. The cubs are blind for up to 35 days, and the juvenile fur is dark and fine. The cubs stay in the breeding holt up to 8 weeks and are nursed for about 4 months. The cubs remain with the mother for quite some time, probably until the following autumn prior to the next mating taking place. Until comparatively recently, otters have seldom bred regularly in world zoos. N. Duplaix-Hall, after observing nearly 150 otters in 25 zoos over the course of an 8-year period, believes that breeding success is linked to three factors: the enclosures, the diet and the otters themselves. 'Before building an enclosure, one must eradicate two preconceived ideas immediately: (a) that an otter needs as much water as a seal, and (b) that it can live quite cheaply on fish. An otter is an expensive animal to house and to feed if one is to succeed in keeping it alive, let alone breeding it. Otters eat up to 20% of their own weight daily due to a high metabolic rate and a rapid digestion. Usually an adult eats no more than 500 g of food at a time, so it is preferable to divide the daily rations into two or three' (Duplaix-Hall, 1975).

A diet low in unsaturated fats or vegetable oil is often responsible for poor coat conditions, for when an otter's fur is waterlogged, the guard hairs are clamped together. Lack of sufficient dry grooming areas can cause a similar poor coat condition, which if it remains unchecked will more often than not result in the loss of the animal.

In Duplaix-Hall's studies, it is advocated that the minimum requirement for one pair of *Lutra lutra* should be an enclosure measuring 15 x 10 m with a land/water ratio of 4 : 1; as this species is a very nimble climber a fence 1.80 m high with a 80 cm smooth overhang is essential. The two most important attributes of the den are quiet and privacy.

When birth is imminent the *Lutra* female rejects the male forcibly, not allowing him to enter the den, so the males are best removed at such times. Thus if intensive captive breeding programmes are envisaged, the male can be removed when mating has been observed and another female introduced to him, thereby increasing the reproductive potential by taking advantage of the otter's polyoestrous cycle.

Now that guidelines for the breeding in captivity of *Lutra* species have been established, successful captive propagation is on the increase and multiple generation births have recently been recorded. In captivity otters can attain an age of 19—20 years, although a lifespan of 12—15 years is more normal.

Population   Although otters are on the decline they still occur throughout the majority of their former distribution. As recorded by C. J. Smit and A. van Wijngaarden (1976), there were estimated to be a total of 300 specimens in the Netherlands in 1965; 40—60 in Switzerland in 1951—2; about 500—1000 in the German Federal Republic in 1974 (but more recently no more than 500 and declining rapidly); and about 700 in Sweden. Every year about 200 otters are killed in Denmark, about 650 are shot in Norway, and less than 50 in Sweden, and some years ago about 400 specimens were taken annually in Rumania.

Until recently the otter has remained widespread in Britain and Ireland in spite of persecution by fishing interests and by the hunt. But there is evidence of a considerable decline in lowland rivers in recent years. Western counties, especially in Wales and the Lake District, have no lack of otters which may alternate between sea and freshwater habitats. Scotland is well populated, with many marine-living animals around the Hebrides, Orkney and Shetland. Density is never very high and, in the opinion of some hunters, 1 per 6 miles of stream is normal.

In 1973, there were 45 European otters in captivity in 23 different collections throughout the world.

Distribution   Otters are very widely distributed in every continent except Australia. The European species is to be found throughout Europe and Asia as far north approximately as the Arctic Circle and as far south as Morocco and Algeria, but it is absent from the Mediterranean islands, except Sicily and Corfu, where it may have been introduced; in Asia it extends westwards through Siberia and Manchuria to the Kuriles and Japan, but the southern limit of the specific race is ill-defined, typical *Lutra l. lutra* intergrading with *Lutra l. monticola* in northern India and Tibet, and with *Lutra l. chinensis* in northern China.

Conservation   Otters have always been trapped for their fur as well as persecuted for their depredations on fisheries and hunted for sport. But they are also affected as river boards clean up cover on the banks, urban districts spread, and drainage and land reclamation occur, and by the regulation of streams and the building of dams, hydro-electric schemes, and sluices. So the natural habitat of the otter is year by year reduced.

Although disturbance by recreational activities such as power boats takes its toll too, water pollution from industrial waste and high levels of pesticides are undoubtedly the otter's chief adversaries. In the remoter parts of its range, where conditions are suitable, it seems likely that the otter will continue to hold its own, but in areas with a high proportion of the most polluted and sluggish streams it remains to be seen whether the measures now being taken to reduce pollution will be sufficient to result in an increased population.

There has always been great controversy about the damage otters do to fishing interests; probably the normal density is too low to cause serious loss in most habitats, although it is recognised that in fish hatcheries at spawning time otters may cause havoc among trout and salmon stocks. Some studies have shown that although a fair proportion of their total diet is made up of many minor food groups, the majority of the fish that they take are coarse fish, and they may well be more useful than damaging in trout and salmon streams, by killing eels which devour the eggs of both these fish.

Similar controversy has also been rife as to the extent of the inroads made by otter hunts on their population. A report in *Oryx* (1969) from the British Mammal Society shows it to be clear from the otter hunt figures given that, other things being equal, the cull did not cause any significant decrease in the population between 1900 and 1937. Nor, even with the reduced numbers of the 1960s, would an annual kill of 50 be significant. A second report in 1974 shows that in some countries, in the four years 1968–71, otters have held their own or increased

slightly; but in the Midlands especially the decline continues, and the otter can truthfully be described as a locally endangered species.

In 1976, the Council of the Scottish Wildlife Trust expressed its strong opposition to otter hunting on the Hebridean island of Mull, where a pack of imported otter hounds pursued this non-traditional Highland sport during the summer of 1975.

Otters are not protected by law in some of the European countries including the Netherlands, both of the German Republics, Sweden, Switzerland, Czechoslovakia and Bulgaria. There are hunting restrictions in the U.S.S.R. and in Norway (including total protection in the south).

Now that we have understood the basic differences between the several species, and met their necessary requirements, otters should not be difficult to breed regularly in captivity. Recently, Mr Philip Wayre, owner of the Norfolk Wildlife Park, Norfolk, England, became the Honorary Director of the newly founded Otter Trust, whose aim is to save the world's nineteen species of otter. The Trust already has 21 otters belonging to five different species.

As recently as 1977, the Nature Conservancy Council considered the otter's status in England and Wales to be endangered, and for this reason the otter is soon to be added to Schedule One of the British Wild Creatures and Wild Plants Act 1975.

Apart from measures to protect the otter by law in all countries where its numbers are found to be dwindling, there is a further clear need: in the interests of the survival of many aquatic species, the fight against water pollution must be intensified and a network must be formed of suitable well-managed nature reserves in which the otters can live unhindered.

Bourlière, F. (1967): *Natural History of Mammals.* **Corbet**, G. B. (1974): *Changing Flora and Fauna of Britain.* **Davis**, J. A. (1971): 'Dying species – the otters'. **Duplaix-Hall**, N. (1975*b*): 'River otters in captivity', in *Breeding Endangered Species in Captivity.* **Graf**, J. (1968): *Animal Life of Europe*, pp. 29–31. **Harris**, C. J. (1968): 'Otters, a study of the recent lutrinae', in *The World Naturalist.* **Neal**, E. G. (1962): 'Otter', in *Animals of Britain, 8.* **Oryx** (1969–74): 'The otter in Britain' (first and second reports). **Southern**, H. N. (1964): *Handbook of British Mammals*, pp. 381–5. **Smit**, C. J. and **Wijngaarden**, A. van (1976): 'Threatened mammals'. **Walker**, E. P. (1964): *Mammals of the World, Vol. II*, p. 1215.

European Wildcat

Felis silvestris

Status: Although rare in some parts of its range, in other areas its numbers have increased during the last thirty years

Description   The problem in identifying wildcats is to distinguish them from wild domestic cats and hybrids. The domestic cat, which is believed to have been derived from the wildcat of Egypt, has certainly received contributions from the European wildcats as well. It is still fertile with European wildcats so it must be presumed that all populations of the wildcat have an admixture of domestic blood. Although *Felis silvestris* was once regarded as a species with forty sub-species, distributed over Europe, Africa and most of Asia, it has now become customary to deal with the wildcat under three main types: the European wildcat *Felis silvestris silvestris*, the African wildcat *Felis silvestris lybica*, and the Asiatic steppe or desert wildcat *Felis silvestris ornata*.

The pure-bred wildcat differs from most domestic cats in that it is larger and has a shorter tail (40–45% of head and body length) which is very bushy, with thick black bands and blunt at the black tip as if it has been shorn off; it also has horn-coloured nails. Although sometimes bearing a resemblance to a fine specimen of the domestic 'tabby', a wildcat immediately impresses the beholder with its more powerful build: it is about a third larger than a domestic cat.

The head is heavy and broad, with a distinct forehead, and the ears are small and project horizontally. The eyes are greenish-yellow, the nose pale brown and the whiskers long. Wildcats have thirty teeth and their claws are sharp and retractile, the paws being pale in colour. The ground colour of the dense, soft, long-haired fur is yellowish-grey, darker and more greyish on the back, more yellowish or almost cream on the underside. There is sometimes a little white on the chest. Four or five longitudinal dark stripes run from the forehead to the nape, merging into a more or less distinct dorsal line which ends at the root or on the upper side of the tail. From this dorsal line, a number of transverse bars run down to the belly and the legs also have transverse stripes.

The variation found between individuals sometimes makes it difficult to decide which, if any, of a population being observed are hybrids. However, as David Jenkins, of the Institute of Terrestrial Ecology, Banchory, Kincardineshire, states: 'there is no reason to suggest that a large flat-skulled, bushy-tailed, striped wild tabby cat recorded in the hills of Scotland is not as true a specimen of *Felis silvestris* as can be found in any part of the species' range'.

The head and body length has a range of 47.5–80.0 cm; tail length 26.0–37.0 cm; hind foot 12.0–14.5 cm; height at shoulder 35.0–40.0 cm. Weight ranges between 5.0 and 10.0 kg, although an exceptional weight of 14.8 kg was recorded from the East Carpathians in 1953. The females are smaller than the males: out of 107 specimens killed during the winter of 1943 in Scotland the average head and body length of the male specimens was 58.9 cm, whereas the average female measured 57.1 cm. The other measurements taken also confirmed that the females are smaller.

Habitat   In Scotland wildcats are nowadays mostly found in the grouse-moor and sheep-farming country of the lower hills. They cross from one valley to another, and their tracks have been seen in snow at over 2000 ft; but they are commoner below 1500 ft and are mostly found below 1000 ft. The chief limiting factor is probably food, and they are seldom found away from places where there are rabbits. They are probably equally common in woodland and in the open; rocky gorges and cairns are favourite hiding places.

On the European continent, extensive and varied forests with plenty of undergrowth, rocky outcrops and small clearings are the forest wildcat's main habitat. Being highly adaptable, it often visits other types of country, such as more open forests, heaths, moors and marshlands, and it may even settle there if it finds conditions suitable. In southern Europe it is often found in the scrubby type of bush known as *macchia*. In Germany and adjoining countries the wildcat favours coniferous forests, while in the Caucasus it prefers the broad-leaved forest zone.

Behaviour   Wildcats do not always avoid human habitation, and tracks are sometimes found round houses and even on windowsills. They will enter buildings, including chicken-houses where they sometimes kill fowls, but they rarely stay inside them, differing here from wild domestic cats. They will climb trees, and are known to make their dens in hollow tree-trunks, but according to some writers are less inclined than domestic cats to climb, escaping instead between rocks or down holes. Wildcats are mainly active in the evening and early morning, often taking a rest in the middle of the night. They occasionally move about in daytime, for they like to sun themselves on a branch or on a secluded boulder, and they share with many other members of the cat family a dislike for rain and water.

The wildcat is a solitary, territorial animal, each individual keeping to an area of approximately 150 acres. Its territory is marked by urine and probably also by faeces (which are usually black and are not buried as in the domestic cat) and by claw-sharpening which may be assisted with secretions from glands in its feet. The animal also rubs its posterior against its marker trees, presumably discharging its anal glands. The usual evidence of a wildcat is the track of paw marks, typically in a straight line, in snow or mud. A wildcat may travel several miles in a night, and its trails have been traced from rabbit-hole to rabbit-hole, suggesting that it may have a regular beat. The male defends its home range against other toms, but does not hesitate to pass far beyond its boundaries when forced to do so by shortage of prey or in order to find a female at mating time.

The hunting technique depends upon stealth and surprise rather than speed. J. G. Millais, the naturalist painter, describes this well: 'Emerging at dawn and before sunset, this stealthy animal creeps in and out of the forest growth and rocks, looking for its prey. When the victim is discovered it is carefully stalked by sight alone until closely approached, when the cat rushes in with a series of immense forward bounds. So swift is this final attack that four-footed game finds it impossible to escape, even if its terror-paralysed nerves did not benumb its muscles.' In one observation of such a killing, the cat was observed to dispatch a hare by jumping on its back and giving it a bite in the neck — typical feline tactics.

Diet Wildcats eat a wide range of food from mice to deer fawns, although individuals that kill larger animals are considered to be specialists and do not represent the norm. Though they may bury uneaten parts of their kills, they are apparently not usually carrion eaters.

In Scotland, David Jenkins remarks that small rodents, rabbits and birds make up the bulk of the prey, even though a certain number of mountain hares and grouse are taken, as well as the odd roe deer fawn or wild-grown lamb. Smaller prey such as voles and small birds are eaten whole; but in the case of hares or deer fawns, the head may be torn off and only the brains and tongue, and perhaps liver and spleen, are eaten. Like foxes, wildcats may bite off the flight feathers of grouse before eating them. Prey caught at night may be eaten where it is killed, but in daytime it is the rule for wildcats to take their prey to shelter — hence the only signs of a kill may be some scattered fur or feathers. They will kill shrews, moles and water-voles, but rarely eat them, for unlike foxes they do not salivate over these items of distasteful prey. Cockchafers and fish are sometimes caught and eaten, but snakes are usually avoided. Unlike domestic cats, wildcats do not play with their prey before killing and eating it.

C. A. W. Guggisberg describes the dominance of small rodents among the forest wildcat's prey, as exemplified by the stomach contents of 28 eastern Carpathian specimens examined: mice and dormice, 65%; squirrels, susliks and other medium-sized rodents, 12%; hares and rabbits, 5%; roe deer fawns, 1%; capercaillie, black cock, hazel hen and other game birds, 8%; small birds (up to the size of a jay), 6%; unidentified, 3%. There are regions where mice and voles make up almost 100% of the prey; and a wildcat shot in the Jura Mountains in 1953 was found to have eaten at least 10 voles.

Breeding   In Scotland, mating seasons are reported to occur at least twice a year, one about the first half of March and the second in May or June. By contrast, German authorities report that the wildcat breeds once yearly, coming into oestrus in late February or March.

The courtship is reported to be a very rowdy affair, accompanied by a lot of mewing and screeching. Several toms may sit for hours around a female, howling almost incessantly, trying to approach her one after the other. After one of the rival suitors has established its supremacy over the other toms, the female eventually signifies her readiness by rolling around on the ground, and then she crouches down so as to let the solicited tom stand over her. At the moment of mating, like so many other members of the cat family, he bites the back of her neck. The act is of very short duration and is repeated many times in succession.

The naturalist Alfred H. Cocks, who had had a lot of experience at the turn of the century in breeding many of the rarer native mammals of Great Britain, recorded that the usual gestation period for the wildcat was 68 days, although giving a range of 65—68 days. In more recent years it has been found that 66 days is the average gestation period for the wildcat, with a minimum period of 63, and a maximum of 69½ days. By contrast, the average gestation period for a domestic cat is 58 days and they have breeding seasons throughout the year.

There are 2—4 kittens born normally in May, and the father plays no part in bringing them up; the female rears her family away from the male who if present is known to kill them. The kittens are usually born in a nest in a cleft in rocks, in a hollow tree or in a fork in a tree, as well as sometimes in an abandoned fox den or badger sett. The kittens are guarded securely by the ferocity of their mother, who is almost unapproachable while they are still confined to the nest; even kittens will spit and fight if handled. For this reason very few have ever been taken alive at this stage, and those few have proved untameable.

Millais describes the wildcat in captivity as a most unsatisfactory pet, owing to its savage and intractable disposition. It never becomes docile, even to those who feed it, and a 'growling swear' is the usual reply to a proffered advance. Lynxes, leopards and lions may all become amenable to discipline, but the wildcat always has his back to the wall, ears down, eyes glittering and paws ready to strike. Well-named, it is the real untamed and untameable savage. Millais's sentiment is partially endorsed by my own experience with the Scottish wildcat's related form in Africa. I had excavated an aardvark's earth only to find a remarkably unsociable wildcat kitten, which, becoming entangled in my net, hissed, spat and struck out wildly with its claws with all the ferocity of a tornado. Although I had the kitten for almost three months, in spite of every overture of goodwill on my part, it showed not the remotest sign of becoming any friendlier, so it was released.

New-born kittens weigh about 40 g and are blind until 9—10 days. Young individuals are more distinctly marked than adults and have a tapering tail as opposed to the adult's blunt one. Lactation lasts about a month. The kittens emerge from the den at 4—5 weeks and play with the mother; they are taught hunting techniques and start to hunt at about 3 months. They are weaned a month later, and the family breaks up at 5 months. At 10 months they are almost fully grown though a further slight growth may occur up to two years. Sexual maturity is attained a year after birth when mating first occurs. The mortality rate among kittens is high, with most deaths occurring between the second and fourth months. Lifespan is given as up to 12 years, although one longevity of 16 years has been recorded.

Population   With an animal as secretive and as widely scattered as the wildcat, it is almost impossible to arrive at even a tentative estimate as to its population; however, in the German Federal Republic its numbers are at present being put at 2000 and in Czechoslovakia the total number is estimated at 700 specimens.

In David Jenkins's recent study of the status of the wildcat in Scotland, the wildcats were reported to be present or formerly present on 100 out of 135 estates and forests in 11 counties. Some of these estimates were backed by figures and the survey must be one of the most accurate yet made for a member of Felidae.

An isolated population that persisted in Glen Doll in upper Glen Clova in Angus was being killed during the 1940s at a rate of about 100 each year, which goes to show that there must originally have been a sizeable population of wildcats. On one estate in mid-Sutherland the records show that the wildcats increased very quickly in the late 1920s, from only an occasional one killed by a large staff of keepers up to 25–35 a year.

J. G. Millais reported that the Earls of Seafield always took great interest in the wildcats and afforded them full protection. In 1879, the old Earl took much pride in showing Millais his wildcats and their families, which were confined to stout wooden cages on his Scottish estate. Eight or ten of the cats were always kept, and they had on several occasions bred and reared their young.

In 1973, world zoos recorded the successful rearing of some 35 wildcats in 16 different collections.

Distribution   In the Pleistocene age the wildcat ranged over the whole of England and Scotland, although apparently it did not reach Ireland and the outer islands of Scotland. In Europe it lived in all wooded regions south of the Netherlands and the German, Polish and Russian lowlands.

Its former presence in southern Britain is shown by its numerous remains in the brick earths of Grays (Essex), the caves of Bleadon and Uphill (Mendips), Cresswell Crags (Derbyshire), Kent's Hole (Torquay), Ravenscliffe (Glamorganshire), the Vale of Clwyd, and in a fissure in the Wealden Rocks, Ightham (Kent). Wildcats were found in west Lincolnshire, and were said to have survived in Yorkshire until 1840. In the Lake District they appear to have lingered until 1843, when the last undoubted specimen was killed near Loweswater. There is no evidence to show when the wildcat became extinct in southern and central England, but probably it lingered until the forests were destroyed to provide land for cultivation. By the end of the nineteenth century there are no further records of the wildcat occurring in England, Wales or southern Scotland.

After World War I the species recovered in the Scottish Highlands, and began to spread southwards. A further increase was reported by David Jenkins in the 1950s and was most marked in two of the chief centres of game preservation, Angus and Moray. Wildcats more recently were recorded as far south as Stirlingshire in the drainage area of the River Forth, and it seems that this population expansion is still continuing.

In Germany the forest wildcat was officially declared as 'vermin' in 1848, and within a short time it became extinct in Pomerania, Wurtemburg, Baden and

Saxony, where the last one was killed as early as 1850. The species hung on precariously in a few restricted areas until protection throughout the year was once more afforded it in 1934, and since World War II its numbers have increased significantly.

Wildcats still occur over the Iberian peninsula in Spain and Portugal; and in France (eastern Pyrenees, Orleans, Ardennes, Champagne, Lorraine, Vosges), Belgium (Ardennes), Italy, Greece, Yugoslavia, Austria, Czechoslovakia and Poland (in the Carpathians). The species occurs in the forested parts of the central mountains of Hungary and Rumania. In Russia it is at present common in the Caucasus and Talysh, as well as being found in many other regions. On Sicily, wildcats only occur in the mountains in the north and south-east. On Sardinia, the sub-species *Felis silvestris sarda* occurs.

Conservation   Because wildcats are considered to be harmful to game, they are persecuted by hunters and therefore rare in large parts of their range. Apart from man, the most dangerous enemy of the forest wildcat must be the lynx, which is said to hunt and kill it whenever it has a chance.

Wildcats have been maintained and bred in captivity, and there is reason to assume that extensive captive breeding programmes could be undertaken for this species, if the conservation necessity ever arose.

According to David Jenkins, wildcats are still widely regarded as vermin in Scotland. Many are still trapped, mainly after tracking them in snow, and others are snared and shot. The reasons for the comparatively sudden increase of wildcats in eastern Scotland are unknown, although many fewer cats were killed after the outbreak of myxomatosis, prior to which wildcats were often killed accidentally by trappers catching rabbits. In 1975 Dr Jenkins stated that he was planning new research into the behaviour of this species, which will undoubtedly shed further light on its status in the Scottish highlands. In 1973 the Forestry Commission, which usually affords protection to the wildcat, carried out a survey on the presence of the wildcat in its own forests in Scotland; this data will no doubt be kept up to date. It is encouraging, to say the least, that although the Scottish wildcat is not officially protected it is probably more abundant now than at any time in human memory.

The wildcat is protected by law in some parts of Austria and in Switzerland, Germany, Spain, Poland and the western part of Czechoslovakia. In order to ensure its survival in areas where it is now rare, protection should be extended to the other countries in which it is still found.

Boorer, M. (1969): *Wild Cats*, p. 50. Burton, M. (1962): *Systematic Dictionary of Mammals of the World*, p. 177. Corbet, G. B. (1966): *Terrestrial Mammals of Western Europe*, pp. 156–7. Denis, A. (1964): *Cats of the World*, pp. 90–4. Duplaix-Hall, N. (1975a): 'Species of wild animals bred in captivity during 1973'. Eaton, R. L. (1973): 'The world's cats'. Graf, J. (1968): *Animal Life of Europe*, p. 23. Gray, A. P. (1971): *Mammalian Hybrids*, p. 37. Guggisberg, C. A. W. (1975): *Wild Cats of the World*, pp. 23–4. Jenkins, D. (1961): 'The present status of the wildcat in Scotland'. Jenkins, D. (1975): *in litt.* Millais, J. G. (1904): *Mammals of Great Britain and Ireland, Vol. I*, pp. 169–80. Rowe, J. J. (1975): *in litt.* Smit, C. J. and Wijngaarden, A. van (1976): 'Threatened mammals'. Southern, H. N. (1964): *Handbook of British Mammals*, pp. 385–90. van den Brink, F. H. (1973): *A Field Guide to the Mammals of Britain and Europe*, p. 142.

Lynxes

European Lynx and Pardel or Spanish Lynx

Lynx lynx   *Lynx pardina*

Status: Protected by law and on the increase in some countries; in others hunting restrictions must be provided to prevent its extermination. The population of the Spanish race relies for its survival on the enforcement of established protective laws

Description   Not all zoologists agree over the number of species of lynx which should be recognised. In matters of this sort, there are always two schools of thought: the 'lumpers' and the 'splitters'. The lumpers, making full allowance for the great range of individual animal variation, set their boundaries wide: the lynxes of southern Europe, northern Europe and Asia, and northern North America, form but one species *Lynx lynx*. Even though fossil evidence and colour differences between typical examples from each population can be striking, the variations are rated as being mostly those of different sub-species. The splitters, on the other hand, recognise three distinct species: the Pardel or Spanish lynx *Lynx pardina*, the northern lynx of Eurasia *Lynx lynx* and the Canadian lynx *Lynx canadensis* of North America.

However, both schools of taxonomists agree that North America has a second, more southern and rather smaller species of lynx, the bobcat *Lynx rufa*. F. Otto Hohn states that the latter, when seen in the wild, can really only be distinguished from the lynx by the colour of its tail (the tip of the tail in the bobcat is black above and white below, in the lynx it is black both above and below); but it also has much narrower footpads and a rather different skull. Moreover, where the ranges of the two species overlap (roughly along the U.S./Canadian border) intermediate forms are not found, for there is no record of interbreeding taking place. As far as those lynxes inhabiting Europe are concerned, there does not appear to be sufficient justification to treat them as separate species; it seems more reasonable to regard them as two separate sub-species.

The lynx is a medium-sized cat, powerfully built, with a lithe, compact body and sturdy legs with large paws; the latter are furred so densely in winter that a remarkably efficient snow-shoe effect is created. It has pointed ears topped with black tufts of hairs and a stubby tail, looking as if docked, with a black tip. The mane-like cheek fringes are short in summer, long in winter, and there are long, stiff whiskers. The lynx has thick soft fur, with colouring varying from sandy to rufous-grey mixed with white on top, scattered with round rufous and grey-brown spots everywhere. The inside of the legs, front of the neck, lips and surrounds of the ears are white, the face reddish, and the winter fur is slightly tipped with white. The southern animals are smaller than the northern race, more heavily spotted and with shorter fur. It is maintained that the male is always paler and larger, particularly about the head, neck and whiskers, and he makes bigger pugmarks.

The northern race, being larger, ranges between 80 and 130 cm (the southern race 85–110 cm), tail length 11–24.5 cm (12.5–13 cm), hind foot 19–22.5 cm (17–19.5 cm), height at shoulder 60–75 cm (60–70 cm). The weight range is 18–38 kg.

Habitat   The species is found in mountainous areas, in the taiga, but also in mixed deciduous forests. Throughout the greater part of its vast area of distribution, the lynx shows a preference for old, high-timbered forests with dense undergrowth and windfalls. Like many other cats, however, it is adaptable enough to colonise a variety of other types of habitat. In Mongolia and the Gobi Altai, the lynx is a rock dweller, partial to places where stony outcrops alternate with shrubs. Whereas the northern race is primarily a forest dweller, the chief distinction of the Spanish race is that it lives in the rather open woods of pines, pistachio scrub and junipers which cover parts of the great dunes, or in the belt dominated by 'jaguarzo' (*Halimium*), a pale-foliaged shrub with striking yellow flowers. This area lies between the woods and the open marshes or *marismas* and is stubbled with old cork oaks and interspersed with stretches of heath, bracken and grassland and with dense thickets of brambles, broom and gorse which are almost impenetrable to man and make splendid hideouts for the lynxes. In general this habitat is like that occupied by the caracal in North Africa; and as the two species could be considered to replace each other geographically, the caracal can be referred to as the African lynx.

Behaviour   Like the European wildcat, the lynx is usually a solitary, nocturnal animal, restricting its activities to the hours of darkness and the twilight of dawn and dusk. When prowling about it is very much on the alert. Its acute vision and hearing give it plenty of warning of a person's approach, enabling it simply to hide where it is by crouching down, or to withdraw into cover if necessary. It is credited with being a good swimmer, a tireless walker and a very good climber. In Europe each individual maintains a territory with an area of 1000–2500 hectares.

The visual power of this animal justifies the expression 'lynx-eyed', as shown by some fairly recent experiments conducted in Germany on lynxes reared in captivity. These could spot a buzzard in flight up to nearly 4 km away, and when a stuffed brown hare was moved on a background of snow by pulling a string, they would notice it up to 297 m away. The hearing of the young lynxes was also found to be better than that of humans or even average dogs. A lynx reacted to a police whistle up to 4.5 km away, while a dog could hear the whistle only up to 2.9 km and a human up to 2.4 km away.

The usual way a lynx makes a kill is to use all available cover, and when that gives out to crawl flat on the ground until close enough to spring. If it misses, which is not often, it does not give chase. As a rule, the lynx is a lone hunter. A favourite method when after rabbits is for the lynx to stalk silently to the edge of a clearing where they are feeding and then wait for one to come within range. When attacking young deer, it leaps at the throat if the fawn is standing or jumps on its neck if it is lying down.

Diet Like the caracal, the lynx hunts game birds, chiefly the red-legged partridge. One account of such a hunt relates how a covey flew over a lynx which was near its drinking place; it jumped up and seized a bird in the air with its claws, then carried it off in its mouth. Apparently the prey is always taken away from the killing point. If it is small enough, it is held with the captor's head high, the tail also jauntily vertical and switching from side to side. Heavier loads are dragged; a red deer calf was moved about 137 m and a rabbit with its trap — lynxes often poach along trap and snare lines — over 0.8 km (½ mile).

The Spanish race is reputed to eat only parts of its victims. In spite of the flesh on them, the legs as well as the back and entrails of a rabbit are usually left; the head, neck, breast, legs and wing muscles of a partridge are eaten, but the lynx will also sample the shoulder and neck of a deer, or perhaps a bit of the hindquarters. After its meal it covers the rest of the kill with sand and litter, making a characteristic mound nearly a foot high; but it does not return to it, for the lynx does not make a habit of eating carrion, and foxes frequently benefit from the leavings.

The European lynx's diet consists mainly of rabbits, hares, rodents, ground birds and young ungulates including domestic animals (sheep and goats), as well as deer, in particular roe deer.

In the North American forests it is the 'varying hare', also known as the snow-shoe rabbit, that forms the main prey of the lynx. Mice are also taken, as well as grouse, ducks, stranded fish, young deer and an occasional mountain sheep. Yet so dependent is the lynx on the hares, that its numbers increase and decrease with the regular fluctuations — caused by disease — of the snow-shoe rabbit population. Another interesting report is that of a single bobcat killing 38 lambs in one night: this type of destruction is of course quite exceptional, in fact it is a record. The relatively small importance of large animals in the bobcat's diet is shown in the following figures, based on an examination of the stomach contents of over 3500 bobcats. Remains of various types of prey were found in the following percentages: various, 46%; hares and rabbits, 45%; deer, 3%; sheep, goats and a very few pigs, 2%; game birds, 1%. In another very large sample, fish, frogs and reptiles, as well as carrion, formed additional but very minor food items.

Guggisberg states that in the Tatar region of Russian Asia, hares make up 66% of the food taken in the winter, followed by water voles and birds. In the Altai, however, the winter diet consists of 58.9% of roe deer, followed by Asiatic wapiti (maral), 14.3%; musk deer, 8.9%; blue hares, 7.1%; carrion, 5.3%; domestic sheep, 3.5%; and capercaillie, 2.0%. Roe deer top the bill of fare in the Carpathians, and their populations have been noticed to decline sensibly in the presence of lynxes. Hares, chamois, marmots and game birds are fequently taken, with red deer and wild boar much more rarely except when young. Examining the stomachs of 93 lynxes from Bielowiesa and other parts of Poland, the following list of prey was recorded: hares and variable hares, 50%; game birds, 15%; mice and other small rodents, 10%; roe deer, 7%; other mammals (squirrels, marmots, martens, badgers, wildcats, foxes, dogs), 5%; unidentified, 2%. Information collected in Yugoslavia on 14 lynx kills in 1975 showed nine roe deer, three red deer, and two fallow deer. In southern Spain, rabbits are the main prey, with red-legged partridges and fawns of red and fallow deer being taken fairly frequently.

Breeding   It is during the mating season that the lynx, usually a silent animal, is most often heard. The challenging cry of the male has been described as varying from a muted, almost bear-like purr to a loud nocturnal caterwauling. Mating takes place in the early spring from January to March. Several males may court a female, and there are noisy skirmishes and fights among them until one becomes the accepted suitor. The female, after a 2—2½ month gestation period, selects a den in a site such as a hollow log, under the roots of a fallen tree, a natural cave, a badger's sett or under an overhanging rock.

The litter consists of 2—3 cubs (more rarely 1, 4 or 5) each about 70 g in weight. The young are blind at birth; they open their eyes at 16—17 days. They can be weaned at 2 months, but lactation can last up to 5 months. The cubs begin to take meat after the first month. The male is expelled from the lair when the young are born, but he remains in the vicinity and brings food to the den entrance until the young are old enough to follow their mother about. Then he tends to make off for good.

At the age of about 40 days their hunting instincts awaken, and they playfully go through the motions of stalking and catching prey. The lair is not finally left until after 4 months, and the cubs remain with the mother through their first winter until the next mating season breaks up the maternal family. Females attain sexual maturity at an age of 21 months, males not until after 2½ years. In 1898, hybridisation between a lynx and a domestic cat was alleged.

The lifespan of lynxes in the wild is probably 13—15 years at best, although they can live longer in captivity, with one recorded longevity of 17 years.

Population   The lynx has been extinct in Germany since 1846, in Austria since 1872, in Italy since 1910, in Hungary since 1915, in Bulgaria since 1935. In France, the last lynx of the Jura was killed in 1845, the last one of the Massif Central in 1875. In the French Alps, a specimen was taken in 1909, and some were seen in

1913; the last unquestioned record for the French Pyrenées is of a lynx shot on Canigou in 1917.

The number of lynxes in Norway is estimated at 150 individuals, but may be much larger: during an 8-year period, 286 specimens were killed. A census taken in Sweden in 1950 recorded 175 lynxes, 152 of which were from the north. A separate estimate taken the same year for Swedish Lapland gave 53 animals, which by 1957 had increased to 127. In 1963 the population for the whole country was put at 200—300. From 1965 to 1967, the annual kill was put at 45—55 specimens. In Finland in 1963, the lynx population was estimated to be 30—40 specimens. In 1972, it was considered to have increased to 100—200.

In Poland in 1963 the number of lynxes in the country was estimated at 300. In Czechoslovakia in 1963, a total of 80 were killed; by 1965, the numbers had increased to 400—500. In Rumania, between 1956 and 1962, the total population was estimated at 1000—1200; every year about 100—150 are shot. The number of lynxes in Yugoslavia is estimated at 50—70 specimens. In 1972, three pairs of lynx were caught in Slovakia and on 2 March 1973, they were released and reintroduced as a species into Slovenia. In 1970, two pairs of lynx were released into the Alps and the Jura region of Switzerland. Local conservation organisations have also reintroduced lynxes into Germany and Italy.

The total population of the Spanish lynx is unknown, but some reports give the number as high as several hundred, including an estimated 150—200 in the Coto Doñana — which is believed to hold the largest remaining population. However, some authorities have estimated the number in the entire delta region to be as few as 30 specimens, of which only 20 inhabit the Coto Doñana reserve. In 1973, world zoos recorded 5 males and 6 females of this race in 6 different collections.

Distribution   The lynx was once a British mammal, as can be seen from the bones found at several sites in England, Wales and Scotland; but there is no evidence that it survived into historic times. It may not have found the post-glacial Atlantic climate to its liking, for it failed really to establish itself anywhere in westernmost Europe. It has always been rare in the coastal areas of Norway; and in Denmark, where it occurred during the Bronze Age, the lynx does not seem to have been present in historic times. Prehistoric remains of it are scarce in Belgium, and there is no indication that it ever inhabited Holland. Otherwise, however, the distribution of the lynx once included all of Europe, from Scandinavia south to the Mediterranean, the Black Sea and the Caucasus and eastward through the Russian forest-belt to the Ural Mountains.

Spanish lynxes formerly occurred all over the Iberian peninsula, possibly as far north as the Pyrenees, and possibly also in parts of France. Lynxes were also found in Sicily and southern Italy; but these have been exterminated and it is not known to which race they belonged.

At present there are resident lynx populations in the northern, central and south-eastern parts of Norway, and in Sweden, Finland, the Baltic States, Poland, Czechoslovakia, Yugoslavia, Greece, Rumania and the U.S.S.R.

Small populations of the Spanish lynx hold on in Spain in isolated montane regions as well as in the delta of Guadalquivir. In Portugal, the Spanish lynx inhabits several areas in the south and east of the country; and recently traces of a lynx of unknown species were found in the Pyrenees National Park in France.

145

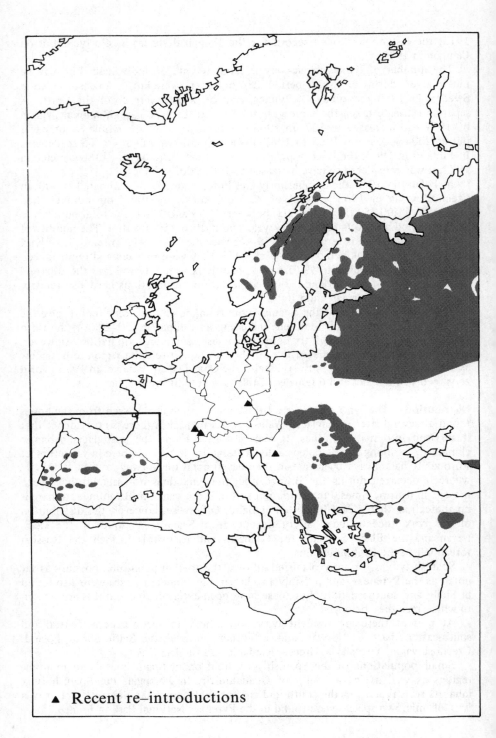

▲ Recent re–introductions

Conservation The chief pressure on the European lynx is continued persecution by hunters; the species is seen as a pest both to game and domestic livestock. Deforestation has also played an important role in the decline of the species, and so has the value put on the lynx's pelt. When it is not being shot at, it is sometimes poisoned instead, or caught with traps. Fortunately, however, the species displays a high degree of biological dynamism, showing signs of recovery just as soon as human persecution is reduced or ceases altogether.

The lynx is numerous in some parts of Russia, although in general the numbers in the south are decreasing. In April 1975, it was reported that in central and southern Sweden lynx stocks were slowly increasing, but sadly this has now aroused the wrath of local huntsmen, who appear to regard lynxes as competitors.

The lynx has been totally protected in Finland since 1968. It is also protected in Switzerland and Liechtenstein. There are hunting laws in Sweden, where there is an open season in December, and in Poland, Rumania, Yugoslavia and Greece where the open season is January. In 1968, the Spanish Government accepted 'ultimate responsibility' for the survival of the Spanish lynx and in October 1973 the Government passed a degree giving total protection to six mammal species and one sub-species which included the Spanish lynx.

Hunting restrictions should be provided by law in all countries on the basis of good management of the lynx population. Bounty systems and the use of poisoned bait and traps should be abolished. As far as the Spanish lynx is concerned, the enforcement of protective laws is imperative for its immediate survival.

Further reintroduction in regions where the species formerly occurred should be considered, for the three pairs of lynx released in Slovenia, Yugoslavia, in March produced four cubs during the 1974 season. By the end of 1975 there were five locations with permanent lynx populations within an area of 600 square kilometres in the Kočevje forest and Inner Carniola; and although one male is known to have died, in 1976 the lynx population in this area was estimated at 15–17. Similarly, in 1973, tracks of at least two lynx cubs were seen in Switzerland where two pairs of adult lynx were released in 1970. In 1973, some three dozen lynx were bred in captivity, thus should the necessity arise, an intensive captive conservation breeding programme could be successfully undertaken for any of the species or races concerned.

Undoubtedly, the most positive step taken so far to protect lynxes was the purchase of approximately half of the Coto Doñana in southern Spain by the World Wildlife Fund from the Spanish Government in June 1965. This large nature reserve of 350 km, the Doñana National Park, is inhabited by a minimum of 10–15 pairs of the endangered Spanish lynx. Ecological studies of the animal are at present being undertaken to bring about a fuller understanding of the long-term requirements of Europe's most endangered carnivore.

Burton, M. (1962): *Systematic Dictionary of Mammals of the World*, pp. 185–6. **Corbet**, G. B. (1966): *Terrestrial Mammals of Western Europe*, p. 157. **Denis**, A. (1964): *Cats of the World*, pp. 94–8. **Duplaix-Hall**, N. (1975a): 'Species of wild animals bred in captivity during 1973'. **Eaton**, R. L. (1973): 'The world's cats'. **Fisher**, J., **Simon**, N. and **Vincent**, J. (1972): *The Red Data Book: Wildlife in Danger*, pp. 79–80. **Graf**, J. (1968): *Animal Life of Europe*, p. 24. **Gray**, A. P. (1972): *Mammalian Hybrids*, p. 36. **Guggisberg**, C. A. W. (1975): *Wild Cats of the World*, pp. 49–63. **Hohn**, O. E. (1973): 'Lynxes'. **Lydekker**, R. (1915): *Wildlife of* *the World, Vol. I*, pp. 392–3. **Oryx** (1970–3): *Vols X–XII*. **Simon, N.** (1966): *Red Data Book: Mammalia, Vol. I*. **Smit, C. J.** and **Wijngaarden, A. van** (1976): 'Threatened mammals'. **van den Brink, F. H.** (1973): *A Field Guide to the Mammals of Britain and Europe*, pp. 142–3. **W.W.F.** (1973–4): *World Wildlife Yearbook*, pp. 121–2; (1976): *Press Releases*, No. 20/1976.

Atlantic Walrus

Odobenus r. rosmarus

Status: In spite of protective legislation, hunting pressure has increased and led to wasteful killing. Some herds, at one time large, have been reduced almost to extinction

Description   The name walrus is from the Scandinavian *valross*, meaning whale-horse. One of the earliest accounts of the species, cited by Maxwell (1967), is given by Ohthere, a Norwegian sailor, who reported to King Alfred the Great in about the year 890 that he had 'made a voyage beyond Norway for the more commodite of fishing horse-whales which have in their teeth bones of great price and excellence'. Ohthere brought some of the 'horse-whale' teeth (walrus tusks) to show the king. Thus as long ago as the ninth century the value of the ivory tusks of the walrus was appreciated; but it was not till many centuries later that the animals were hunted on a commercial basis. Nowadays, in the western world, the walrus is perhaps best known as a figure of fun in cartoon and literature, with its long tusks, Edwardian-like whiskers and enormously fat body.

Two sub-species of the walrus are recognised: *Odobenus rosmarus rosmarus*, the Atlantic walrus; and *Odobenus rosmarus divergens*, the Pacific walrus. The terms 'Atlantic' and 'Pacific' are rather misleading, as both forms are now confined to regions within the Arctic circle. When the skulls of the two are compared, that of the Atlantic animal has shorter tusks, a narrower facial region and wider occipital region than that of the Pacific animal. The walrus species not only constitutes a distinct genus of the Pinnipeds, but is the sole representative of a special family. In many respects the walrus is clearly allied to the eared seals, this being especially shown in the structure of the hind limbs. The hind feet are capable of being turned forwards beneath the body, and are employed in locomotion on land; the three middle toes are much smaller than the outer pair; and the toes of the hind feet terminate in large lobes projecting far beyond the extremities of the bones. These factors, together with the fact that the forelimbs are nearly as large as the hindlimbs, are shared by the walrus and the eared seals.

The walrus is a pinniped, with a thick, swollen body-form, a rounded head and muzzle, a short neck, a tough, wrinkled skin which is almost devoid of hairs except at the muzzle, and large tusks. The eyes are small and the external ears are represented only by a low wrinkle of skin. In 1962, it was observed that whereas the nostrils of the Atlantic sub-species are visible when viewed from the front, one is unable to see the nostrils of the Pacific form when viewed likewise. The fore flippers are long and oar-like and are about one-quarter of the length of the body. All the flippers are thick and cartilaginous, being thickset on the forward (leading) edge. The palms and soles of the flippers are bare, rough and warty for traction on the ice; when walking or running the animal has a somewhat upright carriage. The tail is very small.

Compared to the size of the body, the head of the walrus is rather small. The large array of whiskers consists of some 400 stiff bristles, the roots of which are richly supplied with blood vessels and nerves; these bristles are reported to be sensory in function. The rough wrinkled skin has the appearance of being several sizes too large. King (1964) remarks that the thickness of the skin increases with age, reaching 3.05 cm in an adult, and on the neck of the male as much as 6.35 cm. Under the skin the thickness of the blubber averages 5.08—7 cm in the adult, and this fat may weigh over 409 kg. There is a relatively scanty coat, but in old animals the skin may be nearly naked. There is some evidence that moulting takes place in June and July.

The Atlantic form of walrus has on average smaller tusks than its Pacific counterpart. These long conspicuous tusks are present in both sexes, although more slender in the female. They are in fact the walrus's upper canines, and their great size modifies the whole of the anterior end of the skull. These tusks, or permanent upper canines, erupt when the animal is about 4 months old. They have a small cap of enamel, but this is worn away in about 2 years, so that the wearing surface of the tooth is composed of a thin outer ring of cement surrounding a dentine core. The canines have persistently open pulp cavities, and continue to grow throughout the life of the animal. King refers to the fact that 'the granular nature of the core of dentine filling the pulp cavity is characteristic of walrus ivory, and its presence in carvings is used as a method of identifying the ivory'.

The walrus is thought to use its tusks for prising molluscs from the sea-bed, for

150

levering itself on to the ice, and for defence. The cheek teeth are especially adapted for crushing molluscs, although there is no evidence that crushed shells are swallowed, and the suggestion has been made that shellfish may be sucked from their shells.

The neck of an adult walrus usually contains a pair of pharyngeal pouches: these are not known in any other seal. The pouches open into the pharynx (the portion of the alimentary canal at the back of the mouth); they are inflated with air from the lungs, which is then prevented from escaping by muscular constrictors round the openings. When the walrus is resting in the water, the inflated pouches can be used as 'buoys'.

The bulls of this species reach a length of about 375 cm, a height of 100 cm and an approximate weight of 1500 kg. Usually the females are about two-thirds the size of the males. The tusks can attain a length of 75 cm in the male and 60 cm in the female.

Habitat   Walruses frequent islands, rocky shores and ice-floes, living mainly on the littoral ice, and are seldom seen further than 15 km off-shore. When the ice is dispersed by winds and currents in the summer, the walrus herds haul out on to the land at traditional sites, usually prominent headlands and small islands.

Behaviour   Walruses normally live in mixed herds of cows, calves and bulls, numbering up to a hundred individuals or more. They can swim at about 24 km per hour. They are also able to move over land with remarkable speed; for careless hunters, chased by a walrus, have found that their quarry can run as fast as they can.

The species is chiefly diurnal, but must also be active during the 'Arctic night' hours. Maxwell (1967) reports that during the day, when the herd is out of water, a sentinel is posted, and at the approach of possible danger he gives an alarm call and the whole herd pours into the sea. If one of the herd is attacked, the rest will defend it vigorously, and a slow or clumsy hunter may be badly wounded by tusk slashes.

The Atlantic walrus migrates, but not all animals do so every year. In some regions, in the proximity of Greenland, walruses are present all the year round; but in general, as the ice edge retreats in summer the animals follow it north to their northern limits. In October, when the ice advances again, the walruses move south. Less is known about the movements of the European animals, but authorities state that they may stay closer to the coast in winter.

One report refers to the fact that during migration herds often haul out on small coastal beaches, and great masses of pink walruses have been observed in some secluded spots. The older animals are almost devoid of hair, and the pink colour is thought to be due to a rise in body temperature on leaving the water, causing the blood vessels to dilate so as to prevent over-heating.

Unless molested, the walrus is stated to be gentle and inoffensive in disposition, but when attacked it displays great fierceness and vindictiveness, while its huge bulk renders it a formidable antagonist, especially when its aggressors are afloat in a small boat. Not less noteworthy is the affection of the female walrus for its young and likewise the sympathy of all the members of a herd for a wounded comrade.

The walruses' fondness for each other's company is referred to by Lydekker (1894). Baron Nordenskiold states that curiosity is a distinguishing trait of the walrus, and relates how, when on one occasion he rowed right into the midst of a herd: '. . . part followed the boat long distances quite peaceably, now and then emitting a grunting sound; others swam quite close, and raised themselves high out of the water, in order to take a view of the strangers. Others, again, lay so closely packed on pieces of drift-ice as to sink them down to the water's edge, while their comrades swimming about in the sea endeavoured with violence to gain a position on the already overfilled resting-places, although a number of un-occupied pieces of ice floated up and down in the neighbourhood.'

Ice-floes provide walruses with excellent lazing-grounds, and a whole herd may pile on to a floe in such numbers that the late-comers have to climb on to the backs of the others. By that time the floe may become overloaded and tip up, and the whole herd may find itself back in the water.

When on shore, or on an ice-floe, the various members of a herd of walruses are described as huddling together against one another like pigs. The description of the sound of their voice varies, from being like a repeated 'ahwouk', or a low whistling bellow, to a bellow that sounds like the voice of a St Bernard dog or an elephant-like trumpeting sound. These pinnipeds have fair sight but a poor sense of smell and hearing.

Sunbathing is also reported to be a popular pastime for walruses: they will lie on the ice for hours, scratching continually with their flippers, for parasites are numerous in the folds of their skin. Walruses are also known to sleep in a vertical position in the water, with their neck pouches inflated to keep their heads above water whilst their bodies are submerged.

In September 1971, *Oryx* reported that Soviet airmen found walrus movements provided them with valuable information about weather changes and ice conditions. Herds of walrus will appear at unlikely places, such as near large packs of ice, and within a few days the sea becomes ice-free. Conversely their disappearance from an apparently favourable area will foretell a deterioration in conditions there.

Diet While feeding, a walrus usually sinks to the bottom where it can remain submerged for up to 10 minutes at depths down to 80 m, although it does not often stay down for longer than 4—5 minutes. Although the walrus feeds mainly on molluscs, King (1964) reports that it is only very seldom indeed that pieces of shell are found in the stomach. The tusks are used to stir up the sea bed, and the material thus turned up is examined and sorted out by the walrus's lips and whiskers. The feet and fleshy siphons of the molluscs are then torn off, and swallowed whole — chewed up fragments have not been found. Mussels may be taken into the mouth, the soft parts sucked out and swallowed, and the shell rejected. Shells that have probably been treated in this way often occur around walrus breathing-holes.

Maxwell (1967) remarks that a great deal has been discovered about the diet of walruses by examination of stomach contents. Besides molluscs and crustaceans, large quantities of seaweed have been found. Stones have also been observed in the stomach, but their presence has not been satisfactorily explained. It does not seem likely that they were swallowed accidentally, as the shells of the molluscs are so carefully rejected. Maxwell considered it possible that the stones help crush up the food in the stomach. A peculiarity of the stomach is that it holds no more than a gallon of food, a strikingly small capacity for such a large animal.

Although walruses mostly feed on molluscs, echinoderms and crustaceans, they occasionally do take fish and seals, crushing the seals between their front legs and eating them on the shore or on an ice-floe. In captivity, walruses have thrived reasonably well on a formula of minced clams, heavy cream containing 30% butter fat and a vitamin supplement.

Breeding The bulls are reported to have an annual breeding cycle, but in any one year only about half the adult females produce cubs, and older animals breed even less frequently. Mating probably takes place on land or on the ice-floes where the herds haul out, usually during their migration northwards in May and June, shortly after the birth of the pups. The walrus appears to be polygamous, but there is no evidence of harem formation. After a gestation period of 11—12 months, normally a single calf is born although twin foetuses have been recorded.

The pups are born in April and early May, usually weighing about 60 kg; their skin is dark grey and covered with a coat of silvery grey hair. The young grow very quickly and weigh 225 kg by the end of the first year. They are nursed for 18—24 months, sometimes even longer, and fed with milk until their tusks have developed sufficiently to enable them to dig for their own food. After being weaned the young animals may stay with their mothers for another year or two. This is partly due to their natural gregariousness but probably also to the fact that they are still unable to acquire enough food by their own activities.

The cow's milk is very rich, containing 35% fat and 12% protein. There are four mammary glands, situated low down on the underside of the cow. Before the calf is weaned it travels with its mother, clinging to her neck by its front flippers, and stays in this position even when the cow is swimming or diving.

Cows attain sexual maturity at 4 or 5 years of age and the bulls are sexually mature at 6 years. There is, so far, no exact information about the longevity of the walrus, but it is believed that they can live for at least 16 and probably up to 30 years. Some authorities consider that in their natural habitat walruses can probably attain a longevity of 40 years.

Although the Carl Hagenbeck Tierpark, Hamburg-Stellingen, has successfully raised a number of young walruses obtained by Norwegian seal-hunters in the Arctic, there appear to be no records of this species breeding in captivity.

Population From at least the ninth century onwards, and particularly vigorously from about the seventeenth century, hunting of walrus drastically reduced the numbers of animals. During the years 1868—73 it was reported that whalers alone took at least 60,000 walruses per year. The Gulf of St Lawrence, Spitsbergen and the Pribilof Islands are places where walruses were abundant until exploited by hunters, and just before 1890 up to 5443 kg of walrus ivory a year was being taken from the Pribilof Islands.

In the 1930s, the total number of walruses on the islands in the Laptev Sea eastward to the New Siberian Islands was estimated at 6000—10,000. Present numbers are unknown, but the population is described as no longer numerous. The total number in the Kara Sea in the 1930s did not exceed 3000—4000. In 1954, the number of walruses on Southampton Island, Canada, was estimated at 3000 specimens. The population in the northern part of the Foxe Basin is reported to be probably larger. In the Thule region it was recently reported that 100—130 specimens were shot each year.

In 1964, it was reported that Alaskan Eskimos kill about 1300 animals a year; probably about 4000—6000 a year are taken by the Siberian Eskimos and about 500 a year by Eskimos in Greenland. Fisher *et al.* (1972) record that the average annual kill in the eastern Arctic—Atlantic is estimated at about 2666, of which 90% are taken by the Eskimos. The annual increment in a walrus population has been estimated at 12—20%, which suggests that a minimum population of 23,000 is required to sustain the present rate of kill. The population of the Atlantic walrus was estimated in 1966 as about 25,000.

In 1966, world zoos recorded 4 male and 7 female walruses in five different collections. In 1973, they recorded 3 male and 10 female also in five collections.

Distribution   According to King (1964), William Caxton refers to a walrus taken in the river Thames in 1456. Until the fifteenth century walruses lived on the Scottish coasts, and until 1850 on the Hebrides and Orkneys. Between 1815 and 1954 there were 21 recordings of walruses having been seen or killed, all of them off the Scottish coasts, except one shot in the Severn in 1839, and one seen in the Shannon, Ireland, in 1897. Walruses also occurred on the Norwegian coast; more recently there were 10 recordings of the species off these coasts between 1902 and 1954.

In the sixteenth century they were present on Sable Island off the east coast of Nova Scotia and along the shallow waters of the Gulf of St Lawrence. In the nineteenth century the walrus was exterminated from Bear Island, and in the nineteenth and twentieth centuries it was nearly exterminated on Spitsbergen.

The world population of walruses is reported to occur in four geographically isolated groups. There is one population along the coasts of east Greenland, Spitsbergen, Franz Josef Land and in the Barentz and Kara seas. A second population occurs in the Laptev Sea, north of Siberia, and a third in the eastern part of the Canadian arctic and western Greenland. The largest population occurs in the Bering and Chukti seas between Russia and Alaska.

The distribution of the walrus is governed by the extent of sea ice and the availability of the molluscs that form its principal diet. Walruses that inhabit the Laptev Sea and are apparently resident there throughout the winter are considered by some authorities to be a race in between the Atlantic and Pacific forms. According to another authority, the dividing line between the Atlantic and Pacific races runs north from the Lena River Delta through the Nordenskiold Sea.

Conservation   Man and killer whales are probably the walrus's only real enemies, although polar bears occasionally are known to attack young animals. There are few records of disease.

The walrus plays an extremely important role in the Eskimo economy, and almost every part of the animal is used, for food, shelter or other purposes. Inefficient and wasteful methods of hunting have endangered the existence of the walrus in some localities. However, it is chiefly the commercial exploitation of the walrus for hides, tusks and oil that has caused its decline in numbers. More recently, the availability of firearms and outboard motors has increased hunting pressure considerably and led to a lot of wasteful killing. In spite of a closed season in western Greenland, walrus numbers are still decreasing considerably.

As outlined by Smit and Wijngaarden (1976) the Spitsbergen walruses have been totally protected since 1952; in the U.S.S.R. they have been protected since 1957. They may only be hunted for food by the indigenous populations and by members of Arctic expeditions. In Canada, there have been hunting regulations since 1928.

154

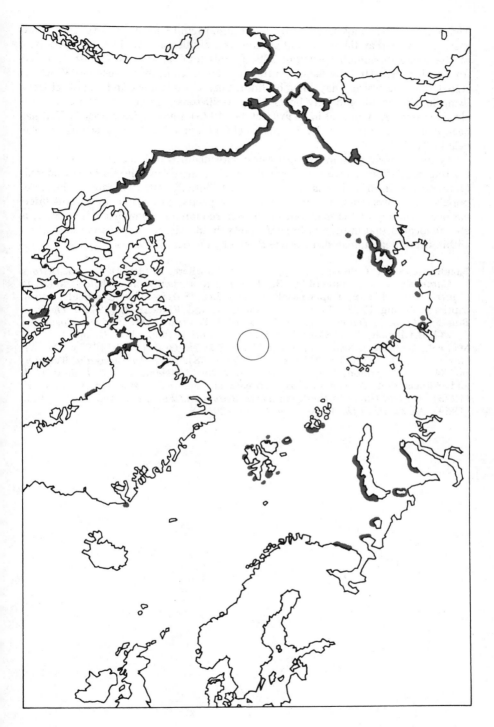

155

The numbers that may be killed by one Eskimo family are limited by law. In the eastern Canadian arctic about 500 specimens are killed a year. In the western part of Greenland this number is about 200. To this total another 30% must be added for hunting losses. In Greenland, hunting regulations came into force in 1957 which stated that the walrus may only be hunted by Greenlanders and Danish citizens living in Greenland, and only boats of up to 40 tons may be used; there is also a closed season. As reported in *Oryx* (October 1973), since 21 December 1972 it has been illegal, under the U.S. Marine Mammal Protection Act, to hunt walrus or polar bear in Alaska.

As the number of walruses in western Greenland is still decreasing despite the hunting regulations already in force there, alternative laws should be considered. More precise information is needed on distribution, potential rate of increase, population movements, and range carrying capacity, as a basis for careful international planning of the management of this economically important species. It is also advocated that important breeding areas should be accorded reserve status, and within these areas human disturbance should be restricted.

Backhouse, K. M. (1969): *Seals*, pp. 12—13. **Bourlière**, F. (1967): *Natural History of Mammals*, p. 69. **Crandall**, L. S. (1964): *The Management of Wild Animals in Captivity*, pp. 423—9. **Duplaix-Hall**, N. (1975*a*): 'Species of wild animals bred in captivity during 1973'. **Fisher**, J., **Simon**, N. and **Vincent**, J. (1972): *The Red Book: Wildlife in Danger*, pp. 89—91. **King**, J. E. (1964): *Seals of the World*, pp. 37—42. **Lydekker**, R. (1894): *The Royal Natural History, Vol. II*, pp. 124—31. **Maxwell**, G. (1967): *Seals of the World*, pp. 69—76. **Oryx** (1971, 1973): *Vol. XI*, Nos 2—3 and *Vol. XII*, No. 2. **Scheffer**, V. B. (1958): *Seals, Sea Lions and Walruses*, pp. 84—6, 139. **Simon**, N. (1967): *Red Data Book: Mammalia, Vol. I*. **Smit**, C. J. and **Wijngaarden**, A. van (1976): 'Threatened mammals'. **van den Brink**, F. H. (1973): *A Field Guide to the Mammals of Britain and Europe*, p. 143. **Walker**, E. P. (1964): *Mammals of the World, Vol. II*, pp. 1296—8.

Ringed Seal

Pusa hispida

Status: An abundant and thriving species as a whole, although two of the European sub-species are threatened. In 1958, the Saimaa seal numbered no more than 40 individuals

Description   The ringed seal is the commonest seal of the Arctic. It represents one of the more diminutive members of the seal family, and its genus, *Pusa*, has retained a more delicate skull structure which sets it apart from its nearest relative, the harbour seal, genus *Phoca*.

Of all the pinniped genera, *Pusa* is perhaps the most difficult to fit into a taxonomic arrangement. Scheffer (1958) remarks that it is a plastic group, whose numbers have encircled the Arctic Ocean and have exploited both marine and freshwater habitats. The wide distribution of the ringed seal has led to its being divided into a number of sub-species. According to some authorities, ringed seals from different geographical areas quite consistently show distinctive colouration and cranial characteristics, and experts are able to separate the varieties with a fair degree of certainty. Other authorities consider that the definition of sub-species may not be justified since the differences are geographical, and that, if used, the sub-specific names provide mainly an indication of distribution. However, whatever the taxonomic puzzle may be, the 'splitters' have yet to decide precisely how many sub-species should be recognised, for these vary from 6 to 12 in number. All however are agreed that two European sub-species, the Saimaa seal *Pusa hispida saimensis* and *Pusa hispida botnica*, are threatened.

Ringed seals are slim and rather small. Like all members of the seal family Phocidae, their hindlegs are fin-shaped, cannot be turned forwards and so are always stretched backwards, thus being useless for locomotion on land. The fur is dense; they have claws on both fore feet and hind feet; and they swim chiefly with their hindlegs, being outstanding aquatic mammals.

Their colour is very variable, but is usually a light grey background spotted, particularly on the back, with black. Many of the spots are surrounded by ring-shaped lighter marks, giving the seal its name, but down the centre of the back the dark spots may be so close together as to be confluent. The belly is usually lighter without distinct markings.

There is little difference in size between the sexes, but the males are slightly larger. The nose to tail length is 120–185 cm (average 140 cm); the weight up to 110 kg (average about 90 kg). The Saimaa seal is slightly smaller than the other races, with a maximum weight recorded at 86 kg.

Habitat   The ringed seal is an animal of the Arctic coasts. It is found wherever there is open water in the land-fast ice, even as far as the North Pole, as well as in fjords and bays, but rarely in the open sea or in floating pack-ice. It is reported rarely to stray more than 16 kilometres away from land or ice (at the very most 130 kilometres).

Bourlière (1967) points out that we know very little about how aquatic mammals tolerate the varying physico-chemical characteristics of the water in which they live. He goes on to state that 'we do know that the manatee lives equally well in fresh, brackish and salt water, and that seals in captivity do very well in river water'. Along the coasts of Europe the common seal lives in salt water as well as in brackish water. Two distinct forms of the ringed seal inhabit the freshwater lakes of Ladoga and Saimaa in Finland. So, as previously mentioned, the ringed seal has exploited both marine and freshwater habitats.

Behaviour   This species is very well adapted to a life on the pack-ice. During the winter the adult seals maintain breathing holes in the ice, which they keep open by frequent use. The Eskimo takes advantage of this behaviour: by approaching very carefully, and listening for the sound of a seal breathing at one of these round holes, he can get near enough to shoot, and then quickly harpoon the animal before it is carried away by the current. King (1964) describes how, in spring, when the seals lie out on the ice, the Eskimo can get close to them by crawling along, pushing in front of him a small sledge which carries his gun, and also a white screen which hides him, and which looks to the seal like an iceberg. This is said to be the easiest form of hunting, and gives a great yield. This deception is similar to the way polar bears prey on the seals (see page 93).

Animals of less than one year old spend the winter at the edge of the pack-ice. Adult animals moult in June and July; during this period they fast and lie on the ice. The species lives solitarily or in small herds. They can dive for a period of up to

158

20 minutes to depths of about 100 m. Ringed seals do not migrate, although they may disperse from the breeding and moulting areas within the limits of the fast-ice throughout the year. On the whole they are silent animals although sometimes one will utter a short bleat or grunt.

Diet   The seals feed on a wide variety of small oceanic amphipods (small crustaceans), euphausians and other crustaceans, and also on small fish. King (1964) relates that 72 food species were identified in the stomachs of seals from the eastern Canadian arctic, and here it was noticed that in shallow, in-shore waters the seals were feeding near the bottom, chiefly on polar cod *Boreogadus saida* (average length of 178 mm) and on the small crustacean *Mysis*, while those in the deeper off-shore waters were catching the planktonic amphipod *Themisto libellula*.

Although feeding largely on planktonic organisms, the ringed seal does not have greatly subdivided teeth like the crab-eater seal *Lobodon carcinophagus*, and there is some evidence that it may pick out the larger animals in a shoal of Themisto, whose size range is 19–63 mm, and catch them individually.

Breeding   Field workers have reported that ringed seal pups are born between the middle of March and the middle of April, are 635 mm in length nose-to-tail, and weigh about 4.5 kg. They are always born on land-fast ice, either in a lair under the snow excavated by the mother, or in a natural hollow in the ice. A breathing-hole opens into the cavity from below, so the mother may reach her pup without being seen.

One authority describes how the pregnant cow digs out a den in the snow that covers the ice, making sure that the entrance to the den is near to the water. The den in which the pup is born is low and spindle-shaped and may be over 3 m long; the heat of the animal's body melts the snow which then freezes into ice so that the roof of the den becomes very strong.

At birth the pup has long, creamy white fur which is shed after 2 or 3 weeks, this moult being completed within 5–6 weeks. It is suckled for nearly 2 months, a rather long period of parental care which probably has come correlation with being born on fast, rather than on moving, ice. Scientists have observed that those seals born on ice which is stable until late in the season are larger than those born on the peripheral ice; they have also found that the most suitable areas for pupping are occupied by the older seals.

The adult males are ready to mate from March until mid-May, although the majority of pups are recorded as being born during the first two weeks of April. During the breeding season the bulls literally stink: they have a very strong and very unpleasant odour, which most likely has an important sexual significance — certainly the young sexually immature bulls do not smell in this way. The cows which are not pregnant are the first to be mated; the cows that have been pregnant are mated two weeks after they have given birth, that is while they are still suckling their pups, but it is not until 3½ months after copulation that the embryo implants in the uterus. This phenomenon is known as delayed implantation. It also occurs in roe deer and many of the Mustelidae such as the badger and the stoat.

In animals in which delayed implantation occurs the embryo which forms after fertilisation in the uterine tube does not become implanted in the lining of the uterus immediately on entering that organ. The blastocyst, as the embryo is called at this stage, remains loose and unattached in the cavity of the uterus and its

159

development is halted. It is not until many weeks or months later that activity and growth are resumed and the blastocyst becomes embedded in the lining of the uterus. This delayed implantation gives an apparent gestation period longer than the period necessary for foetal growth. In the seals, the delayed implantation follows a post-partum oestrus. Scientists consider that delayed implantation must have a selective advantage for the species in making a compromise between the most convenient season for the sexes to mate and the most propitious season for the rearing of the young.

The male is not usually sexually mature until it is 7 years old. Females may ovulate for the first time when 6 years old, but may do so too late for mating that year.

In 1929, a ringed seal gave birth to a hybrid, 73 cm long, which was found dead at the Skansen Zoological Gardens, Stockholm. Its father had been a grey seal *Halicoerus grypus*.

Ringed seals may live to a considerable age, and a male at least 43 years old has been taken, but the badly decayed teeth of old seals may hasten their death. Scientists have found that it is possible to estimate the age of a ringed seal by examining its teeth and claws. During March, April and May the deposition of dentine, the hard tissue that forms the main part of teeth, is less dense than in the following two months. This leads to a ringed appearance in the teeth which provides a reasonably accurate indication of age. The claws, too, have bands which give a clue to the age of an individual seal provided it is under 10 years old. Although Hewer (1962) reported the lifespan of the bull grey seal as being much shorter (10—15 years) than that of the cow, there is no evidence that the same is true of ringed seals, in which male and female longevity appear similar. A female ringed seal lived at the Stockholm Zoo for a period of 15 years, a longevity record for this species in captivity.

Population Taken as a whole, the world's ringed seal population shows it to be an abundant and thriving species. Maxwell (1967) estimates that there are certainly not less than 2½ million of them and probably as many as 6 million. Backhouse (1969) reports that a population of around 5 million has been estimated, and thousands are harvested each year.

The following information about individual ringed seals from different geographical areas can be found in Scheffer (1958): in 1933, it was reported that about 50,000 ringed seals *Pusa hispida ochotensis* were killed annually in the Far East. In 1909, 8968 of the now rare ringed *Pusa hispida botnica* were presented for bounty in Finland. In 1883 it was reported that up to 1000 ringed seals *Pusa hispida ladogensis* were killed annually in Lake Ladoga.

Smit and Wijngaarden (1976) state that there is very little data on the status of the ringed seal *Pusa h. hispida* in the Arctic regions of Europe; however, one report in 1962 recorded the trading of 70,000 skins of this sub-species which was considered to represent most of the annual kill. The sub-species *Pusa hispida saimensis* decreased in 1958 to a total population estimated at 40 specimens, but since then it has been totally protected by law, and the population had increased to 200—250 individuals by the end of the 1960s. Complaints by fishermen resulted in the shooting of 16 specimens in 1965/67 in the area with the densest population.

There are a number of references to ringed seals having been kept in various of the world's zoos, although no recent recordings appear to be available.

160

Distribution   Ringed seals occur in Arctic waters from the North Pole to Arctic North America as far south as Newfoundland, along the entire coast of Greenland, Jan Mayen, Spitsbergen, Bear Island, Franz Josef, and the northern and eastern coasts of the U.S.S.R. as far south as Japan. In the winter they penetrate south along the edge of the pack-ice to northern Iceland. Occasional stragglers may move further south, and have been recorded from the Pribilof Islands, Finisterre, Germany, Netherlands, Ireland, the Isle of Man and Norfolk. They also occur in the Gulf of Finland, the Gulf of Bothnia, Lake Ladoga and the Saimaa lake system.

Seals of the sub-species *Pusa hispida botnica* occur in the area of the Gulfs of Bothnia and Finland. In the spring they are reported to breed on the ice along the Swedish and Finnish coasts. In the summer they wander southward, generally to the line from Norrkoping to the Gulf of Riga. According to one report, they no longer occur in the north-eastern part of the Gulf of Finland.

In Finland *Pusa hispida saimensis* occurs in Lake Saimaa and a series of lakes communicating with it. Saimaa lies at an altitude of 76 m and is cut off from the sea. It drains into Lake Ladoga, 70 m below it, by a stream too swift for seals to navigate. This sub-species is a post-glacial relic which has been living isolated in the lake system for 8000 years.

The brackish Lake Ladoga also has an isolated sub-species *Pusa hispida ladogensis*, which in 1952 was reported to be more numerous in the northern part of the lake.

Conservation   The ringed seal's enemies, apart from man, include polar bears, killer whales and Arctic foxes, and young pups are sometimes eaten by walruses. Parasites include the usual gut infestations of roundworms, thornyheaded worms and tapeworms; roundworms have also been found in the lungs and venous sinuses of the liver.

To the Eskimo, all parts of the animal's body are useful. The flesh is eaten, the blubber is used for oil lamps and also eaten. The liver and intestines are eaten either boiled or frozen. Pup skins may be used for underclothes, fur side inside, and skins of adult seals have many uses: clothes, bags, dog harness and tents are some of the commodities made from them. This utilisation of the ringed seal makes it the mainstay of some Eskimos' economy.

Ringed seals are especially threatened in the Gulf of Bothnia and the Gulf of Finland, due to overhunting by the fishermen. The population in the Saimaa lake system was menaced for the same reason, but since protection was given in 1958 it has been increasing slowly.

Apart from the protection already afforded the Saimaa ringed seal, Sweden protects the ringed seals occurring in the Gulf of Bothnia. Wandering specimens of this population occasionally occur in the Baltic Sea and therefore the German Democratic Republic has also protected the species. International protective measures have been taken for the north-west Atlantic, and agreements have been reached between Norway and the U.S.S.R. concerning the seals in the Barentz Sea.

As reported in *Oryx* (April 1975), British, Dutch, Finnish, German and Scandinavian scientists met at a symposium on Baltic seals at Lidingo, Sweden, in June 1974 and urged the governments of the seven Baltic states to protect the three seal species of the area (ringed, common, grey) and the common porpoise. The measures proposed were: the establishment of sanctuaries, especially in the main breeding areas; intensified scientific research; and a strict control of hunting.

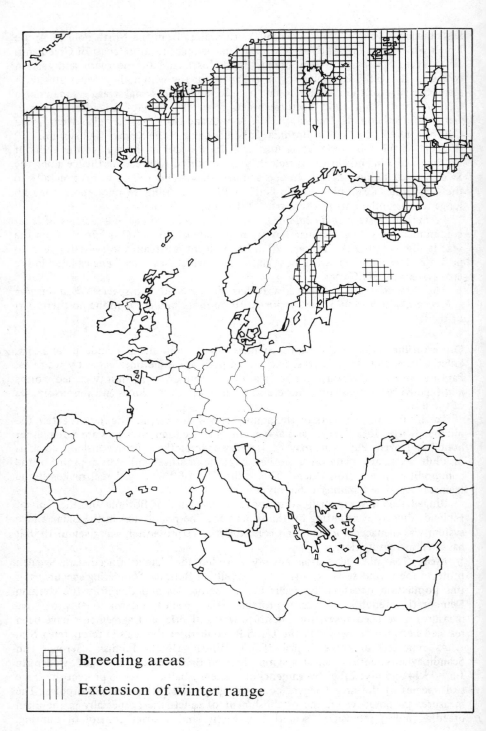

☷ Breeding areas

|||| Extension of winter range

Although both Sweden and the U.S.S.R. now protect the Baltic seals, their efforts are to some extent nullified by the fact that the Finnish Government, pandering to the age-old prejudice of fishermen against seals, until 1976 still offered bounties on seals; however during 1976 the Finnish Government passed a law which discontinues the official bounty of $5 for killing a fox, grey seal or ringed seal.

Protective measures outlined by Smit and Wijngaarden (1976) propose that full protection for the population of ringed seals in the Gulf of Bothnia and the Gulf of Finland is urgently needed. Therefore, hunting by Finnish fishermen should be banned by law. The population of the Saimaa lake system is still vulnerable, especially because parts of the lake system are severely polluted (high residue of mercury have been found in the tissues of some specimens). The pollution of the lake system must be curbed, and a management programme should be developed for the maintenance and regulation of the seal population.

In the World Wildlife Fund's Marine Programme, prepared by I.U.C.N. for W.W.F.'s Marine Campaign 1977/78 *The Seas Must Live*, a global strategy for marine conservation has been outlined. Project 1447 concerns itself with the seals of the Baltic sea, and plans the establishment of a number of reserves for the ringed seal, the grey seal and the harbour seal; population, breeding and pollution studies will also be undertaken to safeguard these threatened species.

Backhouse, K. M. (1969): *Seals*, p. 18. **Bourlière**, F. (1967): *Natural History of Mammals*, p. 261. **Crandall**, L. S. (1964): *The Management of Wild Mammals in Captivity*, p. 432. **Gray**, A. P. (1971): *Mammalian Hybrids*, p. 60. **Hewer**, H. R. (1962): 'Grey seals', in *Animals of Britain*, 7. **I.U.C.N.** (1976): *Monthly Bulletins*, Vol. 7, No. 12. **King**, J. E. (1964): *Seals of the World*, pp. 56–8. **Maxwell**, G. (1967): *Seals of the World*, pp. 121–2. **Oryx** (1975–6): *Vol. XIII*, Nos 1 and 4. **Scheffer**, V. B. (1958): *Seals, Sea Lions and Walruses*, pp. 95–100. **Simon**, N. (1967): *Red Data Book: Mammalia, Vol. 1*. **Smit**, C. J. and **Wijngaarden**, A. van (1976): 'Threatened mammals'. **van den Brink**, F. H. (1973): *A Field Guide to the Mammals of Britain and Europe*, p. 146. **Walker**, E. P. (1964): *Mammals of the World, Vol. II*, p. 1304.

Mediterranean Monk Seal

Monachus monachus

Status: Species on verge of extinction as legal protection has failed to stop its steady decrease in numbers. Population now estimated to be less than 500

Description   The monk seal appears always to have been well known to the inhabitants of the Mediterranean area. Judith King (1956) recalls that Aristotle must have examined one with care, as he gives quite an accurate account in the *Historia Animalium*. The presence of seals gave rise to many stories. The 'half animal fisheaters' on the west coast of Africa were said to have made a pact with the seals not to interfere with each other's fishing. Because of their love for sun and sea the seals were put under the protection of Phoebus Apollo, the sun god, and Poseidon, the sea god. Seals were frequently seen alive in captivity in those days, and their docility and intelligence were noted; Pliny tells how he saw some which answered by growls when their names were called.

The genus *Monachus* consists of three species, all of which are confined to subtropical waters in the Northern Hemisphere, but widely separated from each other: the Mediterranean monk seal, from the Mediterranean and nearby areas, the

West Indian or Caribbean monk seal, *M. tropicalis*, and the Hawaiian or Laysan monk seal, *M. schauinslandi*, from the Hawaiian islands.

Although forming a genus of their own, the monk seals are, nevertheless, closely allied to the four Antarctic seals, with which they share similar skeletal characteristics. As G. Maxwell (1967) remarks, there are also many superficial similarities between the bearded seal of the Arctic and the monk seals: they have four mammae and smooth whiskers, which is unlike other seals, and are fairly sluggish creatures. The monk seals have an unusual skull: the brain case is approximately equal in length and in breadth, and there is a long parallel inter-orbital region. There are just two incisors and five cheek teeth on each side of the upper and lower jaws. Differences among the three monk seal species are slight, and they would be regarded as sub-species if it were not for their immense geographical separation.

The mechanism of swimming in the monk seal is very different from that known in other seals. K. M. Backhouse (1969) remarks that although lateral undulation of the hindlimbs is the main component of locomotion, the forelimbs play their part together with a skulling motion. In this respect the monk seals most clearly resemble sea lions, although the latter use the forelimbs as the prime locomotor units, the hindlimbs usually being trailed close together.

The body is built like all other Phocidae: there are well-developed fore flippers, whereas the hind flippers are small. Nails are present on both the fore and hind flippers; that on the first digit of the fore flipper is about 2.5 cm long, and the others decrease slightly in size towards the fifth digit. The nails on the hind flippers are very small and inconspicuous. The tongue has a notch in its front end. Compared to many pinnipeds the monk seal has a very short alimentary canal, only eight times the body length.

The adult seals are chocolate brown on the back, the brown hairs being tipped with yellow, while the under surface is greyish, sometimes with a centrally placed white patch. Females and immature males are usually lighter in colour than the fully grown male, although there is a certain amount of variation in the colour of the adult seal. The hairs of the adult are very short and bristly and lie close to the body. The whiskers range in colour from light yellow to brown.

The total nose-to-tail length of the monk seal is 278–350 cm, the weight range 300–320 kg.

Habitat   Mediterranean monk seals frequent small beaches on islands and other subtropical coasts of the area with rocks and caves for shelter. In former times they rested on the beaches but the relentless pursuit by fishermen has driven the last remnant populations to retreat into caves, many of which have submarine entrances.

Behaviour   The species used always to live in small herds, but nowadays it is so scarce that it is sometimes found solitarily or in twos and threes. Due to persecution, this once diurnal seal has now adapted to more nocturnal habits, although on the whole it is sluggish and unsuspicious by nature.

The voice has been described as a sharp strong cry from the bottom of the throat; but when it is annoyed, the seal makes a noise like a wounded dog. One report quoted by King (1956) stated that it had a voice 'like that of a hoarse dog and that sometimes it would howl'. The same seal evidently could not tolerate dogs, and would try to drive them away by clapping its teeth. The Mediterranean monk seals kept in captivity have all been noticeably intelligent and docile animals. They become attached to their keeper and will recognise him, follow him about and even to a certain extent obey his orders.

Diet   Little is known of the species' feeding habits in the wild, but the seals in the Black Sea are reported to eat mackerel, anchovy, plaice and flounder, with a particular preference for the last.

The feeding habits, as observed in captivity, are very interesting. King (1956) describes the following occurrences: 'One animal ate about 6 kg of fish daily, and in order to stress the expense of keeping it, inquisitive spectators were told that it ate only the best fish such as eels and trout. It did occasionally receive eels and carp, if paid for by the spectators, but usually it had whiting. It would take the fish either out of the keeper's hands or catch them in its tank, but preferred to eat them in water. It seized the fish by the head, squeezed and shook them a few times, and then swallowed them whole. Often the intestines of the fish were found in the water, and although the keeper thought this was done deliberately, it was suggested that the insides of the fish came out accidentally when it was squeezed.'

The well-known eighteenth-century French naturalist G. L. de Buffon while in Paris saw the same animal that King had described, and said that there it was fed mainly on carp and eels, preferring the latter. The fish were sprinkled with salt, the eels eaten whole, but the carp were crushed with the teeth, allowed to fall and then their bellies were ripped open and the entrails removed. The fish were then seized by the head and swallowed. Further reports also note that the entrails were removed and the fish swallowed head first. King concludes that indeed it seems possible that this method of eating the fish might be the normal one for pinnipeds generally, as it would avoid any injury to the seal by the backwardly projecting fins, scales and spines of the fish.

Two female Mediterranean monk seals were observed to disembowel their fish unless they were very small; they were also unable to pick the fish off the ground, and could eat them only in water. They ate sardines, bonito and octopus – about 12 kg a day. Further reports record that native fishermen along the African coast have seen seals eating fish and lobsters (*Palinurus*), and also that the remains of fish of the genera *Dentex* and *Labrax* had been found in the stomach of a seal captured off Sardinia. The final observation was of a monk seal in the Gulf of Salonika which was seen to be playing with a large fish, tossing it into the air and catching it again.

Breeding   After a gestation period of 11 months, single pups are born on land in alternate years in September and October. The newborn are about 91 cm long and have a black woolly coat which is moulted at weaning time. The pups are weaned at about 6 weeks when they become active outside the breeding caves. Very little exact detail of the Mediterranean monk seal's life history is known, but mating is believed to take place about two months after the birth of the pup. The young stay with the female for 3 years, but do not breed themselves until they are 4 years old.

As detailed observations on reproduction have not been carried out with the Mediterranean species of *Monachus*, it is appropriate to relate some of Kenyon and Rice's findings as related by Backhouse (1969) concerning the closely related Hawaiian monk seal. At birth the pup appears somewhat skinny in spite of weighing some 16–17 kg. It is extremely agile and can swim immediately after birth although usually it does not do so for the first few days. The mother is affectionate and tends to stay with her pup, behaving quite fiercely towards any intruder. The pup also tends to follow the mother around, both on land and in the water; they keep in touch with each other vocally on land. If the cow loses her pup she apparently uses scent to identify it again, having been attracted by its bawling. On finding a pup not her own, her reaction is a simple movement away and not one of threat as so often seen in the grey seal. If a lost or frightened pup finds its mother, she usually calms it by placing her head and neck over it and making deep moaning sounds. But gestures of affection are common at all times during the nursing period, the pup often rubbing and nuzzling the mother's head and neck, and receiving similar treatment from her.

The aggressive behaviour in defence of her pup is very strong: Kenyon and Rice even made use of this to get the female to charge one of them whilst the other nipped in and took the pup for weighing. Having ceased her aggressive acts and finding her pup missing, she then became frantic, dashing about and looking in all directions until it was found again. When a cow and pup were in the sea and the observers on the beach approached the water's edge, the cow would charge to the beach with head held high and then continue some yards up the beach.

At birth the pup is toothless; by 4 weeks all its lower teeth are through, and the remainder arrive by about 6 weeks. For a time after weaning it lives on its fat and its weight drops; at the end of its first year it will still be under its weaning weight. When the moult and weaning period has finished, the pup begins its independent life with a much lighter colouring, being a darkish grey on its back and gradually changing through silver grey to silvery white on its belly.

There is one report of a hybrid between the Mediterranean monk seal and the harp seal. This conclusion was arrived at after an adult female seal was killed in a cave on Corsica in September 1947. It was found to be pregnant and a full-term foetus was removed, but could not be revived. The pup, a female 120 cm long and weighing 17 kg, resembled a pup of *Monachus monachus*, whereas the mother was not considered to be of this species. From a review of the other species of the Phocidae, the conclusion was reached that the female was a hybrid, the result of a cross between a monk seal and, probably, *Phoca greenlandica*. However, the majority of authorities consider it extremely unlikely that such a hybrid could have occurred.

The natural lifespan of the monk seal has not been recorded. Crandall (1964) reports that single specimens of the Mediterranean species were received at the Zoological Gardens of London in 1882, 1894 and 1910, but none survived for more than 4 months. Two West Indian monk seals arrived at the National Zoological Park, Washington, in the summer of 1897, but unfortunately they only survived for 2 months. At about the same time, two animals of this species were received by the New York Aquarium, where they were kept indoors in a large oval pool built in the floor. One lived for 2 years, and the other a little over 5½ years.

Population   Reports cited by King (1956) state that in 1875 the Mediterranean monk seals were very common on the shores of the Balearic Islands, but a further report in 1914 noted their disappearance from these parts. In the late 1940s, various authorities considered that there were still reasonably large colonies of the monk seal along the western coast of Africa down to Cap Blanc; 60 were observed just north of Cap Blanc, and 21 along the coast of Rio de Oro. In 1953, the presence of a herd of about 200 monk seals was observed at Port Etienne. In 1969, the largest existing colony, consisting of up to 200 seals, was reported to be in Rio de Oro.

In Tunisia, where protection is enforced, the largest group of seals had nevertheless decreased from 30 in 1950 to 2 in 1974; and in Algeria, which has the largest population in the area, reports now are usually of seals seen singly, or in twos or threes. *Oryx* magazine reported (October 1975) that in September 1974 a seal in a well-known group of 4 males and 8 females at the Grotte de Novi was shot and the carcase placed in front of the cave in an effort to frighten away the other seals. The colony in southern Spanish Sahara, on the Atlantic coast, is reckoned at 50 in the last census. A small breeding colony of 20—30 in Madeira is reported.

Reliable counts of this species are very difficult, due to its hidden and nocturnal way of life. In former times it must have been very abundant. King (1964) remarked that there were no accurate estimates of the population of this seal though a maximum of 5000 had been suggested. Although Maxwell (1967) has also recorded the population of *Monachus monachus* to be 'less than 5000', A. van Wijngaarden was cited by Simon (1966) in stating as early as 1964 that the entire monk seal population probably did not exceed 500 animals. Twelve years later, in 1976, since less than 50 colonies are known, and the majority of the herds have well under 10 members, even a figure of 500 specimens appears to be an over-estimation.

Distribution   Mediterranean monk seals once lived along the Anatolian coast of the Black Sea (42°N), in the Adriatic Sea (45°N) and the whole Mediterranean, and in the Atlantic Ocean around Madeira, the Canary Islands and the north-west coast of Africa as far as Cap Blanc.

The present distribution is put by Smit and Wijngaarden as follows: Rio de Oro — in two caves north of la Guera, on the Atlantic Coast near Cap Blanc; Morocco — a small colony may exist on the Atlantic coast, a reasonable number of animals live in the caves at Willa Sanjurjo, and monk seals probably also live on the Iles Chaforinas; Algeria — some monk seal colonies are still found, although their exact locations are not recorded; Tunis — a colony is mentioned for the island of la Galite, as well as Cousteau and Dumas; Libya — two colonies were recently discovered near Tolmeitha and Zuetina. On the southern part of the coast of Lebanon a very small colony may still exist. In Turkey, monk seals are reported to occur in a number of places on the southern, western and northern coast of Anatolia. Seven or eight small colonies still seem to be in existence in Cyprus. Two small colonies are still present at Cape Caliakra and Cape Mastence in Bulgaria. For the Greek coasts, only incidental sightings are reported; the seals are still present around Rhodes. In former years monk seals were often seen along the whole Adriatic coast of Yugoslavia; however, it is not known what their present status is there, although in June 1975 there were five or six surviving monk seals reported on the islands of Vis where they have been protected totally.

In Italy, there is reported to be a small but well-protected colony on one of the small islands to the west of Sicily, the exact place being wisely omitted. There are still monk seals on Montecristo, and they apparently are also to be found on Sardinia. The seals are still seen in caves on the coast of Corsica, but whether they are breeding on the island is unknown. In the south-western part of Spain monk seals are still sometimes observed, but breeding colonies no longer exist there. A small colony in Madeira has recently been reported by *Oryx* magazine (October

1975). The largest concentrations occur in Greece (150), Algeria (100), Turkey (50—60) and on the Atlantic Sahara coast (50—100).

Conservation   Nearly all the currently existing monk seal colonies have adopted the practice of living in caves, often with submarine entrances, in order to avoid man. Their population has been reduced to a low level by constant persecution, either for skin, oil and meat or because of their reputed damage to fisheries. Also, a modern factor contributing to the decline is believed to be the disturbance in and around the remaining colonies by skin-diving enthusiasts and tourists.

The animals are, as far as is known, protected in Israel, France, Italy, Yugoslavia, Greece, Bulgaria and Rio de Oro. But on remote coastal stretches it is very difficult to prevent illegal killing.

The Survival Service Commission's Seal Specialist's meeting of the International Union of Conservation and Natural Resources concluded in 1972 that monk seals should be given priority in seal restoration programmes. It urged continued protection, closer surveillance and more detailed study of populations. As a direct result of this meeting, Dr Karl W. Kenyon undertook a most thorough aerial survey, flying over all the Caribbean monk seals' former known habitats, and all likely similar habitats, but reached the conclusion that this species of monk seal had become extinct and probably had been since the last reliable record of it in 1952.

Surveys and studies of the Mediterranean monk seal populations were further developed by the I.U.C.N. in 1974. Through the initiative of Dr D. E. Sergeant, acting chairman of the Seal Specialists' Group, a meeting was arranged in London in October 1974. From the data exchanged it seemed clear that the total population is unlikely to exceed 500 individuals and is declining rapidly. It was recognised that expanding fishing and tourist activities coupled with increasing pollution threats presented difficult conservation problems which were unlikely to be solved with the urgency demanded by the critical plight of the monk seal, and it was agreed that parallel biological and physiological studies be carried out to develop a basis of knowledge for a captive breeding programme — should this eventually prove necessary for the survival of the species.

Recently, it has become all too evident that all forms of legal protection have failed to stop the monk seal's steady decrease in numbers. Its slow reproductive rate does nothing either to assist the rehabilitation of the species. The establishment of a sufficient number of well-guarded nature reserves is clearly essential for safeguarding the remnant population of the Mediterranean monk seal. Unless firm measures are taken to halt the decline, the species can scarcely be expected to survive many more decades. Since the species is on the verge of extinction, a co-ordinated effort of all conservationists is urgently needed if the Mediterranean monk seal is not to go the same way as its Caribbean cousin.

In the World Wildlife Fund's Marine Programme, prepared by I.U.C.N. for W.W.F.'s Marine Campaign 1977/78, *The Seas Must Live*, it was stressed that a major effort would be launched to establish reserves in those parts of the Mediterranean where the monk seal is strongest and/or where the conservation climate is most favourable, and in the Atlantic where pollution problems are not so acute.

Backhouse, K. M. (1969): *Seals, The World of Animals*, pp. 71—8. **Crandall**, L. S. (1964): *The Management of Wild Mammals in Captivity*, pp. 434—5. **Duplaix-**

Hall, N. (1975*a*): 'Species of wild animals bred in captivity during 1973'. **Fisher, J.,** **Simon,** N. and **Vincent,** J. (1969): *The Red Book: Wildlife in Danger,* pp. 92–4. **I.U.C.N.** (1973, 1976): *Monthly Bulletins, Vol. 4,* No. 2 and *Vol. 7,* No. 12; (1975): *Yearbook 1974,* pp. 28–9. **King,** J. E. (1956): 'The monk seals'. **King,** J. E. (1964): *Seals of the World,* pp. 73–7. **Maxwell,** G. (1967): *Seals of the World,* pp. 140–3. **Oryx** (1973–6): *Vol. XII,* Nos 1 and 3, *Vol. XIII,* Nos 2, 3 and 4. **Scheffer,** V. B. (1958): *Seals, Sea Lions and Walruses,* pp. 112–15. **Simon,** N. (1966): *Red Data Book: Mammalia, Vol. I.* **Smit,** C. J. and **Wijngaarden,** A. van (1976): 'Threatened mammals'. **W.W.F.** Press Release, No. 35/1972.

Red Deer

Cervus elaphus

Status: Three of the 12 sub-species of red deer are threatened with extinction due to overhunting, poaching, deforestation and competition from introduced and domestic species.

Description   Red deer have been known to man for thousands of years. A cave painting of this species by a prehistoric artist from Alpera, eastern Spain, is believed to be between 9000 and 6000 years old.

Deer are ruminant mammals closely related to domestic horned cattle, sheep and goats. All deer are included in one family, Cervidae, which belongs to the order Artiodactyla. This family is very extensive, including no fewer than 17 genera, containing 40 different species and over 190 sub-species. Nearly all members of the Cervidae carry bony antlers (the males only except in the reindeer) that are shed and renewed annually throughout life, in contrast to members of the antelope family Bovidae, which possess horns (usually on both sexes) that are unbranched, supported on bony cores, hollow and permanent.

Twelve sub-species of the red deer are recognised, and 8 of these are distributed throughout Europe and the Middle East. Members of the British sub-species *Cervus elaphus scoticus* are considered to be direct lineal descendants of the stags and hinds which crossed the dry floor of the North Sea from Europe at the time when the ice sheets were withdrawing from Britain some 400,000 years ago and great forests were becoming established.

The red deer is a rather large member of the deer family; like all its relatives, it has a body built for rapid movement. The neck is long, the tail short; the limbs are slender, and the ears are long and pointed. The hair of the back is long and coarse, but not to such a degree as the hair of the neck, which in Highland stags is especially long, giving them a noble appearance.

The general colour of the European red deer is a rich reddish brown in summer, which becomes a greyish brown in winter. Animals which seldom, if ever, have access to woodland tend to have lighter-coloured coats, owing to weathering and general fading from sunlight. The 'caudal disc' or rump patch is yellowish brown, and in some animals there is a dark stripe along the back. The face, throat and underparts are a dull grey, while the iris of the eye is straw-coloured in light-coloured animals and brown in dark ones.

Young calves are spotted, but the spots are barely visible after the third month; however, traces of them can sometimes be seen near the back stripe on the adult beast. High up on the outside of the lower hindleg (the cannon bone) there is a gland tuft, and at the approach of the rut the stags develop a mane and the neck swells. Colour abnormalities are said to include white, cream and albino animals; there is also reported to be a white-faced (bald-faced) strain which usually has some white above the knees too. The colour differs slightly from one sub-species to another.

The male's antlers are shed in the spring; the new ones are in velvet in July and are cleaned at the beginning of August. In natural wild populations, the size and shape of the antlers show geographical variation, and so do the body measurements and weight: the biggest and most complicated antlers are found on large beasts in central Europe and the smaller and simpler types at the fringe of the range.

Antlers are described by F. J. T. Page as 'astonishing structures'. They are made of bone and develop in a period of 4 months from outgrowths on the top of the skull called 'pedicles'; from these the previous antlers have been shed. The skin which covers the growing antlers, the velvet, is very sensitive and richly supplied with blood vessels. For about a third of the year, the stag is thus without any means of defence other than its speed in running. The bony core laid down beneath the velvet produces a ring of bones, the coronet, at its base, and this gradually constricts the blood supply. The velvet dies, and the stag rubs it off wherever it can. At this time the antlers look tattered, but later they are burnished until the bone becomes brown or black, with only the tips of the tines a white colour. Antler growth is closely connected with the cycle of reproductive activity.

The finest specimens of the red deer, as regards weight and quality of antler, occur in the east of its range — stags weighing 272—299 kg have been killed in

Poland, Hungary, Yugoslavia and Rumania. Antlers from deer of these countries frequently carry 20 or more points, which weigh on frontal bone over 10 kg and extend to 123 cm in length. Deer specimens found in central Europe reach a body length of 250 cm and a shoulder height of 150 cm. K. Whitehead remarks that if one compares these weights and measurements with those of a good Scottish stag with a body weight of 95 kg, an antler length of 89 cm, an antler weight of 1.8 kg and a shoulder height of 105–140 cm, one is able to appreciate what fine specimens these European stags are. The Corsican red deer *Cervus elaphus corsicanus* is a small race; an average stag will weigh only about 76 kg, and have a shoulder height of 80 cm. In general the hinds of the red deer are much smaller than the stags.

Habitat Red deer are primarily a species of deciduous woodland, including the thicker, montane woodland of the Mediterranean zone and the Asiatic mountain ranges. In Britain, one is inclined to associate red deer with the north and with open mountain and moorland country, for in the Highlands they move seasonally between open moors above the tree line during the summer months and forests and glens on lower ground during the winter.

Excessive numbers of wild herbivores such as deer – often the result of the extinction by man of their natural predators followed by inadequate human control – may have an adverse effect on their habitat by inhibiting partly or completely the successful regeneration of woody species. This is well illustrated by Golley and Buechner (1968) who record that red deer, domestic sheep and repeated moor-burning have between them obliterated the majority of tree regeneration from large areas of the Scottish Highlands. Consequently red deer there are found on open hills, seeking food and shelter in storm-swept glens, and in this respect living under conditions quite different from those natural to the species in other lands. In the Mediterranean area and northern Africa red deer have adapted to the *maquis*, and in mountainous areas to the mountain thickets.

Behaviour This species has a highly developed social life, although the size of the herd varies greatly, depending especially on habitat. G. B. Corbet records that outside the rutting season the hinds and immature stags form the larger herds, which may number about 20 in woodland, but in open country, e.g. in the Scottish Highlands, may exceed 100. Such herds are fairly compact although they may break up into smaller units in summer when, in mountainous country, they usually migrate to higher ground. A distinct social hierarchy can be recognised in these herds. The mature stags form independent herds which are much less stable than those of the hinds and youngsters.

During the winter, the older stags keep very much to themselves while the hinds and younger animals form mixed herds, the female members of which will probably remain together for the rest of their lives, being visited by the stags during the period of the rut (see **Breeding**).

Red deer are not essentially nocturnal when free from interference, but they are most likely to be seen on the move to feeding grounds and watering places in the early morning or during their greatest activity period at dusk. Both the stags and the hinds spend a considerable part of the day lying up on the higher ground or in the deep shade of bracken in the forest. Once settled, they move about very little and are difficult to find, although the stags are sometimes detectable when their antlers show clear against the skyline. Regular migration, sometimes over great distances, is characteristic of these animals. The gait most frequently adopted is a lazy stride or a steady trot which breaks into a gallop when rapid flight is needed.

F. Fraser Darling, in his pioneering study into the behaviour of a herd of red deer, draws attention to the fact that the voice in some animals is a social asset, for however restricted its range may sound to our ears, it plays an important part in animal sociality. His study records that the voice of the red deer has marked sexual differences, not only in type and volume, but in the times and circumstances in which the voice is used. The hind is able to make a sharp staccato bark at intervals of 5–15 seconds. This sound is made only when there is a source of disturbance to the herd, and it is usually made by the leader or by the hind who has discovered the trouble. Immediately, the whole herd is alert, but not necessarily frightened.

The stag usually gives tongue only during the rutting season and for a short period immediately afterward. The sound is a roar, often repeated. He stands squarely on his four legs, extends his neck and head, and the sound rolls forth from a wide-open mouth shaped like an 'O'. The roar is impressive, and doubtless that is what it is intended to be. Fraser Darling describes it as the embodiment of lust and its derivative emotions of challenge, anger and jealousy. By November, the sound has degenerated to a low moan, infrequently given. For the rest of the year the stag is usually silent, though it will bark, like a hind, when frightened.

Being a social species, red deer display remarkable herd organisation in order to detect approaching danger. As Fraser Darling reports: 'In the Scottish Highlands, when a herd of red deer is resting, one or more individuals keep watch in every direction. If, on the other hand, one deer is reposing by itself, it lies with its back toward the wind, keeping watch by sight over the zone in front and by scent over that to the rear.'

Diet   Red deer are both browsers and grazers. They feed on grasses, heather, berries, fungi, lichens, the leaves of most deciduous trees and even bark. When it is available, they eat seaweed. On farmland, they do damage to root crops and vegetables; in forests, young trees may be barked. During the rut, stags are known to consume only very little food.

Breeding   In western Europe the rut takes place between the middle of September and the end of October, which results in the calves being born from late May to early July, after a gestation period of 8 months. In Scotland it has been recorded that 90% of the year's calves are born in a 3-week period in May/June.

The winter grazing areas of the hinds are the traditional rutting grounds where the deer gather in late September. The stags round up as many hinds as they can search out, and defend them from other stags. Fights between rival stags often break out, the stag greeting all challenges with a lion-like roar. Fights have sometimes ended fatally for one of the contestants; and on rarer occasions the antlers have become locked together, resulting in the death of both participants from starvation.

Richard Lydekker (1898) relates: 'owing to the large numbers of red deer gathered on the bare hills, the pairing-season in the Highlands presents a combination of scene and sound without parallel in continental forests. The hills re-echo with the roaring of rival stags, which roam to and fro, restless and defiant, now rolling in the peat-pools, now rounding up their hinds, and now fighting desperate battles. With individual deer the spur of sexual excitement will sometimes totally dispel the fear of man. Contrary to the general opinion, mastership in the herd goes to the weightiest and most vigorous stag without respect to the calibre of his antlers, for so-called "bald" stags are not infrequently masters of large herds. Stags lose condition rapidly during the pairing-season, at the close of which they are usually completely exhausted.'

G. B. Corbet states that the most powerful stags may succeed in monopolising the herd at first but, as they weaken, so they are likely to be supplanted by, or to lose part of the herd to, younger males. The stag retires to his own territories after the rut. There is usually only one fawn at birth, although twins appear occasionally. The spotted fawns lie motionless while the mother is feeding. Weaning begins after about the first month, and fawns are suckled for 8–10 months, and remain with the hind at least until the second autumn. Females are said to remain permanently with their mother's herd and reach sexual maturity in their third year; males leave the herd in their second or third year, but do not normally breed until their fourth year.

The breeding habits and gestation period of the red deer are similar to those of the sika deer, *Cervus nippon*, which has been introduced into parts of the former's range. Interbreeding between the two species occasionally occurs. Hybrids of the red deer with the wapiti *Cervus canadensis* and the Père David's deer *Elaphurus davidianus* have also been recorded in captivity.

The red deer has an average lifespan of 15 years. A stag at 20 years is very old, heavy in belly and neck, broad of shoulder and rump, with shaggy mane and head nodding in a sleepy fashion as it walks. A wild hind was actually known to calve when she was well over 20.

Population   Southern (1964) reports that little is really known about red deer populations in woodland. The Forestry Commission suggest that 1 per 120 acres is the limit above which serious damage can occur. Fraser Darling (1937) states that for Highland deer forests 1 per 40 acres is the limit beyond which vegetation will become impoverished.

Population densities vary considerably, depending to a certain degree on the nature of the environment, and current climatological conditions. A population study by V. P. W. Lowe (1966) on the red deer on the island of Rhum, found that the deer's home ranges, within which individuals lived throughout the year, appeared to be surprisingly constant in size regardless of topographic variation, extending to approximately 988 acres for a hind and 1235 acres for a stag. The limits were not fixed, however, but varied with the year, each home range being based on an area of maximum utilisation, which included the more important winter grazings.

In 1972, the total population of red deer in Britain and Ireland was estimated to fall somewhere between 180,000 and 200,000. Due to a succession of mild winters which subsequently helped the red deer population in Scotland, the Red Deer Commission estimated its numbers in 1975 to be more than 200,000.

In 1965, the Corsican population of *Cervus elaphus corsicanus* was reported to consist of 1 large adult stag, a young stag (about 4 years old), 2 hinds and 1 young. In 1972, it was reported that the last animals have possibly been exterminated since 1968. In Sardinia, 3 to 4 populations of this sub-species are reported; 2 of the populations in the southern part of the island, totalling more than 100 individuals combined, were reported in 1972 to be flourishing.

A closely related sub-species *Cervus elaphus barbarus* is reported to have increased in Tunisia to more than 100 individuals, the original stock having migrated from across the Algeria–Tunisia border in 1962. In 1969, the total number in Algeria was put at about 400.

Distribution Smit and Wijngaarden record that at one time the red deer occurred almost everywhere in Europe; on the British Isles, in the southern parts of Scandinavia, throughout the U.S.S.R. with a northern limit formed by the line Leningrad–Moscow–Sverdlovsk, and from Spain to Anatolia, as well as on the Mediterranean islands of Corsica, Sardinia, Crete, Cyprus and many of the Aegean islands.

The world distribution of the 12 recognised sub-species of red deer covers almost the whole of Europe except for the northern parts of Scandinavia and the U.S.S.R., and they are found on most of the Mediterranean islands, except Sicily; in Algeria and Tunisia; in Anatolia, northern Iran and Afghanistan; in Kashmir, eastern Tibet, and Chinese and Russian Turkestan. Red deer have been successfully introduced into New Zealand, Australia, the United States, Argentine and Morocco.

There is not room in this text to discuss the present distribution of the more or less mixed and introduced populations in central and western Europe; however, following Smit and Wijngaarden for other countries where there are small or threatened populations of known sub-species, the following details are relevant. The sub-species *C. e. atlanticus*, which was formerly widespread in Norway, is now limited to a narrow strip along the west coast, where its population seems to be expanding. There is one report that this sub-species also occurs in the south-eastern part of Norway. In Sweden, the type sub-species *C. e. elaphus* is reported to be found only in Skane. In Denmark, the red deer population is found primarily in Jutland, although it is spreading to other regions. Three original populations have survived in the U.S.S.R., i.e. in the south-western part of Belorussia, in the Carpathians, and in the Caucasus mountains. The sub-species *C. e. corsicanus* occurs on Sardinia. In Tunisia and Algeria the closely related sub-species *C. e. barbarus* is found. In 1973/74 red deer were introduced into Italy's Abruzzo National Park.

Conservation Except where wolves occur, adult red deer have no predators apart from man, but the fawns fall prey to eagles, foxes, jackals, lynxes and wildcats. In the Caucasus no fewer than 60% of the young deer are killed by wolves.

With both sexes, and at all ages, the chief cause of natural death is parasitic disease — lung-worms, intestinal worms and liver-flukes; lung-worms are by far the most destructive and can cause periodically great mortality among fawns. Wet seasons, especially during spring, are associated with high death rates, probably also resulting from parasitic diseases.

Corbet remarks that the history of Britain's native deer has been one of progressive reduction as woodland was destroyed, until by the end of the eighteenth century they had been virtually eliminated from the lowlands, except for some red deer in parks.

In Europe the red deer has been greatly influenced by man. On the one hand, the species has been persecuted severely, whether legally or illegally, and on the

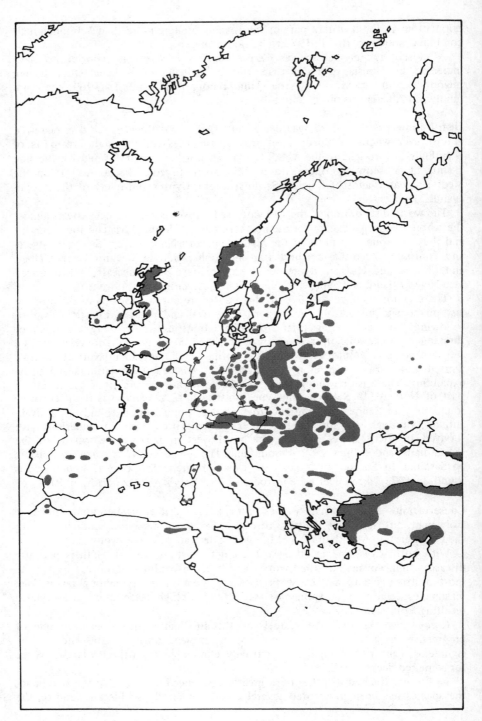

178

other hand it has been guarded, fed, moved, reintroduced, kept behind fences, and bred in zoological parks; it has been transported from one region to another since early times. In large parts of its distribution, the red deer can be considered to be semi-domesticated, and the original form of the indigenous sub-species has been lost. It is, however, considered that 7 out of the 12 sub-species are still pure-bred; 3 of these sub-species *C. e. corsicanus*, *C. e. barbarus* and *C. e. maral*, are threatened with extinction in Sardinia, Algeria, Tunisia and Turkey, due to overhunting and poaching.

In the future, competition with foreign, introduced species, such as the sika, the wapiti and the white-tailed deer *Odocoileus virginianus*, may form an increasing danger elsewhere.

In the United Kingdom, Ireland, Norway, Sweden and Denmark, the populations are protected against the importation of foreign species and sub-species. This is also the case in the Caucasus (U.S.S.R.), Turkey, on Sardinia, and in Algeria and Tunisia. In all of the countries where the species occurs it is protected by hunting laws. None of these populations is in any real danger. However, much more attention should be paid to the small populations in Portugal, Italy, Sardinia, Tunisia, Algeria, Greece and Turkey.

The following protective measures are proposed: continuation of the isolation of the remaining pure-bred populations, enlargement of and better protection for the existing reserves; elimination of competition by domestic sheep and goats; increase of the stock, which will result in a natural spreading of the species towards suitable habitats in the surroundings; restocking, with the original sub-species, of reserves where the red deer has been exterminated; and an effort to reach optimal densities for all populations, after which management as a game species should be applied.

Among old records can be found many indirect glimpses of the esteem in which the chase of the red deer was once held throughout Europe, and especially in Britain, where the deer was considered to be the trophy of kings. The present day emphasis on selective control, and the maintenance of herds of deer as natural components of recently planted forests, is leading foresters, sportsmen and naturalists alike to renew study of these animals. Any person who has had the privilege to witness the red deer in its natural environment will recognise the magnificence of what is in many ways our finest land mammal.

Corbet, G. B. (1966): *Terrestrial Mammals of Western Europe*, pp. 164–6. **Crawford**, M. (1972): 'Conservation by utilisation'. **Darling**, F. Fraser (1937): *A Herd of Red Deer*. **Golley**, F. B. and **Buechner**, H. K. (1968): *A . . . Study of the Productivity of Large Herbivores*. **Gray**, A. P. (1972): *Mammalian Hybrids*, pp. 153–4. **Lowe**, V. P. W. (1966): 'Observations of the dispersal of red deer on Rhum', in *Play, Exploration and Territory in Mammals*. **Lydekker**, R. (1898a): *The Deer of All Lands*, pp. 62–81. **Millais**, J. G. (1906): *Mammals of Great Britain and Ireland, Vol. III*, pp. 91–135. **Oryx** (1975): *Vol. XIII*, No. 2. **Page**, F. J. T. (1962): 'Red deer', in *Animals of Britain, 13*. **Simon**, N. (1968): *Red Data Book: Mammalia, Vol. 1*. **Smit**, C. J. and **Wijngaarden**, A. van (1976): 'Threatened mammals'. **Southern**, H. N. (1964): *Handbook of British Mammals*, pp. 411–17. **Whitehead**, G. K. (1972): *Deer of the World*, pp. 69–71.

Reindeer

Rangifer tarandus

Status: Due to overhunting, introduction of the domesticated reindeer, and climatic change, the areas in which wild reindeer live have become much smaller than in former times. The numbers have also decreased seriously

Description   Reindeer belong to the only genus of the deer family in which both sexes are antlered. Although there is great diversity in the shape of the antlers, and they have been described by E. P. Walker as 'like the boughs of a tree', they are usually long swooping beams with forward-projecting brow tines. The antlers of the female are simpler and generally smaller than those of the male.

The genus *Rangifer* contains only this single species *tarandus* which embraces the reindeer of Eurasia and the caribou of North America; most recent authorities recognise nine sub-species in all. It is a medium-sized member of the deer family, showing a relatively long trunk, long neck and short legs as compared with other species.

Although reindeer present a great amount of racial and individual variation, their colouration is predominantly brownish or greyish with white or light under parts, inner legs and buttocks, the winter coat being somewhat lighter. The muzzle is entirely hairy, the ears and tail are short, and the throat is maned. The coat is remarkable for its density and compactness, and is unspotted at all ages; there is a whitish area in the region of the tail, which includes its sides, but not its upper surface. The main hoofs are short and rounded, the lateral ones very large. The broad, flat and deeply cleft hoofs help the reindeer to walk on soft ground and snow; as they walk a clicking noise is produced by a tendon slipping over a bone in the foot.

Wild or domesticated, the reindeer has had a long association with man, and is almost certainly the first ungulate to have been domesticated. Kenneth Whitehead recalls that it was, in fact, the 'Reindeer Age' that marked the dawn of human history; for in that period, about 25,000—30,000 years ago, the artists of the day, the 'Reindeer Men' of the late Stone Age, painted their animal pictures, which included the reindeer, on the walls of their caves. Whether those men of the late Stone Age ever domesticated any of the animals they drew, and in particular the reindeer, is not known, but Whitehead mentions a reference to domesticated reindeer in a Chinese source dated about AD 499.

In domesticated stock, the colour is said to vary more considerably, especially among those animals with a tame admixture. In these cases the colour is known to range from a dark, greyish brown to a completely white animal. Old bulls have a whitish neck, and by winter should have developed a long white mane. The moult of the adult animal starts in March and continues throughout the summer.

The size of the reindeer varies widely, depending on geographic location. The largest reindeer are found in the eastern part of Siberia; the males here reach a length of 200—220 cm, a height of 110—140 cm, and a weight of 100—220 kg. The reindeer of Spitsbergen are much smaller, with a height at the shoulder of 82—94 cm. However, generally speaking, the reindeer of Eurasia are slightly smaller than the caribou of North America. The average shoulder height of the European reindeer is about 112—119 cm, the females being about 13 cm smaller. A good pair of Scandinavian antlers will measure about 127 cm in length and may bear 28 or more points.

Habitat   Reindeer are the northernmost species of deer, being found throughout the tundra and taiga zones of both the Palaearctic and Nearctic regions.

Smit and Wijngaarden state that the tundra reindeer occur on Novaya Zemlya and in Siberia, living on the treeless lowland plains. In the summer they remain near the coast of the Arctic ocean; in winter they migrate, sometimes over long distances, to the edge of the tundra and forest country. Reindeer are also found living on fjells in Norway where they only migrate over small distances, descending to lower altitudes, especially in the spring. The taiga reindeer inhabit sparsely wooded areas with many streams and lakes; here they live in small herds and do not migrate over long distances.

Edward Topsel's *History of Four-footed Beasts and Serpents* (1658), states that the King of Sweden had 10 reindeer which 'he caused every day to be driven unto the mountains into the cold air, for they are not able to endure the heat'. However, more recent experiences with reindeer have shown that they are capable of tolerating the heat of a Texan summer without any undue distress, provided they are given enough shade and moisture. Reindeer kept at the Dallas Zoo have experienced temperatures between July and September of 32–37°C, and in August these often rise to 43°C.

Behaviour   Reindeer and caribou are highly gregarious, although during certain periods they are sexually segregated. In summer the mature males are solitary, whereas the females and young form herds commonly of 20 or 30 but occasionally more; the mature males join the herds during the period of rut which occurs in September and October. The males shed their antlers soon after the rut and do not start to grow them again until the following April. The females on the other hand retain theirs throughout the winter and only shed them after the young have been born.

Formerly they assembled in herds of hundreds or thousands of individuals for their full migration from treeless tracts to timber areas. They do not necessarily migrate between two distinct areas, but rather wander from place to place. On these migrations, they swim rivers, lakes and streams, and have been recorded to travel at up to 37 miles per hour over a daily distance of about 160 km.

The routes followed by the caribou seem to be much the same from year to year; the herds use trails that are quite visible on the ground and from the air. One field worker observed that when certain streams were crossed, mass drownings could occur which might result in the death of as many as 500 animals. Under some circumstances males may move in compact bands of 100–1000 head; but, as has been established, this segregation of the sexes during migration is not invariable, since copulation takes place during the autumn migration. After the rut, herds tend to unite into larger groups; the males separate from the herds but follow them during their winter movements.

Reindeer are spirited animals, exhibiting both shyness and curiosity; when alarmed, the adults snort, and the fawns bawl. Whereas the Lapps are said to 'herd' their reindeer, herding in this context does not mean driving the animals in a direction in which the deer do not want to go, for normally the reindeer prefer to travel into the wind. The Lapps follow their herds from their summer feeding grounds to their winter grounds and vice versa; their aim is, as far as possible, to maintain the animals in a 'semi-wild' state, the herdsmen ensuring that the deer are on the right pasture at the right times of the year, as well as seeing that the females are undisturbed during calving. Although, as previously stated, the reindeer of northern Europe is the same species as the caribou of North America, experiments in herding caribou in bulk have not been successful. Caribou are said to be difficult to catch but easily handled once caught. Domesticated reindeer are normally very gentle except during rutting when bucks can be dangerous.

Diet   Reindeer moss *Cladonia rangiferina*, a lichen, forms the main diet of the reindeer during the winter months. In its original form before digestion by the deer, it would be indigestible to man; however, after digestion, if the animal is slaughtered, the contents of the stomach are eaten with relish by some of the northern tribes.

182

In the summer the food of the reindeer is composed of herbs, grasses, cotton, grass, leaves and twigs of bushes, bulbs and shoots of shrubs and lichens. When they are near to the coast they are known to consume a considerable quantity of mushrooms during July and August. In the winter, especially before the snow is deep, the lichen *Cetraria* is consumed along with *Cladonia*. In a captive environment, where neither grazing nor browsing are possible, reindeer have thrived well on alfalfa hay, with a herbivorous pellet supplement, some browse items and occasional vegetables.

Bourlière remarks that it is well known that many herbivorous mammals, especially hoofed animals, have a special taste for salt and other mineral substances. Caribou and stag often eat their own horns after shedding, although it has recently been shown that if calcium and other mineral salts are present in the soil then no cast antlers are eaten.

When a herd is feeding, there is a continuous low 'barking' going on among the cows, calves and possibly young bulls.

Breeding As in the red deer, the strongest bulls will hold a herd against intruders, initially, before eventually giving way to other males. During the rutting period the males form a harem, and at this time of the year they utter grunting sounds and roaring. In the autumn caribou bulls are known to fight savagely for a harem of 5—40 cows.

Some elaborate types of prenuptial play have been described in various groups of mammals. The male Baren ground caribou in rut is said to adopt a characteristic stiff-legged gait, lay back his antlers, raise his muzzle, curl up his nose and sniff at the female.

After a gestation period of 190—240 days, the calves, normally one but occasionally twins, are born from about the last days of April until the middle of June. Like the moose or European elk calf, the reindeer calf has no spots, being a uniform brown colour, tending to darken along the back. At birth the calf weighs 4—8 kg; it is able to walk in about 2 hours, nurses for about 2 months and then often joins the rest of the herd in the fall migration. Sometimes it will remain with its mother for longer than the first year, for 2 or even 3 years. The young attain sexual maturity in the autumn of their second year.

In northern Europe reindeer are often kept in a domesticated state. Males older than 4 years are usually castrated, because older and therefore stronger animals might cause too much disturbance in the herd when rutting. Domesticated reindeer are appreciably smaller than wild reindeer.

An attempt to hybridise reindeer with red deer using artificial insemination of two female reindeer with red deer semen was unsuccessful. However, the European reindeer has hybridised in zoological parks with the woodland caribou sub-species on a number of occasions; the result generally is a larger, heavier and more self-reliant animal. Due to the difficulty of herding wild caribou, a great deal of work has been done in trying out reindeer/caribou and caribou/reindeer cross-breeding, so that reindeer farming can be extended and the commercial and economic potential of the deer fully realised.

It has been established that in its native country the reindeer has a high reproduction rate and under the best conditions a domestic herd in which there is no slaughtering could treble itself in 3 years. A reindeer breeder can expect about 90% of the females in the herd of from 2 to 10 years of age to calve every year, whilst older females will calve less frequently. In 1973, world zoos recorded a total of 49 males, 46 females and 10 unsexed calves, born in 36 collections.

The similarity of reindeer milk to that of seals and whales is linked with the growth of the young in regions of cold climates. The chemical composition of the milk is as follows: water, 65%; protein, 11%; fat, 20%; sugar, 2.5%; and ash, 1.5%. During late summer and autumn reindeer milk is produced in very small amounts of about 0.2–0.3 litres per day. The butter fat content of reindeer milk varies according to the month of lactation, and analysis has shown that during the fifth month the fat content averages about 20.8%, with a range of 18.75–22.95%. Small as the quantity is, it has been observed that reindeer milk is about four times as rich in butter fat as ordinary cows' milk. It is used for making into cheese, butter and yoghourt.

The lifespan of the reindeer is about 15 years, although the maximum age reached by domesticated reindeer has been recorded as 25 to 28 years.

Population   Although in Finland the wild reindeer was exterminated in the nineteenth century, a small group of animals re-entered the country from the Karelian S.S.R. in 1950. The first arrivals were mostly males, but females followed. They used to calve in the U.S.S.R. but spend July, August and September in Finland with their calves, mostly in Elimyssalo, in a roadless watershed of virgin spruce forests. In 1967, a doe was found for the first time having calved in Elimyssalo; since then does have calved there in increasing numbers. In January 1972, M. Montonen reported that the permanent wild reindeer population in Finland consisted of perhaps 50–70 animals, but in summer there may be as many as 200. In October 1973, the tracks of about 30 wild reindeer were observed in the Elimyssalo reserve. In eastern Finland altogether a total of 61 females with calves were observed, the highest increase to be recorded so far. In the north, herds of domesticated reindeer occur.

The populations of reindeer in Sweden and Spitsbergen have not been estimated. Norway has reindeer in all mountainous areas; a recent estimate puts the wild reindeer (restricted to south Norway) at around 25,000 animals, while the domesticated reindeer of the north numbered some 150,000. In the U.S.S.R., on the Kola peninsula, reindeer were nearly exterminated in 1930, with only about 100 individuals surviving. Due to conservation measures taken in 1968, their number had increased by 1970 to 20,000. At the end of the nineteenth century there were about 20,000 reindeer on Novaya Zemlya, but as a result of overhunting there are only small populations there at present. The largest number of reindeer in the Old World lives on the Taimir peninsula, where the number in 1970 was estimated to be over 100,000.

In Iceland, between 1771 and 1787, domesticated reindeer from Norway were introduced. The animals went wild, and initially the number increased rapidly. In time, however, the population stabilised at a level of about 3000 individuals, probably due to competition for food from sheep and horses. In January 1972, it was reported that the numbers of wild reindeer in eastern Iceland, having increased in the period 1965–9, dropped by over a third in 1969–70. At the end of 1970 their numbers were estimated at 211 adults and 489 calves. In 1972, it was reported that the numbers had increased in eastern Iceland by approximately 1000 to a total of 3598 individuals.

Between 1952 and 1954, 29 Swedish mountain reindeer were imported to

184

Scotland; more reindeer followed, some of the forest type, and more recently a few were imported from southern Norway. Eighteen years after the first introduction the herd had only increased to about 100, although some had been sold to form other herds.

There have been attempts to introduce reindeer into Germany, Austria and the Orkneys but they were unable to establish themselves and died out soon afterwards.

Outside Europe, the total number of reindeer on Greenland was estimated in 1971 at 25,000–30,000; these have originated from some domesticated reindeer which were introduced in 1952. In 1974, the northern half of Banks Island, Canada, was estimated to have a population of 5300 to 8000. In the same year, on the western Queen Elizabeth Islands there were some 4000 individuals. In the southern hemisphere reindeer occur in South Georgia in the sub-antarctic, where they were introduced in 1908; in 1928 there were 400–500 individuals.

Distribution The former world distribution of the reindeer covered Spitsbergen, Norway, Sweden, Finland, Scotland, the entire European and Asia area of the U.S.S.R. north of 50°N lat., Mongolia, north-eastern China, North America as far south as Idaho, north Dakota, Minnesota, Michigan and Maine, and along the entire southern, western and northern coasts of Greenland.

In Spitsbergen, the Svalbard reindeer was nearly exterminated early in the twentieth century by heavy hunting. In Finland, it was exterminated in the nineteenth century (but see present numbers under **Population**).

The reindeer is generally quoted as having survived in Scotland until the twelfth century. G. B. Corbet remarks that this is based on a single reference in the Orkney Saga to the Earls of Orkney hunting them in Caithness and must be considered very dubious. Subfossil material does not provide any clear evidence of reindeer since the end of the Pleistocene, in early post-glacial times.

Reindeer now occur in Iceland, to the north and north-west of Vatnajokull; in the Cairngorms of Scotland; in the north-western parts of Spitsbergen; in the western and northern parts of Sweden; in Finland in the areas as described (see **Population**); in all mountain areas of Norway; and the entire European and Asian arctic zones of the U.S.S.R. (including Novaya Zemlya, the Yamal peninsula, Severnaya Zemlya and the New Siberian Islands); northern Alaska, Canada (including the Canadian archipelago); the north-western part of the United States, along the north-western coast of Greenland; and in the sub-antarctic on the island of South Georgia.

Conservation Reindeer (or caribou) meat represents the staple diet of many northern peoples of Europe and North America. It is eaten fresh, smoked or dried, and will keep well for long periods. Although there is comparatively little demand for this or any type of venison in Great Britain, it is much appreciated in many countries in Europe and elsewhere; consequently the meat represents a major commercial proposition.

Kenneth Whitehead remarks that there has also always been a demand for reindeer hides in many parts of the world, for they are used to stuff upholstery and also as a component in fine woollen material. Reindeer sinew thread is especially good for sewing canoes or repairing boots because it swells, thus making watertight seams, and it will neither rot nor tear the leather. Skin from the head cape is said to produce a non-skid leather which is useful for the soles of shoes intended for

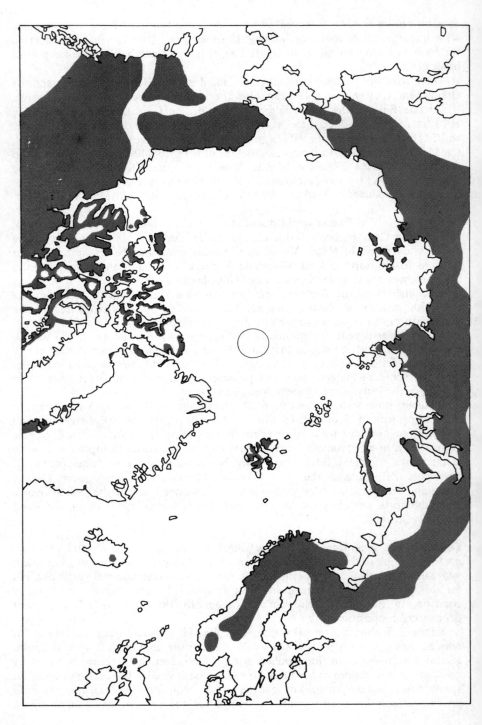

walking on ice. Even the tails have been used in the making of shaving brushes. The antlers have been put to many uses, ranging from household utensils to aphrodisiacs.

The practical value and economic importance of the reindeer have caused it to suffer greatly: its numbers have decreased seriously from overhunting, and the area in which wild reindeer occur has become much smaller than it was in former times. Further reasons for its decline are the introduction of the domesticated reindeer, the general development of the North, and various climatic changes.

Apart from man, the chief predator of the reindeer is the wolf, which in the northern part of its range preys extensively on the species. Reindeer calves are sometimes also attacked by lynx, gluttons, eagles or ravens.

In Spitsbergen reindeer have been protected since 1925, and in Norway since 1902 (a quota system is now practised). In the U.S.S.R. they have been protected since 1957, although local residents are allowed to hunt them. In Canada, the laws differ in the various provinces. In Alaska, the species is only protected in the Mount McKinley National Park. There have been hunting laws in Greenland since 1927.

Smit and Wijngaarden outline the following protective measures: 'Since the number of pure-strain wild reindeer in Europe is very low (they probably occur only in the eastern part of Finland, in the U.S.S.R. and on Spitsbergen), a reserve with undisturbed virgin forests should be created on both sides of the U.S.S.R./ Finland border. Protection for the species in the U.S.S.R. should be continued, perhaps not only by hunting laws but also by the establishment of reserves. Wherever wild reindeer still occur, interbreeding with domesticated animals should be avoided.'

Bourlière, F. (1967): *Natural History of Mammals*. Corbet, G. B. (1966): *Terrestrial Mammals of Western Europe*, pp. 168–70; (1974): 'Distribution of mammals in historic times', in *Changing Flora and Fauna of Britain*, pp. 179–202. Crandall, L. S. (1964): *The Management of Wild Mammals in Captivity*, pp. 602–4. Duplaix-Hall, N. (1975a): 'Species of wild animals bred in captivity during 1973'. Fontaine, P. A. (1962): 'Reindeer ... at the Dallas Zoo'. Gray, A. P. (1972): *Mammalian Hybrids*, pp. 160–1. Lydekker, R. (1898a): *The Deer of All Lands*, pp. 32–49. Montonen, M. (1972): 'Finland's reindeer'. Oryx (1973–5): *Vols XII–XIII*. Smit, C. J. and Wijngaarden, A. van (1976): 'Threatened mammals'. Topsel, E. (1658): *History of Four-footed Beasts and Serpents*. Walker, E. P. (1964): *Mammals of the World, Vol. II*, p. 1402. Whitehead, G. K. (1972): *Deer of the World*.

European Bison or Wisent

Bison bonasus

Status: Extinct in the wild state, but captive or semi-captive specimens are steadily increasing in number

Description   The European bison or wisent is the largest land-animal in Europe, being in the main less clumsily built than its American cousin the North American bison *Bison bison.*

A bison is unmistakable in appearance with its short and broad forehead, heavy head, short neck, high, humped shoulders, and tufted tail. A pelage on the head, neck, shoulders and forelegs is long, shaggy, and brownish black, and there is usually a beard on the chin. The remainder of the body is covered with short, lighter-coloured hairs. In summer, the long hair, together with the short somewhat curly lighter hair on the rest of the body, is shed in large sheets, and is at first replaced by quite short mouse-grey hair which makes the skin look almost bare. Young calves are reddish-brown. The horns borne by both sexes are short, upcurving, and sharp.

The two members of the genus are so closely related that the wisent is best described by pointing out the characteristics in which it differs. The wisent has a shoulder height of 180–195 cm, with adult bulls weighing 770–900 kg, and is 270 cm in length; it stands a little higher and wider in the hips, with much more powerful hindquarters than the American bison. The horns are more slender and have been recorded up to 50 cm long; the forehead is less arched, the hair and the forequarters not so long and close, and the tail longer and less bushy than in the American bison — which, because of its masses of hair, appears to be a much more formidable animal than is really the case.

Habitat   Whereas the American bison is primarily an animal of the open prairies and a grazer, the wisent is essentially a woodland animal and a browser. Its chief haunt is swampy forests.

Behaviour   The wisent is active at night and partly during the day, but it usually rests during the afternoon. It has poor eyesight, but is keen of scent and is a wilder and more wary animal than its American cousin.

Diet   As a browser, the wisent lives principally on leaves, twigs and bark.

Breeding   Wisent live in small herds numbering from 15 to 20 in summer, increasing in winter to 30 or 40, and consisting of cows and young bulls. Mature bulls join the herds in August or the beginning of September, when the majority of the pairing takes place. At this time the bulls utter a loud short roar, meant as a challenge, and they often indulge in fights with their rivals, which can end in the death of one of the combatants. A lifespan of 18—22 years can be expected.

Parturition has been recorded throughout the year at Bialowieza, but most births take place from May to July after a gestation period of about 9 months (260—270 days). Nursing takes place for nearly a year, and the calf normally stays with its mother until it is 3 years old, at which time it usually mates and becomes independent. The International Studbook reported for 1973 the births of 159 (77 male, 82 female) calves. Taking into consideration the deaths that occurred during the same year, this meant a population increase of 82 individuals.

The various breeding programmes have been greatly assisted by the sex structure of the world herd, since it exhibits a constant predominance of females. The average value for the sex ratio for a 20-year period is calculated by Dr J. Raczyński as 0.85 (range 0.74 to 0.91).

Population   Caesar found bison in Germany and Belgium. King Augustus III of Poland shot 42 on a great bison hunt in the primaeval forest of Bialowieza on 27 September 1752. One killed in East Prussia in 1755 had probably strayed from Lithuania. In 1865 the Duke of Hochberg established a reserve as a breeding centre for bison in the Pszczyna forest in south-western Upper Silesia. By 1921 the Pszczyna herd numbered more than 70, but only 3 animals (2 male, 1 female) survived the political upheavals in Upper Silesia in that year.

By the beginning of the twentieth century the only surviving truly wild herd was in the Bialowieza Forest in Poland, on the border of the U.S.S.R. In 1914 there were 737 animals in the Bialowieza herd, but all were slaughtered during World War I. The International Association for the Preservation of Wisent was founded on 25 August 1923; a year later the following report was made on the world population of specimens, all of Bialowieza origin, which some years previously had been distributed among various zoological gardens of Europe: 24 adult males (3 unfit for breeding), 22 adult females (3 unfit for breeding), 2 males and 5 females born in 1922, 7 male calves and 6 female calves born in 1923. The total was thus 33 males and 33 females.

In 1929, the 3 survivors of the Pszczyna herd, together with 2 cows purchased from Sweden and another bull from Germany, were sent to Poland. There they were kept under semi-captive conditions in a part of the Bialowieza Forest in a special fenced enclosure of 507 acres, of which 74 acres were cleared and sown to pasture grasses. These 3 pairs formed the basis of the various herds that have since been re-established in that country.

By 1939 there were 30 animals in Poland, and 35 in Germany. In spite of heavy losses, World War II was not as disastrous for the wisent breeding centres as World War I had been, and 46 animals were recorded as surviving in Poland in 1946. At that time no more than a dozen remained in Germany. It was not until after the war that international co-operation began to produce any visible signs of success. The effect of this co-operation has been rapid growth of herds, especially in recent years, and the formation of an increasingly large number of breeding centres. The turning point in the work of restitution was the initiation in 1952 of a free-living herd of wisent in the Bialowieza primaeval forest. Organisation of free-living herds has been continued successfully in successive years in both Poland and the Soviet Union.

By the end of 1962 the free-living herd numbered 57, almost 60% of which had been born since the release. The International Studbook for the European Bison or Wisent (held by Dr Jan Raczyński, Mammal Research Institute, Bialowieza, Poland), recorded for the year 1973 862 (378 male, 484 female) specimens in captivity, and 652 (305 male, 347 female) specimens in the Bialowieza Forest. A total of 1514 individuals.

Distribution   In prehistoric times the closely allied extinct species *Bison priscus*, which preceded the wisent, ranged over the greater part of Europe, and was by no means rare in Germany, Switzerland, Italy, France and England. Fossil remains apparently indicate the former existence of bison in Russia and perhaps also in Alaska.

In more modern times the European bison or wisent, which was once widely distributed in central Europe, is divided into two sub-species: the Lithuanian (or lowland) bison *Bison bonasus bonasus*, and the Caucasian (or mountain) bison *Bison bonasus caucasius*. The latter race became extinct about 1925, whereas the only free-living herd of the former race is that reintroduced in the Bialowieza Forest, Poland.

Conservation   The depletion and almost total eradication of the wisent could have ended in tragedy. The species' severe decline and then almost miraculous rise in population does however provide an excellent example of how an animal which has become completely extinct in the wild can be saved by the establishment of self-sustaining breeding groups in captivity.

The experiment of liberating animals that for several decades had been living in semi-captivity, and giving them the opportunity to adapt themselves to a wholly wild existence, has had encouraging initial results. The free-ranging herd in the Bialowieza Forest, the home of the last wild bison, is in excellent condition (better than that of the semi-captive herd), and calves born once again in the wild state have developed admirably.

J. Raczyński reports that the free-ranging breeding centres are of importance not only from the point of view of quantity, but also with respect to quality. Free

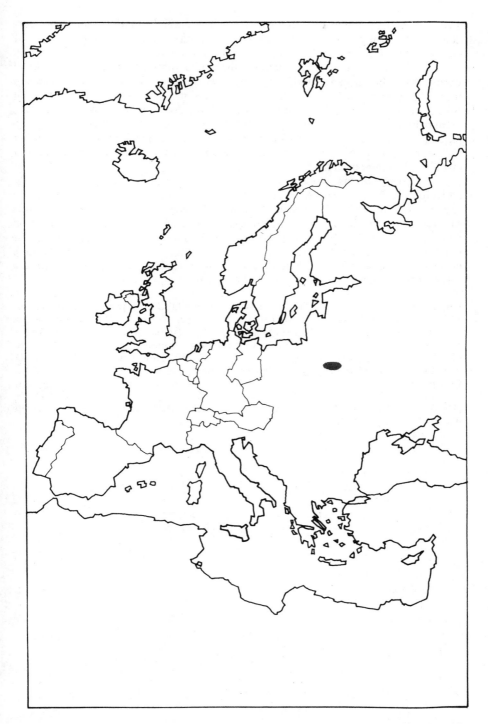

mating of animals under conditions closer to the natural situation, and reconstruction of the form of herd life proper to this species, eliminate a large number of unfavourable phenomena which occur in centres of the enclosed type.

In addition to the pure-bred wisent, there is a substantially larger number of wisent that contain genes both from the now extinct (1930) Caucasian race and from the typical Bialowieza race, as well as some with a small admixture of American bison genes. The wisent will also hybridise with domestic cattle. It is extremely important for propagation programmes to confine their activities to pure-bred stock, and the International Studbook for the species makes every effort to monitor the movement of animals and so prevent hybrids being moved and introduced to pure-bred herds.

The recovery of the wisent from near extinction to a population of 1500—2000 individuals reflects the success of the protection measures already taken. When the situation of this species is considered on a world scale, it is obvious that the results so far obtained by breeding wisent provide genuine possibility for its reproduction above what Raczyński considers to be the threshold number of 2000 animals, in the not too distant future. However, to attain this objective the release of wisent on a larger scale is desirable if suitable localities can be found, and it is essential for the various captive breeding programmes to be continued and expanded.

Duplaix-Hall, N. (1975*a*): 'Species of wild animals bred in captivity during 1973'. **Fisher**, J., **Simon**, N. and **Vincent**, J. (1972): *The Red Book: Wildlife in Danger*, pp. 143—5. **Fitter**, R. (1968): *Vanishing Wild Animals of the World*, p. 52. **Krasinska**, M. (1971): 'Hybridisation of European bison with domestic cattle'. **Lydekker**, R. (1915): *Wildlife of the World, Vol. 1*, pp. 389—90. **Mochi**, U. and **Carter**, T. D. (1974): *Hoofed Mammals of the World*. **Mohr**, E. (1967): 'The studbook of the European bison'. **Raczyński**, J. (1975): 'Progress in breeding European bison in captivity', in *Breeding Endangered Species in Captivity*, pp. 253—62. **Simon**, N. (1966): *Red Data Book: Mammalia, Vol. 1*. **Walker**, E. P. (1964): *Mammals of the World, Vol. II*, p. 1433.

Wild Goat

Capra aegagrus

Status: In many of the regions in which it was once found, the wild goat has been exterminated by hunting and poaching

Description The wild goat is particularly interesting as it is the chief ancestral stock from which the various breeds of domestic goats are derived. This species is characterised by the long scimitar-like horns of the males, which curve backwards, much compressed, with their inner front edges sharp keeled for some distance above the base, and above this bear several bold widely-separated knobs. On the inside the horns are nearly flat, externally they are convex, and behind rounded; the tips are generally convergent, but occasionally divergent; throughout they are faintly striated and in colour are nearly black. The horns of the does are much smaller with an even front edge.

The bucks have a rather long beard. R. Lydekker remarks that in old males the beard occupies the whole width of the chin, while in younger animals it is confined to the middle. In the winter, the hair on the neck and shoulders is rather longer than elsewhere, and in the colder areas of the animals' habitat, a coat of woolly underfur is developed beneath the hair.

The general colour of the upper parts is brownish-grey in winter, tending in summer to rufous brown or reddish-grey, the under parts and the inner sides of the buttocks being light-coloured in both sexes. In the older bucks, however, the general colour is paler. There is a dark brown stripe down the back; the tail, the chin, throat and beard, the front of the legs with the exception of the knees, and a stripe along the flanks are all dark brown as well. There is also some white on the lower parts of the legs. A certain amount of individual variation is displayed in regard to the extent of the dark and white markings. In the female the colouration is generally somewhat paler and there is no beard.

The buck's impressive horns are usually 50–60 cm long, although they have been recorded to measure as much as 130 cm. The horns of the much smaller doe go up to 15 cm. Bucks can attain a length of 150 cm and a height of 95 cm, but the size and weight can differ considerably among the various sub-species. In some areas bucks reach a weight of 35–38 kg and does 26–30 kg, in other areas the bucks weigh 70–80 kg. Measurements of the feral goat *Capra hircus* found in the remote parts of the western Scottish Highlands record an average length of 75 cm, and a horn-span of 75 cm (with a record of 111.5 cm).

Habitat Wild goats live in the *maquis* – wild, bushy and rocky terrain – in mountainous areas with steep slopes, usually near forest-clad uplands. During the summer, the old bucks keep to the higher mountains, often being encountered at snow level, while the does and kids frequent lower ground.

In the winter, both sexes descend to lower altitudes, living at elevations of 700–1000 metres on rocky ground among bushes or scattered pines. In certain parts of their distribution, they may even descend almost to sea-level.

Behaviour An extremely active animal, mainly in the early morning, late afternoon and evening, the wild goat chiefly frequents craggy and rocky districts, taking leaps of great length with unerring precision. Its agility among rocks has been described by one authority as little short of marvellous, although if driven down to the lowlands it is said to be easily caught by dogs. During the day it withdraws to caves or inaccessible places to rest or ruminate.

In T. H. White's translation of a twelfth-century Latin bestiary, Caper the Goat is described as an animal who gets called this because she strives to attain the mountain crags (*aspera captet*): 'These linger on the highest mountains and can recognise approaching people from far away, distinguishing the wayfarer from the sportsman. Thus Our Lord Jesus Christ is partial to high mountains, i.e. to Prophets and Apostles, for it is said in the Song of Songs: Behold my cousin cometh like a he-goat leaping on the mountains, crossing the little hills, and like a goat he is pastured in the valleys'.

The wild goat is found either solitary or in small parties or herds. During the greater part of the year the males and females live apart in herds of 3–7; in the autumn and winter sometimes even as many as 20–30 individuals are seen together.

Although at other times extremely shy and wary, during the pairing season wild goats can sometimes be approached with ease. If surprised, they utter a kind of short snort, and immediately make off in a canter. When danger threatens, the oldest male takes command of the herd, and carefully surveys the line of advance or retreat before permitting the others to follow. One authority remarks that sentinels are almost always posted to warn the flock, these being relieved at short intervals, and it appears that this sentry-duty is undertaken according to seniority, the youngest animals commencing first, and the oldest buck taking his turn last. In Asia Minor the wild goats are hunted both by driving and by stalking, but they are so cunning that the former method is not generally very successful.

Diet Although primarily browsers, goats are well known for the variety of fodder, often of very poor quality, on which they are capable of subsisting, as G. B. Corbet remarks. Their agility amongst rocks enables them to reach food that is inaccessible to most other species and they will not hesitate to climb trees if the trunk is leaning at a convenient angle (which is often the case on rocky mountain-sides).

Wild goats feed mainly on low-growing vegetation, i.e. twigs, herbs and grasses. In Asia Minor, grass, the young shoots of dwarf oaks and cedars, and berries, are said to constitute their staple diet. In the Bamu protected region of Iran, M. E. Taylor has observed the local movements of the wild goats. They spend the summer on the northern slopes of their mountain reserve, but when the snow builds up in the winter, they travel to the south-facing ones where the snow melts rapidly. They also change altitude, moving up a mountain as spring advances because the vegetation at lower altitudes starts growing first. By midsummer, most of the rapid growth associated with winter rain is over, and the wild goats tend to remain on the higher slopes. In winter they obtain water by eating snow or by drinking from holes in the rocks filled with rain or melted snow, and in summer from natural springs.

In the twelfth-century Latin bestiary, the wild goat (Caprea) was described as having the following peculiarities: 'that he moves higher and higher as he pastures, that he chooses good herbs from bad ones by the sharpness of his eyes, that he ruminates these herbs, and that, if wounded, he runs to the plant Dittany [= Ditany, Dittander, Pepperwoort], after reaching which he is cured.' As recently as 1974, it was reported that a game scout in Iran attributed the wild goat population's freedom from parasites to their eating certain plants. It has been recorded that the bezoar-stone, a concretion found in the stomach of the wild goat (which is also known as the bezoar goat) is highly esteemed as an antedote to poison by some humans; they are also known to utilise it as a remedy for several diseases.

Breeding The Latin bestiary recalls: 'Hyreus the He-Goat is a lascivious and butting animal who is always burning for coition. His eyes are transverse slits because he is so randy.'

During the rutting period, which is usually in November, the bucks fight among themselves. One or two, occasionally even three, kids are born, usually during May or June, but in some areas they can be produced somewhat earlier. J. C. Greig remarks that despite the feral goat's long history in Britain, the goats have not yet adapted to the long daylight of northern latitudes. As light affects the onset of the breeding season, the goats rut earlier in the north than in the south, and in some areas the kids are born in early January. The wild and feral goats' ability to survive and multiply in a variety of temperature extremes gives some indication of their hardy qualities.

The young are able to follow their mothers within 2–3 days of birth and are reported to stay with them for 7–12 months. Females reach sexual maturity at 1–2 years of age, males when they are 3–4 years old.

Hybridisation between the wild goat and the markhor *Capra falconeri*, and between the wild goat and the domestic goat are both recorded, the hybrids being fertile in both sexes. The lifespan of the wild goat is put at 10–15 years.

Population   There are considered to be few populations of the wild goat that have not been affected in some way or another by interbreeding with feral domestic goats.

The following populations are referred to by C. J. Smit and A. van Wijngaarden. In Italy, wild goats are numerous on the small island of Montecristo, which is a nature reserve. In Greece, in March 1963, the following numbers were recorded: western Crete, 300; islands around Crete where they have been introduced: Theodoru, 55, Agii Pantes, 20, Dia, 20; and the Parnitha reserve (Peloponnesus), 6. A population of 100 were recorded on Erimomilos (belonging to the Cyclades) and 120–150 in south-western Samothrace.

Cross-breeding between wild and domestic goats occurs on the island of Giura which has an estimated population of 600 individuals. The species has been introduced into the Oros Iti mountains near Lamia, with 55 specimens recorded, near Atalantonisi, with 20, and on the island of Psili, with 6 individuals. The goats on the island of Erimomilos are not all pure-strain – only 100 out of the population of 400–500 are considered to be of true wild stock.

The U.S.S.R. has an estimated population of several thousand wild goats in the northern part of the Caucasus, but authorities consider it to be less numerous than 50–100 years ago. In Czechoslovakia, in 1963, crosses between the wild goat and domestic goat were introduced into a reserve area. In 1964, 14 individuals were counted. In the Bamu protected region, Iran, M. E. Taylor (1974) recorded that a conservative estimate of the wild goat population was in the region of 500 individuals. However, such observations are difficult, owing to the shy, almost secretive disposition of the wild goat.

In 1973, world zoos recorded the presence of some 70 individuals belonging to three separate races of the wild goat, a high proportion of which were captive bred.

Distribution   The wild goat occurs on Montecristo (Italy), Crete, the Greek archipelago, in Asia Minor, northern Lebanon, western Syria, Iran, the north-western part of Iraq, Georgian S.S.R., Armenian S.S.R., the northern part of Turkmenian S.S.R., Afghanistan and the West-Sind and Beluchistan regions of Pakistan. Recently a population of wild goats was discovered in the western Hajr of Oman. Its former European distribution included all mountainous areas around the Mediterranean and many of the islands.

196

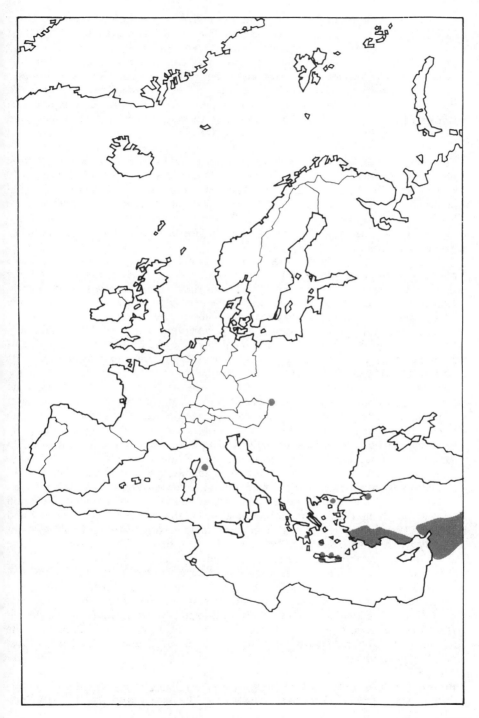

197

Most of the domestic breeds of goat are descended from *Capra aegagrus*. There are no traces of the wild goat to be found in the British Isles, while the earliest remains of domestic goats are found in settlements of the Neolithic period. Since that time they have always been kept by man, and have assumed a considerable variation in size, pelage and horn-growth. For as long as they have been domesticated, goats have escaped into mountainous regions and established themselves in the wild. Such feral populations of long standing now exist in many parts of the British Isles, in north Wales, the Cheviots, Galloway, the Scottish Highlands and Ireland, especially on small islands.

Conservation In their insular retreats, wild goats are now almost immune from predators, but on the Asiatic mainland it is likely that they are, or were, heavily preyed upon by the larger carnivores. However, notwithstanding the lack of animal predation, in many of the regions they inhabit, human hunting and poaching have led to the wild goats' extermination. Recently, for example, their numbers are known to have decreased dramatically in the northern part of Iraq, as a result of severe overhunting.

Wild goats are protected in Italy, Greece, Turkey, in the Bamu protected region of Iran and the U.S.S.R. Crete has a reserve of 3000 hectares in which in 1974 the Zoological Societies of New York and San Diego were reported to be jointly financing a field project by Nicolas Papageorgeiou to study the ecology of the Cretan wild goat. The island of Erimomilos is also a reserve area.

Wild goats will breed readily in a captive environment. In April 1965 and May 1967 the State of New Mexico Department of Game and Fish imported 1 male and 5 female wild goats, as part of a project to establish captive breeding herds of several non-indigenous species of exotic hoofed animals, and eventually to release their progeny in the wild in order to increase the variety of New Mexico's big game animals. The State Department of Game and Fish made a special agreement with Albuquerque Zoo to undertake the management of the Department's breeding groups of hoofed animals. In June 1966 and May 1967 the first two females to be imported reared 3 and 4 kids respectively. The success which the Albuquerque Zoo has achieved in acclimatising and breeding exotic hoofed animals goes to prove that with proper animal management zoos can readily breed sufficient numbers of animals to establish viable herds in wild or semi-wild conditions.

Surveillance is extremely difficult in isolated mountain regions, and there is still a lot of poaching, despite the protection afforded the wild goat in both Greece and Turkey. There is one report that helicopters have been used to hunt wild goats in Turkey where this species urgently requires better protection. Conservationists have advocated the establishment of reserves in suitable areas in Turkey and the Middle East, and that poaching in these areas should be prevented by regular surveillance.

Protective measures, including the prevention of cross-breeding with feral domestic goats and the culling of hybrids, should be continued in Greece, Italy and the U.S.S.R. The introduction of wild goats into suitable areas should be considered as well as the provision by zoological institutions of further facilities to increase the numbers of pure-bred animals by the introduction of selective and methodical breeding programmes.

Burton, M. (1962): *Systematic Dictionary of Mammals of the World*, pp. 240–1. Corbet, G. B. (1966): *Terrestrial Mammals of Western Europe*, p. 177. **Duplaix-**

Hall, N. (1975*a*): 'Species of wild animals bred in captivity in 1973'. **Gray**, A. P. (1972): *Mammalian Hybrids*, pp. 129–32. **Greig**, J. C. and **Cooper**, A. B. (1970): 'The "wild" sheep of Britain'. **Lydekker**, R. (1894): *The Royal Natural History, Vol. II*, pp. 239–40; (1898*b*): *Wild Oxen, Sheep and Goats*. **Millais**, J. G. (1906): *Mammals of Great Britain and Ireland, Vol. III*, pp. 213–14. **Oryx** (1974): *Vol. XII*, No. 3. **Roth**, J. P. and **Bowman**, M. M. (1969): 'Management of antelopes at Albuquerque Zoo'. **Smit**, C. J. and **Wijngaarden**, A. van (1976): 'Threatened mammals'. **Taylor**, M. E. (1974): 'Wildlife of a mountain reserve in Iran'. **White**, T. H. (1954): *The Book of Beasts*.

Ibexes

Alpine Ibex and Spanish Ibex

Capra ibex   *Capra pyrenaica*

Status: The Alpine ibex was on the verge of extinction, but thanks to the enforcement of protective measures has been saved. The population of the Spanish species is still at a very critical level

Description   Ibexes, turs, markhors and sheep all belong to the sub-family Capridae in the family Bovidae. Thus separating the sheep from the goats is not always as easy as it may sound, for they are closely allied. Among the characteristic goat features are the following: both sexes have horns, and the horns have a triangular base; in the adult male the horns rise close together on the head and are of considerable length, compressed and angulated, rising above the plane of the forehead either in a scimitar-like curve or in a spiral; in the female the horns are smaller and further apart at the base; there is usually a beard, and members of the goat genus *Capra* do not have sex glands in the face or feet, but do have them under the tail. Goats also show certain skeletal differences from sheep.

In western Europe there are only two species of wild goat, the Alpine ibex and the Spanish ibex. Although it is clearly recognised that these animals represent two distinct species, their basic biology is alike and they are treated together in this text for the benefit of comparison.

The two ibexes are somewhat similar in appearance, but can be distinguished by the broader shoulders and dark grey back stripe of the Spanish species. The general colour of the coat of the Spanish ibex is grey or greyish-brown, the belly is greyish-white. The beard is confined to the chin – long and narrow in old males in the winter pelage, but in the summer pelage and in young males at all seasons, reduced to an insignificant tuft. In summer the coat is fine and short, in winter longer and more shaggy. The coat of the Alpine ibex is brown, some parts of the body being yellower, others greyer; the belly is also greyish-white.

The Alpine ibex is characterised by its big curved horns, which can reach a length of 75 cm, and short beard. The males reach a length of 130–150 cm and a weight of 65–100 kg, the females 105–125 cm and 40–70 kg. The height is 70–90 cm, tail length 12–15 cm. The shape of the horns of the Spanish ibex differs from that of the Alpine species. Spanish bucks of 12–15 years can have horns with a length of 75–85 cm. The males reach a length of 125 cm and a weight of 70–80 kg. Southern Spanish forms are even smaller than those from the Pyrenees.

Habitat   Ibexes dwell on steep cliffs, and display remarkable powers of climbing and jumping. In this respect they differ markedly from most of the larger sheep, which usually prefer open rolling valleys and plateaux.

The Alpine ibex inhabits mountain areas with steep rocks at altitudes of between 2500 and 3500 m. In the winter, and especially in the spring, it descends to lower altitudes. The Spanish ibex also lives in mountain areas but at altitudes of 1500–2500 m. In the winter it too moves to lower areas.

Behaviour   Alpine ibex are mostly active during the night, i.e. mainly several hours before sunrise and sometimes also during the evening, and they may take periods of rest during the day. The animals live in herds and usually only move over short distances. The composition of the herds varies during the year. Females tend to withdraw more often into inaccessible districts, whereas the bucks are more often found in open areas. Solitary individuals are generally old, sick or wounded animals, and probably some unmated males.

Spanish ibex are reported to be active in the late afternoon and during bright nights, when they graze on mountain meadows. During the period when they were hunted intensively, they were only active during the night. The males and females live in separate herds most of the year, the young animals (up to 3 years) staying with the females.

Herds of bucks can become very large, having up to 50 individuals – although at the end of the last century, R. Lydekker wrote that the flocks then often comprised 100–150 head each. During the spring and summer months, when the old rams are said to be on the highest peaks, the younger members of the same sex and the ewes frequent the warmer southern slopes of the mountains. And in winter, under the pressure of cold and hunger, these latter will descend at times even to the near neighbourhood of the higher villages.

When in bush-covered country, hunters have reported that it is impossible to bag adult males without resorting to driving: the hollows in the rocks and the abundant vegetation by which they are covered render it almost impossible to detect the game.

Diet Ibexes are both grazers and browsers, and they feed on herbs and grasses in mountain meadows. These animals may feed throughout the night. In spring they move upward to new areas for feeding, and in winter they leave the deep snows and severe weather to seek lower levels and a food supply that is more accessible.

Breeding Old bucks are said to keep apart from the does and younger bucks throughout the year, except during the rutting season which takes place during October and November. The kids are born in the latter part of April or the early part of May, after a gestation period of from 20 to 22 weeks. Very soon after birth they are able to trot after the does which at this season resort to the southern slopes to avoid the cold winds prevailing in other situations. The mother protects her young by fighting with her horns or by decoying the intruder. Females become sexually mature at the age of 3–6 years, and usually give birth to one young every year.

Hybridisation between members of the genus *Capra* is quite frequent. The Alpine ibex has hybridised with the markhor *Capra falconeri* and the domestic goat *Capra hircus*. J. Dorst notes that the introduction of mammals related to native forms may be followed by hybridisation of the two, with unfortunate consequences. In 1901 the ibex *Capra ibex*, the wild goat *Capra aegagrus* and the Nubian ibex *Capra nubiana* were introduced into the Tatra Mountains. The resulting hybridisation upset the entire population since the reproductive period was affected and the young were born in midwinter.

One advantage of being able to determine the age of a mammal is that it is then possible to gain an indication of the proportion of reproductive individuals in the total population. Although it is generally very difficult to do so, in the case of the ibex and some other closely related species determining the age is fairly straight-forward: the horns are permanent and consist of a bony axis covered with a corneous sheath which groves faster in the lush seasons than in the dry periods of the year. Thus these animals have their age inscribed on their horns — every time the growth of the horns is retarded or halted a distinct transverse streak with loosened edges results. The maximum age reached by the Spanish ibex is 15–20 years, the Alpine ibex can attain an age of 12–18 years.

Population C. J. Smit and A. van Wijngaarden refer to the populations of the Alpine ibex as follows. About 150 years ago, some 60 specimens lived in the Parco Nazionale del Gran Paradiso in the Val d'Aosta in the north-western part of Italy, which is considered to be the only place in Europe where pure strain animals had survived. In 1958 they occurred in two areas in Italy, in Gran Paradiso, where there were 3000 specimens, and in Valdieri Enraque in the province of Vueno where there were 200 specimens.

In 1959, there were 20 specimens in the Grand Casse mountains of Savoie, France. These animals had crossed the border and originated from the Gran Paradiso population. In the 1960s a reserve was created in this area, the Parc de la Vanoise, where 200 specimens were counted in 1971. There are populations occurring in three other locations in this area.

Alpine ibexes were exterminated in Switzerland in 1840, but were reintroduced at the end of the nineteenth century. In 1952 there were 10 colonies with 1100 specimens; in 1961, 33 colonies with 2600 specimens.

A few Alpine ibex have occurred in Liechtenstein since 1972. The species was exterminated in Austria around 1720; at the end of the nineteenth century specimens from zoological gardens were reintroduced, but were considered not to be pure-bred animals. Others were imported from a breeding institute in Italy. In 1959 there were reportedly 7 colonies with approximately 150 specimens. In the German Federal Republic, there is one colony living along the Austrian border, with about 20 specimens.

In Yugoslavia, about 40 specimens were reported to be living along the Loibl Pass on the Austrian border in 1959. Early in this century, this colony had a high proportion of mixtures of Alpine ibexes and domestic goats, but due to selective shooting the population is now said to be relatively pure. In 1949, 6 specimens were introduced into the Crimea, but this population is now extinct. Two sub-species of *Capra ibex* live in the Caucasus; one of these, *C. i. caucasia*, was estimated to number about 15,000—20,000 individuals in 1966.

Four sub-species of the Spanish ibex have been described. The sub-species *C. p. lusitanica* was exterminated between 1890 and 1892. The type species *C. p. pyrenaica* is said to number fewer than 20 specimens. *C. p. victoriae* was nearly exterminated around 1900. In 1905, when the Sierra de Gredos was declared·a royal hunting reserve, there were still about 12 specimens in this area. Due to the protection given after that year, there are now about 2500—3000 specimens. Some 2000 specimens of the sub-species *C. p. hispanica* occur in the reserve of Sierra de Gazorla, about 500 in Sierra Nevada, about 1500 in the mountains between Marbella and Ronda, and 500—600 in Los Puertos de Tortosa. Outside the reserves they occur in the mountains between Malaga and Granada, the region west of Valencia, and in the Sierra Morena. Eight specimens from the Sierra de Gazorla were introduced into the Covadonga National Park in 1957 and 1958. In 1972, it was reported that ibexes from the same area were also introduced into the Panticosa's Balneario. There are also reports that the Spanish ibex occurs in Portugal, but no information about the localities or numbers is available.

In 1973, 21 world zoos recorded the total captive populations of the alpine ibex as 85 males, 94 females, of which 80 males and 88 females had been bred in captivity. The Spanish ibex was recorded to be confined to two zoos, Barcelona and Madrid, where 1 male/2 female and 0 male/1 female were represented respectively.

Distribution The world distribution of the Alpine ibex, including several sub-species, is given by Smit and Wijngaarden as follows: the Italian, French and Swiss alps, Austria, the German Federal Republic and Yugoslavia, the Caucasus, the mountains of Russian Turkestan and central Siberia, Mongolia, Chinese Turkestan, Kashmir, the northern Punjab, Afghanistan, Israel, Arabia, Egypt, the Sudan and Ethiopia. The localities of the present European distribution can be seen under **Population**.

203

The Spanish ibex occurs only in the Iberian peninsula, mostly in Spain, although in 1968 there was one report that it also occurred in Portugal. The type species, *C. p. pyrenaica*, used to occur on both the French and Spanish sides of the Pyrenees and probably in the Cordillera Cantabrica as well. Today, it occurs only in the Parc National de Ordesa in the province of Huesca. The sub-species *C. p. lusitanica* used to occur in the north-western part of the Iberian peninsula in Galacia and northern Portugal but became extinct at the end of the nineteenth century. *C. p. victoriae* occurred in the mountains in the central part of the Iberian peninsula from Toledo to the Sierra de la Francia; in present times it has survived in the hunting reserve of the Sierra de Gredos, as well as being successfully introduced into the Panticosa's Balneario, not far from Ordesa. *C. p. hispanica* was found in the mountains from the north of the Ebro River to Andalusia and the Sierra Morena; its present distribution is included with the estimated numbers of this sub-species under **Population**.

Conservation The continuous improvement of hunting weapons, expanding industrialisation, and the rapid increase in human population adversely affected many animal populations during the nineteenth century. The population of European herbivores dwindled at an alarming rate, and the ibex was hunted to such an extent that certain races restricted to Spain and Portugal have disappeared.

Overhunting brought the Alpine ibex to the verge of extinction. However, thanks to the protection given to a few remaining individuals in the north-west corner of Italy — firstly by the Italian kings who made the area a hunting reserve and more recently by the Italian Government who converted the reserve to the Gran Paradiso National Park — the Alpine ibex has been saved.

With these few remaining ibexes, one of the most remarkable examples of a successful animal reintroduction was accomplished. Vinez Ziswiler remarks that at the beginning of this century the St Gallen Animal Park Association in Switzerland decided to take the breeding of the Alpine ibex into its own hands. After some initial failures, an original breeding stock of some 34 animals materialised; these animals had been bred in enclosures before any attempts to release them in the wild were risked. In 1911, the first of this stock was released in the mountains of St Gallen. Of the subsequent releases, a few failed; the majority, however, led to a successful re-establishment. The most successful colonies developed so favourably that they soon became 'mother colonies' and supplied animals for further reintroduction. Since their establishment, the three large colonies in Grisons, Berne and Valais together have yielded more than 1000 animals to be released in other areas. Presently, there are reputed to be about 40 established ibex colonies in the Swiss mountains, totalling more than 3700 animals. Through migration and by the conscious efforts of man, ibex bred in Switzerland are now enriching the alpine regions of several other countries. The species is completely protected by law in Italy, France, Switzerland, Austria, the German Federal Republic, Yugoslavia and Israel.

Persecution by hunters and poachers has brought the Spanish ibex to a low level. In October 1973, the Spanish Government passed a decree giving total protection to six mammal species and one sub-species, which included *Capra pyrenaica*.

In 1968, there were no more than 150 of the walia ibex *Capra walie* in the world, and all of these were confined to the Simien mountains in Ethiopia. In 1969, the Simien Mountain National Park was officially proclaimed; subsequently, thanks

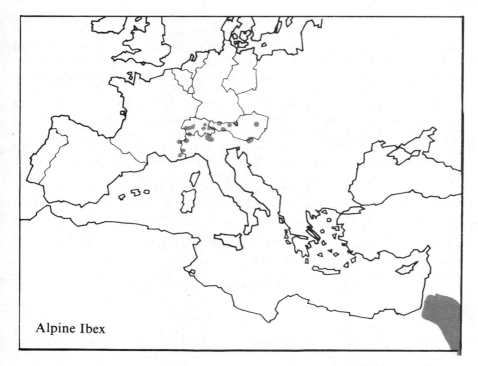

Alpine Ibex

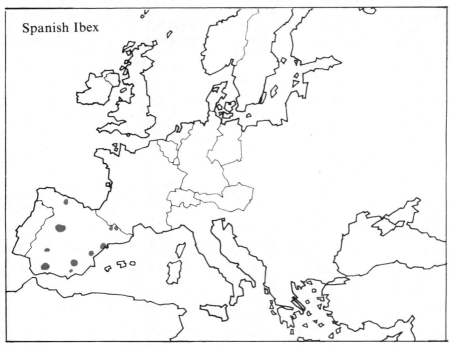

Spanish Ibex

205

to the introduction of conservation measures, poaching has almost disappeared and in 1974 the population of the walia ibex was reported to have risen to 300 individuals. Although the numbers of walia ibex have seriously declined compared with those of 40—45 years ago, the residue is considered to be adequate to ensure the survival of the species and to allow it gradually to reoccupy its former range provided adequate protection is given while the opportunity still exists.

Now that the Spanish ibex has been afforded total protection, it is hoped that its population will make a similar recovery and increase in the same way as the walia ibex. With the introduction of proper conservation measures and supervision, poaching can be brought to the minimum, and sound management can prevent cross-breeding between sub-species. The possibility of reintroducing the species in additional suitable areas should also be considered.

The Vienna Zoo and the Museum of Zurich University are responsible for the International Studbook of Capra ibex. (Studbooks and world registers are maintained in order to facilitate the planned breeding of rare species.) In 1973, world zoos recorded the successful rearing of some 40 Alpine ibexes. As the various species of ibex thrive and reproduce well in a controlled environment, it is hoped that, should protective measures in the wild fail, captive breeding programmes for these sub-species of ibex that are still below the critical level will be introduced before they follow the fate of *C. p. lusitanica*, and are lost forever.

Bourlière, F. (1967): *Natural History of Mammals.* **Dorst**, J. (1969): *Before Nature Dies.* **Duplaix-Hall**, N. (1975*a*): 'Species of wild animals bred in captivity during 1973'. **Fisher**, J., **Simon**, M. and **Vincent**, J. (1972): *The Red Book: Wildlife in Danger*, pp. 165—6. **Gray**, A. P. (1972): *Mammalian Hybrids*, pp. 132—3. **Lydekker**, R. (1898*b*): *Wild Oxen, Sheep, and Goats.* **Oryx** (1969—74): *Vols X—XII.* **Simon**, M. (1966): *Red Data Book: Mammalia, Vol. I.* **Smith**, C. J. and **Wijngaarden**, A. van (1976): 'Threatened mammals'. **van den Brink**, F. H. (1973): *A Field Guide to the Mammals of Britain and Europe*, p. 184. **Ziswiler**, V. (1967): *Extinct and Vanishing Animals.*

Mouflon

Ovis musimon

Status: In all the original areas, numbers have been considerably reduced without exception by overhunting and competition from domestic sheep

Description   The genus *Ovis* includes the domestic sheep, their wild ancestors the mouflons, the argali of central Asia and the bighorn of North America. (As was pointed out in the discussion of ibexes (page 200), sheep and goats are very closely allied, and it is difficult to decide, with some species, which they are.) Separating wild sheep from wild goats is more difficult than with domestic breeds, which are quite distinct. The zoologist and naturalist Ivan Sanderson recalls how he narrowly escaped serious trouble in one part of Africa after giving an animal to a native chief under the impression that it was a sheep – a most acceptable gift – only to learn that the majority of that dignitary's retainers declared it to be a goat, which happened to constitute a dire insult in that country.

Sheep do not have beards, they have scent glands on the face and feet, but not under the tail. Their horns tends to be more circular in the cross-section (not triangular as with goats) and spiral outwards and forwards (not curved back or spirally up as in goats).

The exact number of mouflon species of sheep is not clear. There are many local forms varying widely in build and in the shape of their horns. Compared with many domestic breeds, the mouflon is a rather small sheep with a short non-fleecy coat.

Its hair is close and thick, elongated in winter on the throat of the rams to form a distinct fringe, and it has a thick coat of woolly underfur at the same season. The horns of the male are fairly large, stout and strongly wrinkled; the front surface is markedly distinct from the outer one, with the outer angle rounded off, but the inner one sharp. The curvature of the horns forms a close spiral of about one complete circle, with the tips bending forwards and outwards so as to be situated almost immediately below the eyes. The ewes are usually hornless.

The general colour of adult rams in late or early autumn is greyish to reddish brown, becoming chocolate-brown on the head and face. There are numerous black markings: the sides of the neck, the throat, the chest, a line on the flanks, a streak down the withers, a saddle-shaped patch on the back, the front and sides of the forelegs above the knees, and the front and inner side of the hindlegs above the hocks. The ears are greyish externally, and white on the margins and part of the interior, muzzle and chin are greyish-white, passing into a greyish-rufous patch in the centre of the black area on the throat. The rear border of the black saddle is marked by a broad band grizzled with white. All the under-parts except a narrow dark streak between the forelegs and the buttocks are pure white, which stands out in brilliant contrast to the black band on the flanks.

There is a narrow white streak on the hind surface of both pairs of legs above the knees and hocks; the lower portion of the forelegs is white, with a variable amount of black on the front surface between the knees and the pasterns. The hindlegs below the hocks are similarly coloured, but with less of pure white. In winter the general colour of the coat darkens and tends more to chestnut-brown, while the saddle-like patch becomes larger and squarer, and takes on at the hind edge a yellowish or whitish tint, which is apparently most marked in the very old rams. The face-glands below the eyes are comparatively small. The description of the autumn colouration is cited by Lydekker in 1898, and taken from a very fine mounted ram in the British Museum which had been shot in the mountains of the interior of Sardinia.

The body length is 110–120 cm, height at the shoulder 65–75 cm, tail length 3.5–6.0 cm. The rams' curved horns may attain a length of 85 cm. Their weight range is 25–50 kg.

Habitat   Mouflon are generally restricted to mountainous areas in their native islands, where they usually inhabit only the higher parts, sometimes selecting peaks where they can take a wide survey of the surrounding country. They frequent broken ground, many of the valleys being filled with forests of ilex. Because of the dense *maquis* which covers the hills in a lot of the regions where they are found, the mouflon can only be observed when they come to graze in natural clearings.

The Cyprian mouflon is found in the Paphos forest, which is a mountainous region rising to a maximum height of about 1400 m (4619 ft), with eleven valleys radiating more or less from the centre of the area. During the summer, mouflon occupy the higher sectors of the range, moving down the valleys during the winter. For the greater part of the time they are said to remain within the forest, but on rare occasions emerge and cause damage to orchards and vineyards.

Some authorities have inferred that it is probable that the mouflon originally was just as much a species of the steppes as of the mountains, including the lightly wooded steppe of the Mediterranean region. Introductions of mouflon into many parts of Europe have mostly been in forest, and they have apparently adapted well to what G. B. Corbet describes as a 'deer-like existence' in quite thick forest, although they still feed predominantly by grazing in clearings. Corbet goes on to state that sheep of Soay, one of the islands of the St Kilda group in Scotland, are a feral race of domestic (but unknown) origin which closely resemble the wild mouflon in many aspects. They live on exposed tree-less islands, but without competition from any other herbivore.

Behaviour   Mouflons live in small flocks showing a distinct seasonal migration, grazing in the winter on lower altitudes, each flock occupying a clearly defined territory. Mature rams join the female flocks at rutting time, but in the autumn they retire to join the male flocks again, for outside the rutting period the males live in separate flocks from the ewes and young. Occasionally, mouflon have been known to desert their own kin in order to live among tame sheep, while sometimes a motherless domestic lamb has been known to seek companionship among a flock of mouflon.

All wild sheep are constitutionally restless and never remain long in one place. F. Bourlière points out that adult sheep and cattle, and probably ruminants in general, have been shown to take short periods of lying at rest, interspersed with periods of standing and rumination. These animals rarely close their eyes and seem even then not to lose consciousness.

When mouflon are alarmed, they are said to have a habit, or at least the rams have, of placing themselves in the middle of a bush of *maquis*, or in the shadow which it casts. The ewes, who are naturally less conspicious, are known to take similar evasive action but to a less degree. The mouflon are also assisted by their wonderful alertness of vision, which enables them to detect exceedingly slight signs at a moderate range. When startled they are known to whistle in a similar fashion to the chamois.

Diet   Wild sheep are predominantly grazers, feeding on a variety of ground vegetation including sedges and heaths as well as grasses and herbs. Unlike feral goats and domestic sheep, they are reputed to cause little or no harm to the forest.

Breeding   The rams engage in fierce conflicts among themselves for supremacy during the rutting season, and during the months of December and January the mountains are said to re-echo with the sound of the blows as one ram rushes against the head of another.

After a gestation period of 150–170 days, one or two lambs are born during April or May. The lambs are able to follow their dams almost immediately. The female normally attains sexual maturity by the age of 15 months, although females have been known to reproduce within their first year. Males reach maturity when they are about 18 months. In 1964, the mortality among infants and juveniles of the Cyprian mouflon was estimated at about 20–30%.

In 1972, M. E. Taylor deduced from observations made in the Bamu protected region of Iran that lambing lasted for 2–3 weeks, up to 27 April. He also found that a high proportion of lambs (about half), were twins; exact figures were difficult to calculate, because a few days after parturitition the mother and lamb(s) usually joined 'sterile' females and formed little parties, in which the true ratio of lambs to mothers could not be accurately estimated.

Mouflon rams mate readily with ewes of domestic breeds. The hybrids of both sexes are fertile and their fleece is generally of intermediate character, with a tendency to hairiness. Hybridisation between mouflon and the bighorn sheep *Ovis canadensis*, as well as between mouflon and urial *Ovis orientalis*, has also been recorded on frequent occasions. The lifespan of the mouflon is 12–14 years.

Population   Mouflons are still present on Corsica where in 1967 the total number was estimated probably not to exceed 200 individuals. In 1950, the mouflon population of Sardinia was put at 3000 to 4000 specimens. The original population is, however, extinct. The only population now present on the island is descended from an imported group. In May 1973, the population on Sardinia was estimated to number only 700 individuals.

In Cyprus, by 1937, the Troodos population was exterminated and all that remained of the Cyprian mouflon was a small herd of 15 animals in the Paphos forest. Swift remedial action in 1938, making the entire Paphos forest a game reserve, undoubtedly saved this sub-species. In 1963 it was estimated that 300 animals were in the Stavros forest on Mt Olympus, in the north-western part of the island. However, a further estimate in 1970 of this population established no more than 200 individuals.

In Turkey, only one mouflon population survives in the whole of Anatolia. It occurs in the Konya-Bozdag reserve, and in 1974 was reported to have 80–100 animals. In the U.S.S.R. the population in the Aragaz mountains has been exterminated. The only surviving population is found in the mountains in the south-eastern part of the Armenian S.S.R. and the Nakhichevan A.S.S.R.

In Iran, during two one-day censuses in the spring of 1972, carried out in the Bamu protected region, 1274 and 1170 were recorded on each day respectively. In a one-hour aerial census, 1246 individuals were counted. M. E. Taylor considered that these figures represent no more than 50% of the total population.

In other parts of the mouflon's distribution, no information about their numbers is available.

Distribution   According to Smit and van Wijngaarden, the world population of mouflon is to be found in the mountains of Corsica, Sardinia and Cyprus in the Mediterranean (but it is not known whether they also inhabited the Italian and Balkan peninsulas in the past), and in all the mountain chains of Antolia, Iran, Transcaucasia and the whole of central Asia including Tibet, Outer Mongolia and the Transbaikal region. Because the mouflon is restricted to mountainous areas, the distribution is split into many small populations and as a result many sub-species have developed. In general the body and horn size of the population increases from west to east.

At present, wild indigenous forms of this species are confined to Corsica, Sardinia, Cyprus, and to the mountains of Asia from Turkey to Mongolia. In addition to the three European populations, introduced mouflons now occur in many places in Europe and are managed as a game species. According to a study cited by Smit and van Wijngaarden (Pfeffer, 1967), mouflons originating from Corsica and Sardinia have been successfully introduced into the following countries: Austria, Belgium, Bulgaria, Czechoslovakia, Denmark, Finland, France, the German Democratic Republic, the German Federal Republic, Hungary, Italy, Luxembourg, the Netherlands, Poland, Rumania, Spain, Switzerland, the U.S.S.R.

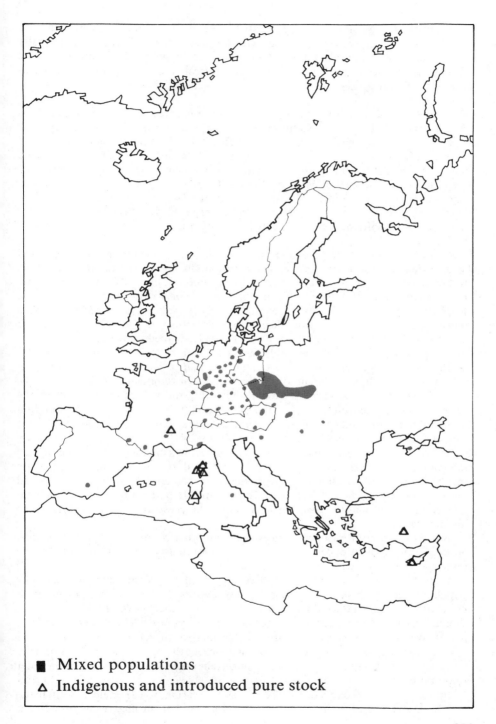

■ Mixed populations
△ Indigenous and introduced pure stock

211

and Yugoslavia. Most of these populations are, however, not pure-bred and are considered to be the result of crosses with other species of wild and even domestic sheep; the total number is put at 25,000. However the population living in the Parc naturel de Caroux is descended from pure Corsican ancestors and is estimated to number 120 individuals.

Conservation   Throughout the original distributional area the number of mouflons is decreasing rapidly due to overhunting and competition from domestic sheep.

On Corsica, the species is protected in the Reserve de Bavella and the Reserve d'Asco. The desperate state of the rarer wildlife species in Sardinia and the horrifying rate of habitat destruction and 'development' particularly in the west of the island was described in 1973 by Franco Tassi, Director of the Italian Abruzzo National Park: 'The mouflon, found mainly in the Gennargentu Mountains and on Monte Alto, is becoming increasingly under pressure due to a proposed winter sports development, with lifts and cableways, and the construction of a road to the highest peaks.'

In 1938, a representative of the Fauna Preservation Society visited Cyprus and investigated the status of the Cyprian mouflon. In the same year the game laws were strengthened to make the preservation of mouflon more effective, and certain forest guards and police were given the full-time responsibility of enforcing the law. In 1939, the entire Paphos forest, extending to 148,500 acres, was declared a game reserve in which it was made illegal to carry firearms for any purpose. The expulsion of goats from the forest in 1930—40 also helped to protect the mouflon. The population of the Cyprian mouflon has risen from 15 in 1937 up to 150—200 at the present time; in 1970, it was reported that 18 were kept in captivity in Cyprus as a breeding group. In 1967, the Cyprus Government signed the I.U.C.N. form of acceptance of ultimate responsibility for the remaining mouflon in the Stavros forest. Ironically, despite the protection this afforded to the mouflon against illicit poaching, the unexpected natural hazard of fire was reported to have caused destruction to these forests in December 1974.

In Turkey, the last surviving population is protected in the Konya-Bozdag reserve (area 40,000 ha). In the Bamu protected region of Iran, mouflon are regularly hunted throughout the year, the main objective being the large horned males. Hunting is however controlled by the Department of Environmental Conservation through the issue of licenses and the presence of game scouts in the hunting parties.

No information on protective measures from other countries is readily available, although in most European countries where mouflons have been introduced as a game species, they are protected by hunting laws.

Protective measures already proposed include the optimal management of the population in the existing reserves in Corsica, Cyprus, Turkey and Iran. In addition, populations of introduced animals on the Continent, known to be pure-bred, should be given an opportunity to expand as soon as possible and used to restock places where the species has been exterminated in recent times. When the population as a whole reaches an optimal level, the species could be normally hunted. Shooting within populations of uncertain origin should be selective in order to promote the original type.

In 1973, world zoos recorded the successful rearing of 183 males, 219 females and 36 unsexed mouflon in 89 collections. What numbers of these were pure-bred is not recorded; however, these breeding results illustrate the fact that mouflons will reproduce well in a captive environment.

At present, the Cyprian mouflon is the only sub-species of *Ovis musimon* to warrant a sheet in the I.U.C.N.'s *Red Data Book* of endangered species. With more systematic protection of the animal both from natural disasters, such as forest fires, and from man-made predation, along with education of people to appreciate the aesthetic value of the mouflon as a potential tourist attraction, it is hoped that the Cyprian mouflon's population will continue to rise in numbers away from the brink of extinction.

Bourlière, F. (1967): *Natural History of Mammals.* **Corbet**, G. B. (1966): *Terrestrial Mammals of Western Europe*, pp. 175–6. **Duplaix-Hall**, N. (1975*a*): 'Species of wild animals bred in captivity during 1973'. **Fisher**, J., **Simon**, N. and **Vincent**, J. (1972): *The Red Data Book, Wildlife in Danger*, pp. 168–9. **Gray**, A. P. (1972): *Mammalian Hybrids*, pp. 141–4. **Lydekker**, R. (1894): *The Royal Natural History*, *Vol. II*, pp. 225–7; (1898*b*): *Wild Oxen, Sheep and Goats*, pp. 154–66. **Millais**, J. G. (1906): *Mammals of Great Britain and Ireland, Vol. III*, pp. 209–11. **Oryx** (1970, 1973): *Vol. X*, No. 5 and *Vol. XII*, No. 1. **Sanderson**, I. T. (1955): *Living Mammals of the World*, p. 272. **Simon**, N. (1966): *The Red Data Book: Mammalia, Vol. 1.* **Smit**, C. J. and **Wijngaarden**, A. van (1976): 'Threatened mammals'. **Taylor**, M. E. (1974): 'Wildlife of a mountain reserve in Iran'. **van den Brink**, F. H. (1973): *A Field Guide to the Mammals of Britain and Europe*, pp. 163–4.

Bibliography

A.A.Z.P.A. (1975): *American Association of Zoological Parks and Aquariums*, Vol. XVI, Newsletter No. 4, U.S.A.

Allen, G. M. (1939): *Bats*, Dover Publications, New York.

Ariagno, D. and **Delage**, R. (1970): 'Oiseaux et mammifères du Haut-Vercors', *Alauda*, *38*, France.

Baal, H. J. (1950): 'Some bats of Jersey', *Bulletin of the Société Jersiaise*, Vol. XV, Part II, Museum, Jersey.

Backhouse, K. M. (1969): *Seals, The World of Animals*, Arthur Barker, London.

Bassett, C. F. (1957): 'The mink', in *The UFAW Handbook on the Care and Management of Laboratory Animals*, 2nd ed., U.F.A.W., London.

Blackmore, M. (1963): 'Bats – noctule, leisler's and serotine', in *Animals of Britain*, *18*, ed. L. Harrison Mathews, Sunday Times, London.

Boorer, M. (1969): *Wild Cats*, Paul Hamlyn, London.

Bourlière, F. (1967): *The Natural History of Mammals*, 3rd ed., Alfred A. Knopf. New York.

Burton, M. (1962): *Systematic Dictionary of Mammals of the World*, Museum Press, London.

Canivenc, R. (1966): 'A study of progestation in the European badger (*Meles meles* L.)', in *Comparative Biology of Reproduction in Mammals*, ed. I. W. Rowlands, Academic Press, London, for Zoological Society of London.

Chernyavsky, F. B. (1970): 'The snow bighorn (*Ovis nivicola Esch.*) of Chukotka, U.S.S.R.', *Byvll. mosk Obshch, Ispyt. Prir.*, *75*, No. 1 (in Russian, English summary).

Collins (1975): *Collins Encyclopedia of Animals*, ed. A. R. Waterston, Collins, London.

Corbet, G. B. (1966): *The Terrestrial Mammals of Western Europe*, G. T. Foulis, London.

Corbet, G. B. (1974): 'The distribution of mammals in historic times', in *The Changing Flora and Fauna of Britain*, Vol. 6, ed. D. L. Hawksworth, Academic Press, London.

Cranbrook, Earl of and **Crowcroft**, P. (1968): 'The white-toothed shrews of the Channel Islands', in *The Annals and Magazine of Natural History, Ser. 13,* Vol. 1, London.

Crandall, L. S. (1964): *The Management of Wild Mammals in Captivity*, University of Chicago Press, Chicago and London.

Crawford, M. (1972): 'Conservation by utilisation', *Oryx, Journal of the Fauna Preservation Society*, Vol. XI, No. 6, London.

Crowcroft, P. (1957): *The Life of the Shrew*, Max Reinhardt, London.

Crowcroft, P. (1963): 'Shrews', in *Animals of Britain*, *17*, ed. L. Harrison Mathews, Sunday Times, London.

Darling, F. Fraser (1937): *A Herd of Red Deer: A Study in Animal Behaviour*, Oxford University Press, London.

Davis, D. G. (1967): 'A brief note on the birth of wolverines *Gulo gulo* at Colorado Zoo', in *International Zoo Yearbook*, Vol. 7, ed. Caroline Jarvis, Zoological Society of London.

Davis, J. A. (1971): 'Dying species – the otters', *Anim. Kingd.*, *74*, No. 2.

Denis, A. (1964): *Cats of the World*, Constable, London.

Dorst, J. (1969): *Before Nature Dies*, Collins, London.

Dorst, J. and **Dandelot**, P. (1970): *A Field Guide to the Larger Mammals of Africa*, Collins, London.

Duplaix-Hall, N. (1975*a*): 'Census of rare animals: species of wild animals bred in captivity during 1973', in *International Zoo Yearbook*, Vol. 15, Zoological Society of London.

Duplaix-Hall, N. (1975*b*): 'River otters in captivity: a review', in *Breeding Endangered Species in Captivity*, ed. R. D. Martin, Academic Press, London.

Durrell, G. M. and **Mallinson**, J. J. C. (1970): 'The volcano rabbit *Romerolagus diazi* in the wild and at Jersey Zoo', in *International Zoo Yearbook*, Vol. 10, Zoological Society of London.

Eaton, R. L. (1973): 'The world's cats', *Ecology and Conservation*, Vol. 1, World Wildlife Safari, Oregon.

Fisher, J., **Simon**, N. and **Vincent**, J. (1972): *The Red Book: Wildlife in Danger*, Collins, London.

Fitter, R. (1968): *Vanishing Wild Animals of the World*, Midland Bank, London.

Fitter, R. (1972): 'Whales: the next step?', *Oryx, Journal of the Fauna Preservation Society*, Vol. XI, No. 6, London.

Fitter, R. (1974): 'Future for whales', *Oryx, Journal of the Fauna Preservation Society*, Vol. XII, No. 5, London.

Fitter, R. (1975): 'Whales and whaling: a dance of death', *Oryx, Journal of the Fauna Preservation Society*, Vol. XIII, No. 2, London.

Fitter, R. (1977): 'International whaling: eating the seed corn', *Oryx, Journal of the Fauna Preservation Society*, Vol. XIII, No. 5, London.

Fontaine, P. A. (1962): 'Reindeer (*Rangifer tarandus*) at Dallas Zoo', in *International Zoo Yearbook*, Vol. 3, Zoological Society of London.

Fuente de la, F. R. (1972): *World of Wildlife*, Vol. 5, Orbis Publishing, London.

Fuente de la, F. R. (1974): *World of Wildlife*, Vol. 10, Orbis Publishing, London.

Godfrey, G. K. (1976): 'The ecological distribution of *Crocidura suaveolens* in Jersey', in *Twelfth Annual Report, Jersey Wildlife Preservation Trust*, Jersey.

Golley, F. B. and **Buechner**, H. K. (1968): *A Practical Guide to the Study of the Productivity of Large Herbivores*, I.B.P. Handbook No. 7, Blackwell Scientific Publications, Oxford.

Graf, J. (1968): *Animal Life of Europe*, Frederick Warne, London.

Gray, A. P. (1971–2): *Mammalian Hybrids*, 2nd ed., Commonwealth Agricultural Bureaux, Slough, England.

Greig, J. C. and **Cooper**, A. B. (1970): 'The "wild" sheep of Britain', *Oryx, Journal of the Fauna Preservation Society*, Vol. X, No. 6, London.

Guggisberg, C. A. W. (1975): *Wild Cats of the World*, Taplinger Publishing Company, New York.

Hamilton, B. Count (1962): 'Keeping beavers *Castor fiber* in captivity', in *International Zoo Yearbook*, Vol. 4, Zoological Society of London.

Harrington, C. R. (1965): 'The life and status of the polar bear', *Oryx, Journal of the Fauna Preservation Society*, Vol. XIII, No. 3, London.

Harris, C. J. (1968): 'Otters, a study of the recent lutrinae', in *The World Naturalist*, ed. Richard Carrington, Weidenfeld and Nicolson, London.

Harrison Mathews, L. (1952): *British Mammals*, Collins, London.

Harrison Mathews, L. (1963): 'Baleen whales', in *Animals of Britain, 24*, ed. L. Harrison Mathews, Sunday Times, London.

Hediger, H. (1947): 'The breeding of field hares *Lepus europaeus* Pallas, in captivity', Zoological Garden, Basle, Switzerland.

Hewer, H. R. (1962): 'Grey seals', in *Animals of Britain*, 7, ed. L. Harrison Mathews, Sunday Times, London.   7

Hohn, O. E. (1973): 'Lynxes', *Animals Magazine*, Vol. 15, No. 6, Nigel Sitwell, London.

Holloway, C. W. (1971): 'I.U.C.N.'s second working meeting of polar bear specialists in Morges, Feb. 2–4, 1970', *Biol. Conserv.*, *3*.

Hooper, J. H. D. (1962): 'Horseshoe bats', in *Animals of Britain*, *2*, ed. L. Harrison Mathews, Sunday Times, London.

Hooper, J. H. D. (1964): 'Bats and the amateur naturalist', *Studies in Speleology*, Vol. 1, Part 1, Devon, England.

Hurrell, E. (1962): 'Dormice', in *Animals of Britain*, *10*, ed. L. Harrison Mathews, Sunday Times, London.

Hurrell, H. G. (1963): 'Pine martens', in *Animals of Britain*, *22*, ed. L. Harrison Mathews, Sunday Times, London.

I.U.C.N. (1973–6): *International Union for Conservation of Nature and Natural Resources Monthly Bulletins, New Series*, Morges, Switzerland.

I.U.C.N. (1975): *I.U.C.N. Yearbook 1974*, Morges, Switzerland.

I.Z.Yb. (1974): *International Zoo Yearbook*, Vol. 14, ed. N. Duplaix-Hall, Zoological Society of London.

Jackman, B. (1977): 'Why persecute the badger?', in *Sunday Times*, London.

Jacobi, E. F. (1968): 'Breeding facilities for polar bears *Thalarctos maritimus* (Phippe, 1774) in captivity', *Bijdr. t. Dierk.*, *38*, Amsterdam.

Jacobi, E. F. (1975): 'Breeding of sloth bears in Amsterdam Zoo', in *Breeding Endangered Species in Captivity*, ed. R. D. Martin, Academic Press, London and New York.

Jenkins, D. (1961): 'The present status of the wild cat (*Felis silvestris*) in Scotland', *The Scottish Naturalist*, Vol. 70, No. 2.

Jenkins, D. (1975): *in litt.* (Institute of Terrestrial Ecology, Banchory, Kincardineshire).

King, J. E. (1956): 'The monk seals (Genus *Monachus*)', Bulletin of the British Museum (Natural History), *Zoology*, Vol. 3, No. 5, London.

King, J. E. (1964): *Seals of the World*, Trustees of the British Museum (Natural History), London.

Krasinska, M. (1971): 'Hybridisation of European bison with domestic cattle', Part 6, *Acta Theriol.*, *16* (Polish summary).

Larousse (1972): *Encyclopedia of Animal Life* (Léon Bertin's text revised and adapted by Maurice Burton), Hamlyn, London.

Larson, T. (1971): 'Polar bear: lonely nomad of the north', *Nat. Geogr. Mag.*, *139*, U.S.A.

Lockie, J. D. (1966): 'Territory in small carnivores', in *Play, Exploration and Territory in Mammals*, ed. P. A. Jewell and Caroline Loizos, Academic Press, London, for Zoological Society of London.

Lowe, V. P. W. (1966): 'Observation of the dispersal of red deer on Rhum', in *Play, Exploration and Territory in Mammals*, ed. Jewell and Loizos.

Lydekker, R. (1894): *The Royal Natural History*, Vol. II, Frederick Warne, London.

Lydekker, R. (1894–5): *The Royal Natural History*, Vol. III.

Lydekker, R. (1898*a*): *The Deer of All Lands: A History of the Family Cervidae, Living and Extinct*, Rowland Ward, London.

Lydekker, R. (1898*b*): *Wild Oxen, Sheep and Goats of All Lands, Living and Extinct*, Rowland Ward, London.

Lydekker, R. (1915): *Wildlife of the World*, Vol. 1, Frederick Warne, London.

Lyon, M. W. (1903): 'Classification of the hares and their allies', *Smithsonion Misc. Collections*, Vol. 45, Washington, D.C.

McNutty, F. (1974): *The Great Whales*, Doubleday, New York.

Mallinson, J. J. C. (1975): 'Notes on a breeding group of Sierra Leone Striped Squirrels *Funisciurus pyrrhopus leonis* at Jersey Zoo', in *International Zoo Yearbook*, Vol. 15, Zoological Society of London.

Maxwell, G. (1967): *Seals of the World*, Constable, London.

Millais, J. G. (1904): *The Mammals of Great Britain and Ireland*, Vol. I, Longman Green, London.

Millais, J. G. (1905): *The Mammals of Great Britain and Ireland*, Vol. II.

Millais, J. G. (1906): *The Mammals of Great Britain and Ireland*, Vol. III.

Mivart, St G. (1890): *Monograph of the Canidae: Dogs, Jackals, Wolves and Foxes*, R. H. Porter, London.

Mochi, U. and Carter, T. D. (1974): *Hoofed Mammals of the World*, Lutterworth Press, Guildford and London.

Mohr, E. (1967): 'The studbook of the European bison', in *International Zoo Yearbook*, Vol. 7. ed. Caroline Jarvis, Zoological Society of London.

Montonen, M. (1972): 'Finland's reindeer', *Oryx, Journal of the Fauna Preservation Society*, Vol. XI, London.

Mowat, F. (1963): *Never Cry Wolf*, Dell Publishing Company, New York.

Neal, E. G. (1962*a*): 'Badgers', in *Animals of Britain*, *1*, ed. L. Harrison Mathews, Sunday Times, London.

Neal, E. G. (1962*b*): 'Otters', in *Animals of Britain*, *8*, ed. L. Harrison Mathews, Sunday Times, London.

Ognev, S. I. (1962): *Mammals of Eastern Europe and Northern Asia*, Vol. II, The Israel Program for Scientific Translations, Jerusalem.

Ognev, S. I. (1963): *Mammals of the U.S.S.R. and Adjacent Countries*, Vol. V, The Israel Program for Scientific Translations, Jerusalem.

Ognev, S. I. (1964): *Mammals of the U.S.S.R. and Adjacent Countries*, Vol. VII, The Israel Program for Scientific Translations, Jerusalem.

Olney, P. J. S. (1976): 'Species of wild animals bred in captivity during 1974' and 'Multiple generation captive births', in *International Zoo Yearbook*, Vol. 16, Zoological Society of London.

Oryx, (1965–77): *Oryx, Journal of the Fauna Preservation Society*, Vols VIII–XIII, London.

Overend, E. D. (1976): 'TB in British badgers'; in *Oryx, Journal of the Fauna Preservation Society*, Vol. XIII, No. 3, London.

Page, F. J. T. (1962): 'Red deer', in *Animals of Britain*, *13*, ed. L. Harrison Mathews, Sunday Times, London.

Pedersen, A. (1962): *Polar Animals*, George Harrap, London.

Pernetta, J. C. (1973): 'The ecology of *Crocidura suaveolens cassiteridum* (Hinton) in coastal habitat', *Mammalia*, *37*, No. 2, Paris.

Peyre, A. (1956): 'Ecologie et biogeographie du desman (*Galemys pyrenaicus G.*) dans les pyrénées francaises', *Mammalia*, *20*, No. 4, Paris.

Puissegur, C. (1935): 'Recherches sur le desman de pyrénées', *Bull. Soc. Hist. Nat.*, *67*, Toulouse, France.

Racey, P. A. and **Stebbings**, R. E. (1972): 'Bats in Britain — a status report', *Oryx, Journal of the Fauna Preservation Society*, Vol. XI, No. 5, London.

Raczyński, J. (1975): 'Progress in breeding European bison in captivity', in *Breeding Endangered Species in Captivity*, ed. R. D. Martin, Academic Press, London and New York.

Richard, P. B. and **Viallard**, A. V. (1969): 'Le desman des pyrénées (*Galemys pyrenaicus*) premières notes sur sa biologie', *La Terre et la Vie*, Paris.

Richard, P. B. (1973): 'Le desman des pyrénées (*Galemys pyrenaicus*), mode de vie, univers sensoriel', *Mammalia, 37*, Paris.

Rood, J. P. (1975): 'Observations on population structure, reproduction and moult of the Scilly shrew', *Journal of Mammology, 46*, England.

Roth, J. P. and **Bowman**, M. M. (1969): 'Management of antelopes at Albuquerque Zoo', in *International Zoo Yearbook*, Vol. 9, Zoological Society of London.

Rowe, J. J. (1975): *in litt.* (Forestry Commission, Farnham, Surrey).

Sanderson, I. T. (1955): *Living Mammals of the World*, Hamish Hamilton, London.

Scheffer, V. B. (1958): *Seals, Sea Lions and Walruses: A Review of the Pinnipedia*, Oxford University Press, London.

Schmidt, F. (1943): 'Naturgeschichte des Baum-und des Steinmarders', *Mongr. Wildsaüget, Lpz. 10*, 1–258.

Sherman, H. B. (1930): 'Birth of the young of *Myotis austroriparius*', *Journal of Mammology, 11*, England.

Shorten, M. (1962): 'Red squirrels', in *Animals of Britain, 6*, ed. L. Harrison Mathews, Sunday Times, London.

Simon, N. (1966): *Red Data Book: Mammalia*, Vol. I, Survival Service Commission of I.U.C.N., Morges, Switzerland.

Slijper, E. J. (1962): *Whales*, Hutchinson, London.

Smit, C. J. and **Wijngaarden**, A. van (1976): 'Threatened mammals — mammals in need of special protection in the member states of the Council of Europe', a Council of Europe report prepared by the State Institute for Nature Management, Netherlands, for the European Centre for Nature Conservation, Strasbourg.

Southern, H. N. (1964): *The Handbook of British Mammals*, Blackwell Scientific Publications, Oxford.

Spencer-Booth, Y. (1963): 'A coastal population of shrews (*Crocidura suaveolens cassiteridum*)', *Proc. Zool. Soc. London, 140*.

Stebbings, R. E. (1970): 'Bats in danger', *Oryx, Journal of the Fauna Preservation Society*, Vol. X, No. 5, London.

Stebbings, R. E. (1975): *in litt.* (Inst. Terr. Ecol., Huntingdon).

Taylor, M. E. (1974): 'Wildlife of a mountain reserve in Iran', *Oryx, Journal of the Fauna Preservation Society*, Vol. XII, No. 3, London.

Thorburn, A. (1920): *British Mammals*, Vol. 1, Longmans, Green, London.

Topsel, E. (1658): *The History of Four-footed Beasts and Serpents*, E. Cotes for G. Sawbridge, London.

Valverde, J. A. (1971): *El Lobo Espanol* (Distributional status, Spain) *Canis lupus signatus, Montes, 27*.

van den Brink, F. H. (1973): *A Field Guide to the Mammals of Britain and Europe*, 3rd ed., Collins, London.

218

Vlasak, P. (1972): 'The biology of reproduction and post-natal development of *Crocidura suaveolens* Pallas, 1811 under laboratory conditions', *Biologica, 3*, 1970: 207–92, Mort, 1972, Acta Universitas Carolinae, Prague.

Walker, E. P. (1964): *Mammals of the World*, Vols I and II, Johns Hopkins Press Baltimore.

Watson, A. and **Hewson**, R. (1963): 'Mountain hares', in *Animals of Britain, 23*, ed. L. Harrison Mathews, Sunday Times, London.

White, T. H. (1954): *The Book of Beasts: a Translation from a Latin Bestiary of the Twelfth Century*, Jonathan Cape, London.

Whitehead, G. K. (1972): *Deer of the World*, Constable, London.

W.W.F. (1972–7): *World Wildlife Fund Press Releases*, No. 35/1972, No. 3/1976, No. 20/1976 and No. 3/1977, World Wildlife Fund, Morges, Switzerland.

W.W.F. (1973–4): *World Wildlife Yearbook*, ed. Peter Jackson, World Wildlife Fund, Morges, Switzerland.

W.W.F. (1976): *The World Wildlife Fund, News Feature*: 'World wildlife fund launches $10 million campaign for the seas', Morges, Switzerland.

Ziswiler, V. (1967): *Extinct and Vanishing Animals*, Longmans, Springer-Verlag, New York.

Useful Organisations

Council of Europe
Environment and Natural Resources
Dept
67006 Strasbourg, France

European Information Centre for
Nature Conservation
Strasbourg, France

International Union for the
Conservation of Nature and Natural
Resources (I.U.C.N.)
1110 Morges, Switzerland

The World Wildlife Fund
CH 1110 Morges, Switzerland
and
29 Greville Street, London EC1

British Mammal Society
62 London Road
Reading, Berks

Nature Conservancy Council
19 Belgrave Square
London SW1

Fauna Preservation Society (F.P.S.)
Zoological Gardens
Regents Park, London NW1

Society for Promotion of Nature
Conservation (S.P.N.C.)
(National Association for County
Naturalists Trusts)
The Green, Nettleham, Lincoln

Council for Nature
Zoological Gardens
Regents Park, London NW1

Countryside Commission
1 Cambridge Gate
London NW1

Institute of Terrestrial Ecology and
Biological Records Centre
Monks Wood Experimental Station
Huntingdon

Jersey Wildlife Preservation Trust
(J.W.P.T.)
Les Augrès Manor
Trinity, Jersey, C.I.

General Index

Abruzzo National Park, 81, 84, 85, 89, 90, 177, 212
Albuquerque Zoo, 198
Allen, G. M., 21, 22
Aristotle, 164
Arran, Lord, 125
Augustus III, King of Poland, 189

Backhouse, K. M., 160, 165, 166
Badger Bill (1973), 125, 126
Barcelona Zoo, 89
Basle Zoo, 28
Beinn Eighe National Nature Reserve, 101
Boitari, L., 84
Boras Zoo, 115
Bourlière, F., 28, 47, 65, 158, 183, 209
British Mammal Society, 17, 123, 131
British Museum, 208
British Wild Creatures and Wild Plants Protection Act (1975), 19, 24, 63, 104, 126
Buechner, H. K. see Golley, F. B.
Buffon, G. L., Comte de, 166

Canadian Wildlife Service, 95
Canivenc, R., 122
Caxton, W., 154
Cocks, H., 137
Colorado Zoo, 115
Corbet, G. B., 10, 26, 43, 53, 55, 100, 104, 174, 176, 177, 185, 195, 209

Dallas Zoo, 182
Darling, F. F., 175, 176
Dorst. J., 202
Duplaix-Hall, N., 130

Edinburgh Zoo, 123

Fauna Preservation Society, 63, 77, 212
Fisher, J., 154
Fitter, R., 77
Forestry Commission, 176
Fuente, de la, F. R., 71, 101, 102

Godfrey, G. K., 2, 3
Golley, F. B. and Buechner, H. K., 174
Gray, A. P., 103
Greig, J. C., 196
Guggisberg, C. A. W., 136

Hagenbeck, C., 153
Hare Coursing Act (1975), 31
Harrison Mathews, L., 60, 70, 71, 72
Hediger, H., 28
Helsinki Zoo, 54, 115
Hewer, H. R., 160

Hewson, R. see Watson, A.
Hochberg, Duke of, 189
Hohn. F. O., 142
Hooper, J. H. D., 14, 15
Hurrel, H. G., 99, 100, 101, 102, 103

Institute of Terrestrial Ecology, 135
International Council for the Protection of Endangered Bats (I.C.P.E.B.), 19, 24
International Union for Conservation of Nature and Natural Resources (I.U.C.N.), 82, 84, 95, 163, 170, 212, 213
International Whaling Commission (I.W.C.), 76. 77

Jackman, B., 126
Jefferies, D. J., 125
Jenkins, D., 135, 136, 138, 140
Jersey Wildlife Preservation Trust (J.W.P.T.), 28, 36

Kenyon, K. W., 170
King, J. E., 150, 154, 159, 164, 165, 166, 167, 168

Lemmenjoki National Park, 117
Linnaeus, C. von, 40
Locke, J. D., 101, 102
London Zoo, 167
Lowe, V. P. W., 176
Lydekker, R., 50, 87, 108, 151, 175, 194, 201, 208

McNutty, F., 72, 76
Marine Programme (W.W.F.), 163, 170
Marineland Aquarium, Florida, 73
Maxwell, G., 149, 151, 152, 160, 165, 168
Millais, J. G., 22, 33, 35, 101, 103, 104, 120, 122, 136, 137, 138
Ministry of Agriculture, 123, 125, 126
Montonen, M., 184
Mowat, F., 80

National Centre of Scientific Research, Artiège, 10
National Zoo, Washington, 167
National Environment Research Council (N.E.R.C.), 125
Nature Conservancy, 125
Neal, E. G., 119, 120, 122, 123, 125
New York Aquarium, 167
New York Zoo, 198
Nordenskiold, Baron of, 151
Norfolk Wildlife Park, 42, 122, 133

Ognev. S. I., 55, 59, 101, 102, 119, 120, 121, 122

220

Ohthere (sailor), 149
Orkney, Earl of, 185
Oryx (magazine), 74, 89, 90, 123, 125, 131, 152, 156, 163, 168
Otter Trust, 133
Overend, E. D., 126

Page, F. J. T., 173
Pescasseroli Zoo, 81
Pest Infestation Control Service, 125
Peyre, A., 10
Pimlott, D., 84, 85
Pliny, 26, 164
Point Defiance Zoo, 81
Polar Bear Specialist Group, 95
Posnan Zoo, 54

Racey, P. A. and Stebbings, R. E., 17, 19, 22
Raczynski. J., 189, 190, 192
Red Deer Commission, 176
Richard, P. B. and Viallard, A. V., 10
Rood, J. P., 2

San Diego Zoo, 198
Sanderson, I. T., 65, 207
Scheffer, V. B., 158, 160
Schmidt, F., 100
Scottish Wildlife Trust, 133
Sea Specialists' Group, 170
Segnestam, M., 85
Sergeant, D. E., 170
Sherman, H. B., 22
Shorten, M., 33
Simon, N., 168
Slijper, E. J., 70, 71, 72, 73, 74, 76
Smit, C. J. and Wijngaarden, A. van, 17, 48, 55, 74, 93, 130, 154, 161, 163, 168, 177, 181, 187, 196, 202, 203, 210

Société Nationale pour la Conservation du Castor, 45
Southern. H. N., 15, 26, 29, 75, 101, 102, 103, 119, 120, 121, 123, 176
Spencer-Booth, Y., 2
Stebbings, R. E., 19, 22; *see also* Racey, P. A.
Stockholm Zoo, 160
Survival Service Commission (S.S.C.), 82, 97, 170
Sweden, King of, 182

Tacoma Zoo, 85
Taylor, M. E., 195, 196, 209, 210
Topsel, E., 181

United States Marine Protection Act (1972), 156

Van den Brink, F. H., 119
Viallard. A. V., *see* Richard, P. B.
Vienna Zoo, 206
Vlasak, P., 2, 3

Walker, E. P., 40, 180
Watson, A. and Hewson, R., 26, 28, 29
Wayre, P., 133
White, T. H., 194
Whitehead, K., 174, 181, 185
Wijngaarden, A. van *see* Smit, C. J.
Wolf Specialist Group, 82, 84, 85
World Wildlife Fund (W.W.F.), 77, 85, 89, 163, 170

Zurien, E., 84
Zurich University Museum, 206

Index of Species

Pine marten, 36, **99—106**
Pinnipeds, 150, 152, 165, 166
Platypsyllus castorsis, 41
Polar bear, **92—8**, 154, 156
Polar cod, 159
Polecats, 50, 55, 100, 103, 104, 107, 109
Porpoises, 70, 77
Pteropidae, 14
Pusa hispida see Ringed seal
Pusa hispida botnica, 158, 160
Pusa hispida ladogensis, 161
Pusa hispida saimensis see Saimaa seal
Pyrenean desman, **7—12**

Rabbits, 25, 26, 28, 114, 121, 129, 136, 143, 144
Rangifer tarandus see Reindeer
Rats, 129
Ravens, 50, 187
Red deer, 185, **172—9**, 183
Red squirrel, **32—8**, 110
Reptiles, 144
Reindeer, 80, 93, 114, **180—7**
Rhinolophus ferrum-equinum see Greater horseshoe bat
Ringed seal, 93, **157—63**
Rodents, 25, 40, 60, 102, 129, 136, 143
Roe deer, 85, 136, 143, 144
Romerolagus diazi see Volcano rabbit
Rorqual whale, 71, 72
Russian desman, 8, 10

Sable, 103
Saimaa seal, 157, 158, 161, 163
Salmon, 129
Sardines, 166
Sciuridae, 32
Sciurus vulgaris see Red squirrel
Sciurus vulgaris leucourus, 36
Seals, 93, 152, 164, 184
Sheep, 80, 121, 135, 143, 144, 174, 200, 207, 209
Short-eared owl, 55
Shrews, 136
Shrimps, 129
Sierra Leone striped squirrel, 36
Sika deer, 176
Skunk, 113

Snails, 129
Snakes, 108, 136
Snowy owl, 55
Snow-shoe rabbit, 143
Sorex, 1, 3
Spanish ibex, **200—6**
Spanish lynx *see* Pardel lynx
Sperm whales, 70
Squirrels, 101, 102, 136, 144
Stoats, 4, 36, 50, 55, 63, 128
Susliks, 136

Tadarida teniotis see European free-tailed bat
Tadpoles, 129
Talpidae *see* Moles
Tayra, 128
Thalarctos maritimus see Polar bear
Tits, 102
Treecreepers, 102
Trout, 129
'Trumpeter rat', 7
Tundra vole *see* Northern vole
Turs, 200

Urial, 210
Ursus arctos see Brown bear
Ursus arctos marsicanus, 89
Ursus arctos pyrenaicus, 89

'Varying hare' *see* Snow-shoe rabbit
Vespertilionidae, 21
Volcano rabbit, 28, 29
Voles, 102, 135, 144

Walia ibex, 204
Wapiti, 144, 176
Warblers, 60
Water voles, 108, 129, 136
Weasels, 4, 55, 63, 118, 128
Whales, 77, 184
White-tailed deer, 179
Wild cat, 177
Wild goat, **193—9**
Wisent *see* European bison
Wolverine, **113—17**, 187
Wolf, 55, **79—85**, 177, 187
Worms, 177
Wrens, 102